# WORLD WAR II FIGHTING JETS

# WORLD WAR II FIGHTING JETS

Jeffrey Ethell & Alfred Price

Naval Institute Press
Annapolis, Maryland

First published in the UK in 1994
by Airlife Publishing Ltd

Published and distributed in the United States of America and Canada by the
Naval Institute Press, 118 Maryland Avenue,
Annapolis, Maryland 21402-5035

**Library of Congress Catalog Card Number 94-65971**

ISBN 1-55750-940-9

This edition is authorized for sale only in the United States, its territories
and possessions, and Canada



Printed in England by Butler & Tanner Ltd.

# CONTENTS

# AUTHOR'S NOTE

In this book German words have been anglicised where appropriate. Thus Günther has been written as Guenther, Köthen as Koethen and Böhlen as Boehlen.

Where measurements are given they are in Imperial measures, with converted figures being rounded out where appropriate.

Where Japanese Navy ranks are stated, they have been translated to their nearest U.S. Navy equivalent.

On several occasions the authors found great difficulty in marrying the British, American, German and Japanese records concerning actions involving jet aircraft. Frequently the claims from one side bear little or no relation in time or place to the losses admitted by the other. For this reason claims and losses have been linked in the text only where there is clear evidence for doing so; where there is no positive link claims have in most cases been omitted.

# ACKNOWLEDGEMENTS

The authors wish to tender their grateful thanks to David Irving for permission to quote from his book *The Rise and Fall of the Luftwaffe*, and to Captain Eric Brown for permission to quote from *Wings of the Luftwaffe*.

In collecting material for this work the authors received generous assistance from numerous friends in several countries. Particular thanks are due to the following: Guenther Wegmann, Rudolf Opitz, Horst Goetz, Hans-Georg Baetcher, Rudolf Schnoerer, Walter Hagenah, Erich Sommer, Rudolf Zimmermann, Diether Lukesch, Peter Kappus, Rudolf Glogner, Arno Abendroth, Jay Spenser, Walter Boyne, Harold Watson, Richard Smith, Eddie Creek, Hanfried Schliephake, Hans Ring, Guenther Heise, Ken Bokleman, Bill Hess, Chris Shores, Robert Mikesh, Harold Andrews, Logan Coombs, Norm Taylor, Nathan 'Rosie' Rosengarten, Ropert Esposito, A.W. 'Tony' LeVier and Ray Wagner.

# PREFACE

This is an expanded version of the authors' earlier book *The German Jets in Combat*, published in 1979. That work limited itself to describing the development and operational careers of three German jet aircraft types that saw combat over a long period during World War II: the Messerschmitt 163, the Me 262 and the Arado 234. The new book covers all of that ground, plus a lot more. It includes descriptions of the development and combat careers of three other jet aircraft types that saw action during the conflict, the British Gloster Meteor, the Japanese Yokosuka Ohka and, by the narrowest possible margin, the Heinkel 162. It also tells the stories of the two American and one German jet aircraft that had entered squadron service and were on the point of going into action when the war ended: the Lockheed P-80A Shooting Star, the Ryan FR 1 Fireball and the Bachem Ba 349 *Natter*.

This work takes the reader through the most rapid period of scientific advance in the history of aviation: from the beginning of the jet age to the period immediately following World War II. It is a gripping story of human endeavour, the essentials of which took place between the beginning of 1943 and the beginning of 1946. At no time before or since have test pilots been confronted with so many, or such difficult, technological and aerodynamic hurdles. First there were the completely new and inadequately developed power plants, the turbojet engines and rocket motors. These pushed the current technologies up to and sometimes beyond their limits, and they could be temperamental to the point of lethality. Secondly there were the airframes of the early jet aircraft; in each case new designs that were liable to suffer the teething troubles that inevitably go with such things. Thirdly, and in the short term more intractable than the other two, there was the little-understood phenomenon of compressibility that manifested itself as speeds nudged ever closer to the invisible 'sound barrier'.

All of this took place against the background of all-out war in which major nations were battling for their very survival. In the certain knowledge that the enemy was also working on these problems, and might find the answers first and reveal their discovery with devastating effect, there was no time for carefully staged test programmes seeking incremental advances in knowledge. It was a callous world in which test pilots, and often service pilots as well, were expected to take risks in order to advance the frontiers of knowledge and bring new aircraft into service quickly. It was a world in which he who dared did not always win, but he who refused to dare would almost certainly lose.

Jeffrey Ethell,
Front Royal,
Virginia,
U.S.A.

Alfred Price
Uppingham,
Rutland,
England.

# THE RATIONALE FOR THE JET ENGINE

Although the ideas that spawned them were by no means new, it was not until the latter part of the 1930s that serious work began on gas turbine engines and rocket motors to power military aircraft. Two factors combined to spur development work in these fields. First, as the war clouds gathered over Europe and other parts of the world, there were strong pressures to improve the performance of military aircraft and in particular fighters. Secondly, and stemming from the first, there was a dawning realisation among aircraft designers that the immutable laws of physics would prevent propeller-driven planes from attaining speeds above 500 mph. The fundamental problem stemmed from the use of the propeller as a means of converting rotational power into thrust: as speed increased, the propeller's efficiency fell drastically.

A few figures will serve to illustrate the point. In round terms, the Spitfire attained a maximum speed of about 300 mph at sea level with an engine that developed 1,000 horsepower. At that speed the propeller was about 80 per cent efficient and the 1,000 pounds of thrust that it produced equalled the drag from the Spitfire's airframe.

Now consider the engine power needed to propel the same airframe at twice that speed, 600 mph. Drag rises with the square of speed, so if the speed was doubled the drag was quadrupled. Thus the 1,000 pounds of drag at 300 mph became 4,000 pounds of drag at 600 mph, and to overcome that the aircraft needed 4,000 pounds of thrust. It can be shown that this was the equivalent of 6,400 horsepower. But at 600 mph the efficiency of the propeller was little over 50 per cent, so a piston engine to drive the aircraft at that speed required not 6,400 horsepower, but 12,000. In 1945 the best piston engines available for fighters produced a fraction over one horsepower for each pound of their weight. Thus a piston engine developing the power to propel our notional fighter at 600 mph would have weighed about 11,000 pounds — about double the all-up weight of an early production Spitfire.

For flight at high speeds the turbojet engine or rocket motor were fundamentally more efficient forms of power plant. They produced their thrust directly, with no conversion losses. The thrust developed by the jet engines remained more-or-less constant throughout the aircraft's speed range. The BMW 003 turbojet fitted to the He 162 delivered 2,028 pounds of thrust for a weight of less than 1,400 pounds, and gave the fighter a maximum level speed of 562 mph. No piston-engine and propeller combination offered a thrust-to-weight ratio that was in any way comparable, and it was clear that their days were numbered for use in high performance aircraft.

The third prototype Me 262, the first to get airborne on jet power alone, being readied for its maiden flight at Leipheim on 18 July 1942. *(Transit Films)*

# CHAPTER 1

# The Messerschmitt 262

In the history of aviation few aircraft have been the subject of greater controversy than the Messerschmitt Me 262. Several commentators have drawn on its history to demonstrate the military ineptitude of Hitler and other German leaders who, it is said, failed to push its development with the necessary vigour or use the aircraft in the right way. Some have even gone so far as to suggest that, correctly used, the Me 262 might have changed the course of the Second World War. Such sweeping statements deserve careful analysis; and to provide that analysis we shall consider not only the technical development of the aircraft but also the military and political background to that development.

The Messerschmitt Me 262 stemmed from the firm's Project 1065, a design study to meet a 1938 requirement from the German Air Ministry, for a research aircraft powered by two of the new P 3302 gas turbine engines under development by the BMW Company. At the time the P 3302 was expected to develop a thrust of just over 1,300 pounds, and BMW confidently expected to have a pair of the new engines available for flight testing by the end of 1939. It proved to be a grossly over-optimistic prediction.

Fritz Wendel boarding the aircraft. *(Transit Films)*

The airframe design produced by Dr Woldemar Voigt and his team was for a low wing monoplane with slight sweep-back on the wing, two jet engines and with the then conventional tail wheel undercarriage. From the start the Messerschmitt team had tried to produce a design suitable for later development into an interceptor fighter, though the Luftwaffe requirement had not mentioned this. In March 1940 the company received a contract to build four examples of the new aircraft, which was now designated the Messerschmitt Me 262; three of the airframes were intended for flight testing and the fourth for static testing.

In the event BMW's timetable for its new engine proved to be wide of the mark. Not until the end of 1940, over a year late, was the first of these bench-tested; and then it was found that it delivered a thrust of only 570 pounds. In the meantime the Heinkel Company had pushed ahead with its own design for a gas turbine; on 27 August 1939, three days before the outbreak of the Second World War, one of these developing 1,100 pounds thrust had been the sole means of power for the specially-built Heinkel He 178 test aircraft.

As a result of the problems experienced by BMW with the novel form of power unit, the first Me 262 airframe was completed long before its engines. In order to test its handling characteristics, therefore, the prototype made its first flight on 18 April 1941 powered by a single nose-mounted Junkers Jumo

The third prototype taking off. *(Transit Films)*

210 piston engine developing 690 hp. Test pilot Fritz Wendel took the aircraft on its maiden flight from the Messerschmitt airfield at Augsburg.

It was not until November 1941 that the first pair of flight-cleared BMW 003 engines (as the P 3302 was now known) arrived at Augsburg for installation in the Me 262. On 25 March 1942 Fritz Wendel took off in the new aircraft on the power of the Jumo piston engine and the two jet units; it was as well that the piston engine had been retained, for shortly after the take-off the jet engines failed one after the other and Wendel was only just able to get the badly underpowered aircraft back on to the runway.

It was now clear that the BMW 003 engine still required considerably more development work. So the Me 262 was modified to take the new Junkers Jumo 004 turbojet, which by the end of 1941 had completed its ten-hour running trial and was developing 2,200 pounds of thrust. On 18 July Fritz Wendel took off for the first Me 262 flight solely on jet power. The flight was normal apart from the take-off; during the run, with the aircraft in the tail-down position, the elevators were blanketed by the wing and were ineffective; so when he reached flying speed Wendel had to touch his brakes to lift the tail off the ground, then the elevators functioned normally and he could get airborne.

Wendel discussing the flight afterwards with Professor Willi Messerschmitt. *(Transit Films)*

Although the Me 262 soon demonstrated a maximum speed of around 500 mph and a climbing performance greatly superior to any other fighter in service, initially there was little Luftwaffe interest in the aircraft. In the summer of 1942 the Focke Wulf FW 190A and the Messerschmitt Bf 109G were equal or superior to anything in service with the Royal Air Force, the USAAF or the Soviet Air Force; Germany was not yet threatened with daylight bombing attacks and the main battle fronts were deep in the Soviet Union and in North Africa. At the primitive forward airfields an entirely new aircraft like the Me 262, with its short-lifed and unproven jet engines which required careful handling and skilled maintenance, would have been of little value. The need was for ever-greater numbers of conventional fighters for the final push to victory, rather than such a temperamental novelty even if it did have a far higher performance. Nevertheless, to keep abreast of the new technology, in May 1942 the Luftwaffe placed an initial order for 15 pre-production Me 262 fighters; in the following October this was increased to thirty. The development of the new fighter was to be pushed ahead to the point where it could be placed into full production, if required.

The mood in the spring of 1943 may be gauged from part of the minutes of the production conference held in Berlin on 31 March, with *Generalfeldmarschall* Erhard Milch in the chair. The Messerschmitt Me 209, a linear development of the 109, was discussed; if the Me 262 was to be placed in large-scale production, it would have to be at the expense of the Me 209. Milch commented: 'Dinort (*Oberst* Oskar Dinort, one of Milch's staff officers) has proposed that the Me 209 should be dropped and everything concentrated on the 262. We have discussed the matter, and I consider such a move premature.' *Generalmajor* Adolf Galland, the inspector of fighters, agreed with him: 'We should not do it.' The Me 209 was to be hastened into production with all possible speed; the Me 262 could replace it in production later — if the war lasted that long.

During the weeks that followed, however, there was a considerable shift of opinion in favour of the Me 262. In May Adolf Galland visited Lechfeld and flew the fourth prototype; he was so impressed that on his return to Berlin he urged that the jet fighter be placed in production as soon as possible, and receive priority over all others. Milch accepted Galland's recommendations; the Me 209 was to be dropped from the production schedule. A few days later, on 28 May, came further pressure to push ahead with the Me 262. Engineer *Oberst* Dietrich Schwenke, head of the department responsible for assessing the latest enemy equipment, informed a meeting in Berlin that a talkative RAF prisoner had let slip that during a visit to Farnborough the previous Christmas he had seen '. . . a propellerless aircraft flying at an altitude of about 1,000 feet and in his opinion it was very fast. This is the first mention of an enemy jet fighter . . .' *Generalmajor* Wolfgang Vorwald, head of Milch's technical department, commented that such a development by the enemy was certainly possible.* It seemed to be an ominous pointer to the future; and for the present things were gradually becoming more and more difficult for the Luftwaffe, as the latest British, American and Soviet fighters proved uncomfortably equal to the best machines the Luftwaffe had in service. Now it was clear that only the Me 262 could provide the jump in performance necessary to overcome the numerical advantage likely soon to be enjoyed by the enemy fighter forces.

At a production conference held in Berlin on 29 June, attended by Willi Messerschmitt, Milch was informed of the current position regarding the planned production of the Me 262:

> Construction of the wings, and final assembly, will take place at Augsburg and construction of the fuselages and tails will take place at Regensburg. By concentrating our effort and if certain suppositions are realised, we can have delivery of the first production aircraft by January 1944. Production will then rise in the second month to 8, in the third to 21, in April to 40 and in May to 60 aircraft. By the middle of May we shall reach the requested number of 100 aircraft and production will run at 60 per month until November . . .'

This was a poor time to play politics with the equipment for the Luftwaffe, but this is what now happened. And the culprit was Willi Messerschmitt. Piqued at the rejection of his firm's Me 209, he now resolved to keep it in production *with* the Me 262 and tried to increase his pool of skilled manpower to bring this about. An inveterate empire-builder, Messerschmitt was able to pull sufficient strings with Nazi party officials to retain the Me 209 in the production schedule for several months after Galland and other senior Luftwaffe officers had said it was no longer needed. But the additional skilled workers

* The machine referred to was the Gloster E 28/39, the first British jet propelled aircraft, one example of which was flying in the winter of 1942.

necessary to tool up two aircraft production lines instead of one were not forthcoming, with resultant delays to both programmes. Not until November 1943 was the Me 209 finally dropped from production, and the Messerschmitt Company's efforts concentrated on the Me 262.

In the meantime the test programme of the Me 262 was gathering momentum. In July the fifth prototype, the first to be fitted with a tricycle undercarriage albeit a fixed one, made its first flight. It was followed in November by the sixth prototype, the first pre-production machine with a retractable tricyle undercarriage and slightly revised engine nacelles.

Up until now the Messerschmitt Me 262 had been considered solely as a bomber-destroyer. But like other fighters in production for the Luftwaffe (and, indeed, those of other air forces), it was planned that the aircraft should be able to carry bombs and be used in the secondary role of fighter-bomber. In view of the frequency with which the story of the Me 262 in the fighter-bomber role has been misrepresented, it is important to examine it now in some detail.

Aircraft 'White 10' was an early production machine belonging to *Erpobungskommando* 262.

During the great air battles fought over Germany in the summer and autumn of 1943 the defences had aquitted themselves well. The available bomber-destroyers, and in particular the heavily armed Messerschmitt 110s and 410s, had demonstrated that they could inflict swingeing losses on the unescorted US heavy bomber formations. At the time it seemed to many Luftwaffe leaders that, given an increase in the number of conventional bomber-destroyers, the threat of the daylight attacks could be erased altogether.

Meanwhile, there could be no doubting that the Western Allies were making intensive preparations for a major invasion operation to be launched the following year, somewhere in north-western Europe. Hitler saw clearly that the battle to secure the beachhead would be decisive to the course of the war: if the German forces could beat off the invasion, the Allied losses would almost certainly be so great as to preclude another attempt for one or perhaps even two years; and in the meantime powerful forces could be released for the Eastern Front. But if the defensive battle was lost and the Allied forces were able to establish themselves ashore, Germany would be squeezed between the Eastern and Western fronts like a nut in a vice. An opposed landing was bound to be fraught with tremendous difficulties and confusion during its first critical hours. How much more difficult would things be if the Luftwaffe had available a hundred or so high-speed fighter-bombers, with which to bomb and stafe the troops coming ashore. A few hours delay in establishing the beachhead might be sufficient for the German Army to move up reserves to defeat the invasion. Hitler's thoughts began to crystallize: what was needed was a ground attack aircraft with the speed to penetrate the powerful fighter defences covering any such invasion. His mind turned towards the only aircraft likely to be available for the task: the Messerschmitt Me 262.

On 2 November Goering, accompanied by Milch and Vorwald, visited the Messerschmitt works at Augsburg to discuss the production of the Me 262. After the *Reichsmarschall* and his entourage had toured the factory complex, Goering mentioned Hitler's requirement for a high-speed fighter bomber and asked whether the Me 262 could carry bombs. Messerschmitt replied: '*Herr Reichsmarschall*, from the very outset we have provided for the fitting of two bomb pylons so it can carry bombs — either one 500 kg or two 250 kgs.'* The head of the company then volunteered

* A stenographer was present at the conversation and the transcript has survived.

A pair of Me 262 fighter-bombers of *Kommando Schenk* taking off, each carrying two SC 250 bombs under the nose. This unit began operations from Juvincourt in France towards the end of July 1944, and was the first to go into action with turbo-jet propelled aircraft. *(via Dierich)*

the information that the new fighter could even carry two 1,100 lb or one 2,200 lb bomb and went on to state, in answer to a question from Goering, that in his view the task of modifying the fighter to carry bombs could be completed in a couple of weeks.

Just over three weeks later, on 26 November, the Me 262 was demonstrated before Hitler at Insterburg. Inspecting the fourth and sixth prototypes on the ground, the Führer repeated his question: could it carry bombs? Again Messerschmitt assured him in the affirmative: it could carry one 2,200 lb or two 1,100 lb bombs without difficulty. That was the answer Hitler had sought. Here was the *Blitz-bomber* he was looking for.

Following Hitler's order to prepare the Me 262 for operations as a fighter-bomber, the tenth prototype was used to test the modifications for this role. In this photograph the aircraft carries a single 250 kg (550 lb) bomb on its port rack, and a pair of solid fuel rockets under the rear fuselage to shorten the take-off run. *(via Schliephake)*

BELOW AND RIGHT:
Close-up of bomb installation on operational Me 262, carrying two SC 250 bombs.

From then on the Me 262 featured prominently in Hitler's counter-invasion plans. At a war conference on 20 December he confidently explained to senior Wehrmacht officers:

'Every month that passes makes it more and more probable that we will get at least one *Gruppe* of jet aircraft. The most important thing is that they (the enemy) get some bombs on top of them just as they try to invade. That will force them to take cover, and in this way they will waste hour after hour! But after half a day our reserves will already be on their way. So if we can pin them down on the beaches for just six or eight hours, you can see what that will mean to us . . .'

With some modifications the Me 262 could certainly have carried out the role Hitler had in mind for it. There is no evidence that at this stage any Luftwaffe officer tried to sway the Führer from his view. But significantly, Messerschmitt did not initiate work on even a prototype bomb-carrying Me 262. This divergence, between Hitler's expressed wishes and the actual course of development of the Me 262, lit the slow-burning fuse of a time-bomb that was to shake the entire project.

For his part Milch acknowledged the importance of the aircraft as a fighter-bomber but, turning a blind eye to Hitler's wishes, he endeavoured to ready the Me 262 for service as a *bomber destroyer* with the minimum of delay. Confirmation of the aircraft in this role came with the maiden flight of the eighth prototype in December 1943, the first to carry armament: it was fitted with a battery of four 30 mm Mk 108 cannon, a low velocity weapon whose explosive shells were very effective against bombers but which was not really suitable for ground attack work. Undoubtedly Milch's attitude at this time was influenced by the disturbing intelligence reports he had received on the new generation of US heavy bombers. At a conference in Berlin on 19 January he reviewed the developments to be expected in 1944: 'In this year the new B-29 and B-32 bombers will come into service. They will attack from altitudes of between 35,000 and 39,000 feet. There is no anti-aircraft gun that can reach such altitudes. The only countermeasure we have is our (future) fighter program. Our present fighters are not able to engage the enemy at such altitudes . . .' In fact the B-29 and the B-32 heavy bombers were never to be used against Germany, and in any case they were incapable of attacking from the '35,000 and 39,000 feet' altitudes predicted by Milch. But the conference minutes provide us with a rare insight into the information (albeit false) on which he was acting. Later in the conference Dr Krome, from Speer's Ministry, asked which was the more important, the V2 bombardment rocket or the Me 262. Milch snapped back 'We need the Me 262 before all else, before U-boats and tanks, because without this aircraft armament production will no longer be possible . . .'

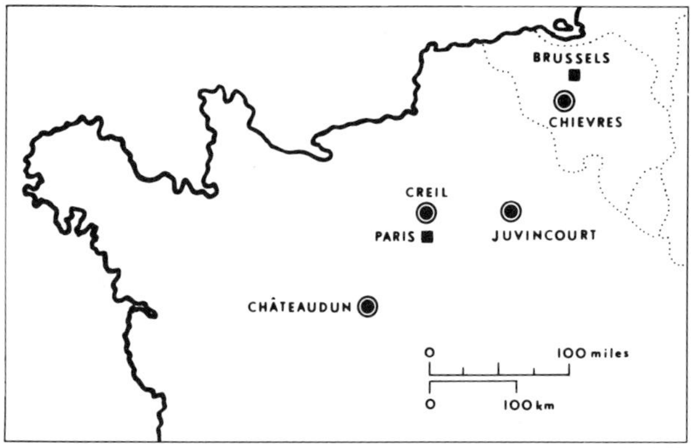

Airfields used by German jet aircraft in France and Belgium.

By the end of January the ninth prototype Me 262 had flown; an additional 23 airframes for the pre-production batch had been completed but lacked engines. Junkers were having considerable difficulty in getting the Jumo 004 into mass production. Not only was the company working very close to the limits of the current technology — the 004 was the first gas turbine in the world to go into large-scale production — but it was having to do so without the steel alloys necessary for high temperature work: chromium and nickel were in desperately short supply in Germany by 1944 and there was insufficient for the mass production of jet engines. Junkers were forced to make an engine that would work using the substitute materials that were available. For example the combustion chambers of the 004 engine were made out of

OPPOSITE:
Two stills from an instructional film on the Me 262, showing the aircraft on jacks for a retraction test of the undercarriage. This is a fighter-bomber version, with bomb racks and ports for only two 30 mm cannon. Just in front of the cockpit is the Edelweiss emblem of *Kampfgeschwader* 51. *(via Bokleman)*

ordinary steel with a spray coating of aluminium baked on in an oven. As a result failures and fires were a common occurrence with the early production engines, which initially had a running life of only about ten hours. Nearly six months were to pass before the essential solutions to the basic problems had been found and reasonably reliable 004s began to come off the production lines in large numbers. The lack of engines, more than any other factor, imposed a rigid limit to the number of Me 262s completed by the middle of 1944.

As a result of the engine shortages deliveries to the Luftwaffe did not begin until April, when the first 16 were received; during the following month there were only seven. At last sufficient Me 262s were available for the formation of a service trials unit, however, and at the end of April *Erprobungskommando* (Proving Detachment) 262 came into being at Lechfeld in Bavaria, commanded by *Hauptmann* Werner Thierfelder. Thierfelder himself, and several of the other pilots, had come from IIIrd *Gruppe* of *Zerstoerergeschwader* 26 which flew the bomber-destroyer version of the Messerschmitt Bf 110. *Oberleutnant* Guenther Wegmann, one of the first to join the trials unit, later recalled that he found the Me 262 an easy machine to fly once he had mastered the problem of throttle handling. With the early engines the throttles had to be advanced very slowly indeed, or they were liable to overheat and catch fire. Similarly, once the pilot had cut his throttles at low altitude he was committed to a landing; if he re-opened his throttles and tried to go round again the engines took so long to build up power that the aircraft was likely to hit the ground first. Otherwise Wegmann recalls having little difficulty with flying the Me 262. It must be pointed out, however, that he had had considerable experience with the twin-engined Messerschmitt Bf 110; and he had been trained in instrument flying — a factor whose significance will become clear later. Certainly less-experienced pilots from single-engined day fighter units found the high-speed short-endurance twin-jet Me 262 much more of a handful.

*Leutnant* 'Quax' Schnoerrer, another of the early pilots, recalled that the usual practice was to tow the Me 262 to the take-off point before each flight:

'With fuel for only 40 to 60 minutes flying, one could not spend 10 of them on the ground taxying. The engines were started up and the throttles advanced very slowly with the wheel brakes on. As soon as the engines reached 8,400 rpm release the brakes, and off we went. Immediately after take-off, at a height of about 10 or 20 metres, bring in the undercarriage and flaps. Once airborne, there was a wonderful feeling of effortless speed and power. But as a result navigation became something of a problem, because by the time one had sorted one's self out after the take-off the aircraft was already several kilometres from the airfield.'

Gradually the pilots of *Erprobungskommando* 262 began to amass experience with the new fighter and its temperamental engines, however, and appreciate the enormous advantages in combat of its superb performance: maximum speed 540 mph at about 20,000 feet, initial rate of climb of 20 m/second (3,935 ft per minute). Moreover, the four Mk 108 cannon could loose off about 96 pounds of high explosive shells in a three-second burst, giving the Me 262 a fire power considerably higher than any other conventionally-armed German fighter.

It seemed, too, that the Me 262 had become available in the nick of time. By the spring of 1944 the long-range American escort fighters, and in particular the Merlin-engined P-51 which had a performance superior to any German piston-engined equivalent, were escorting bomber formations penetrating deep into Germany. This placed the Luftwaffe fighter force on the horns of an uncomfortable dilemma: if its aircraft carried the heavy armament necessary to knock down the tough B-17s and B-24s, they fell as easy prey if they were caught by the American escorts; but if the German fighters were lightly armed, to enable them to engage the escorts on less unequal terms, they lacked the fire power to knock down the bombers even if they did succeed in penetrating the escorts and getting within range. The Me 262, with both the speed to evade the escorts and the fire-power to tear the bombers to pieces, seemed to provide the only answer to this problem.

In the meantime, however, the slow fuse of the time-bomb under the Me 262 project had burned almost to its end. On 23 May Goering, Milch, Galland and other senior Luftwaffe officers, as well as Albert Speer and officials from his armament ministry, were summoned to Berchtesgaden to discuss the latest fighter production programme. For an account of what happened that day the authors are indebted to David Irving*:

"Milch certainly did not suspect the storm was now almost upon him. With *Oberst* Petersen, director of the research establishments, he now joined Goering and Speer in a large unheated room at Hitler's Berghof, with a large picture window overlooking the Alps. Hitler listened absently to the details of the Fighter Staff programme, apparently gazing out over the mountains, until the planning for the Me 262 jet fighter was mentioned. Here he interrupted, 'I thought the 262 was coming as a high-speed bomber? How many of the 262s already manufactured can carry bombs?' Milch told him: 'None *mein Führer*. The Me 262 is being manufactured exclusively as a fighter aircraft.' There was an awkward silence. Milch explained that the aircraft could not carry bombs without extensive design changes, and even then no more than 1,100 lbs.

Hitler lost his composure. He now realized that with the Allied invasion in France due any week, the wonder aircraft on which he had rested a large part of his hopes of defeating it could not possibly come in time. He excitedly interrupted Milch, 'Never mind! I wanted only one 550-lb bomb.' He demanded precise statistics on the loads carried by the fighter version — its armour plate, guns and ammunition. 'Who pays the slightest attention to the orders I give?' he exclaimed. 'I gave an unqualified order, and left nobody in any doubt that the aircraft was to be equipped as a fighter-*bomber*,'"

Not only was Hitler bitterly disappointed at the loss of one of his most important anti-invasion weapons, he was extremely angry at having been deliberately misled about the ability of production Me 262s to carry bombs.

The upshot was that Hitler made Goering personally responsible for getting the Me 262 into service as a fighter-bomber as rapidly as possible, regardless of the effect this would have on the production of the fighter version. During the post-mortem on the day after the Berghof meeting

* Published in *The Rise and Fall of the Luftwaffe*: the Life of Luftwaffe Marshal Erhard Milch, Weidenfeld and Nicolson, London.

A line-up of early production Me 262s of *Erprobungskommando 262* at Lechfeld, probably photographed in July 1944. This unit carried out the trials of this aircraft in the fighter role.

Goering discussed with senior Luftwaffe officers the modifications necessary to ready the Me 262 for the fighter-bomber role. He was told it would mean removing much of the armour plate already in the aircraft, and installing extra fuel tanks under the pilot's seat and in the fear fuselage, as well as installing the bomb pylons. In themselves there were not major modifications, and they could be incorporated in newly-built aircraft relatively easily; but it would be extremely difficult to incorporate these changes to fuselages already built. Goering, who had felt the lash of Hitler's tongue for his failure to ensure the production of the aircraft as a fighter-bomber, now tried to pass on the rebuke: 'The Führer must have the strangest impression of you. From every side, including Messerschmitt, he was left in no doubt about this, right from the start. And then in my presence (at Insterburg) Messerschmitt told the Führer that his company had provided right from the start for it to be manufactured as a fighter-bomber. And now suddenly it is impossible!'

On 27 May Goering telegraphed Milch emphatically: 'The Führer has ordered that the Me 262 aircraft is to enter service exclusively as a high-speed bomber. The aircraft is not to be regarded as a fighter until further notice.' At a meeting a few days later, however, Hitler relented and agreed to allow testing of the fighter version to continue provided this did not delay the entry into service of the bomb-carrying version. And until further orders only the bomber version was to be delivered to operational units.

The first casualty in the rift over the Me 262 was Erhard Milch himself. Hitler had no further confidence in the man whom he blamed for misleading him, and in the weeks that followed Milch was progressively stripped of his various offices; in retrospect it is remarkable that the Führer did no more than that.

Yet whatever Hitler, Milch, Goering or Messerschmitt had or had not done up until now, the fact remains that the basic factor limiting the production of the Me 262 as a fighter or fighter-bomber was the mass production of the Jumo 004 jet engine. And this had yet to begin. Thus when Allied troops punched their way ashore in Normandy on 6 June, just ten days after the stormy conference at Berchtesgaden, less than thirty Me 262s had been delivered to the Luftwaffe and neither the aircraft nor its pilots were ready for action. The golden opportunity for the *Blitzbomber* to influence events, if indeed it was capable of doing so, had passed.

In the meantime, work was belatedly begun to convert the Me 262 into a fighter-bomber. The tenth prototype was modified to carry pylons for two 550-pound bombs under the nose. As well as most of the protective armour plating around the pilot, the main fighter-bomber version lost two of its four cannon; strangely, however, the unsuitable 30 mm MK 108 low-velocity cannon was retained as its gun armament. To extend the radius of action, 132 Imp gallons of fuel were to be carried in an extra tank fitted in the rear fuselage; but this weighed about as much as the two 550 lb bombs slung under the nose, and the rear tank was well to the rear of the aircraft's centre of gravity. It was imperative, therefore, that this fuel be burnt as early as possible during the combat mission; otherwise, if the bombs were released while the tank was full, the aircraft immediately became dangerously tail-heavy. There were other problems: because of its clean airframe the Me 262 built-up speed very rapidly in dive, so it was unsuitable for steep-diving attacks; and because the pilot was unable to see immediately below and ahead of the aircraft to aim his bombs, horizontal attacks from medium or high altitude were likely to be grossly inaccurate. But the Me 262 could be effective at low altitude for horizontal or shallow dive attacks.

For all of its limitations, the Me 262 now fulfilled Hitler's requirement for a high speed counter-invasion fighter-bomber. Its use for this task was to be a temporary expedient, until the more effective Arado Ar 234 bomber became available. This position was confirmed during Hitler's conference on 25 June, after which Albert Speer noted:

'The Führer states again, during a meeting with the *Reichsmarschall* (Goering) his unalterable demand for the immediate production of jet bombers. Until the 234 can be secured in production, series production of the 262 is to be pressed with all speed and it must be made available for this purpose . . .'

By this time the first Me 262 fighter-bomber unit, *Erprobungskommando Schenk*, had formed at Lechfeld under the bomber ace *Major* Wolfgang Schenk. Nominally the unit was part of *Kampfgeschwader* 51, from which many of its pilots had come. The hasty conversion on to the new type took almost exactly one month and, on 20 July, the unit moved to Châteaudun near Orleans in France with nine aircraft and pilots in readiness to mount the world's first jet bomber operations.

This continued concentration on the Me 262 as a fighter-bomber, so long after the Allied beachhead in Normandy had been established, might seem to run counter to Hitler's stated aim of using this aircraft against an invasion during its initial stages. But it should be remembered that at this time many German leaders still thought the Normandy landings to be only a feint, to draw German forces away from the Pas de Calais area where the main invasion would take place. And at this time the Allies were mounting a large-scale spoof operation to strengthen the Germans in this impression. If a second invasion operation did take place, *Erprobungskommando Schenk* was to be ready to meet it.

Schenk's fighter-bombers now began spasmodic operations against Allied ground forces but, as a security measure to conserve aircraft to counter the expected main invasion, pilots had strict orders not to attack from altitudes below about 13,000 feet. Since the Me 262 pilots had no means of aiming their bombs from such an altitude accuracy was poor, and the attacks achieved little. When, in mid-August, the German retreat out of France gathered momentum the detachment, now redesignated 1st *Gruppe* of *Kampfgeschwader* 51, was ordered to pull back to Creil near Paris on 15 August; then to Juvincourt near Rheims on the 22nd, and finally to Chievres in Belgium on 28 August.

It was only on the final day of the withdrawal that Allied fighters made contact with one of the elusive high-speed fighter-bombers. Late in the afternoon of the 28th Major Joseph Myers was leading a flight of P-47s of the 78th Fighter Group, providing top-cover for other aircraft of the Group attacking ground targets. Then, as he later reported:

'While stooging around west of Brussels at 11,000 feet, I caught sight of what appeared to be a B-26, flying at about 500 feet and heading in a southerly direction and going very fast. I immediately started down to investigate and although diving at 45 degrees at 450 IAS (720 kph, indicated airspeed), I was no more than holding my own in regard to the unidentified aircraft. When approximately 5,000 feet above and very nearly directly over the aircraft, I could see that it was not a B-26, although it had the general overall plan of the B-26. It was painted slate blue in colour, with a long rounded nose, but I did not see any guns this time, because at this point he started evasive action, which consisted of small changes of direction not exceeding 90 degrees of turn. The radius of turn was very great and, although I was diving at around 450 IAS, I had very little difficulty cutting him off and causing him to again change direction. He made no effort to climb or turn more than 90 degrees at any time. I closed to within 2,000 feet above him and directly astern and had full power on in a 45 degree dive in an effort to close. At this distance I could readily see the similarity between the aircraft and the recognition plates of the Me 262. With full power on and the advantage of altitude I gradually started closing on the enemy aircraft and drew up to within 500 yards astern and was about to open fire when the enemy aircraft cut his throttle and crash landed in a ploughed field. He hit the ground just as I fired, so I continued firing until within 100 yards of him, observing many strikes around the cockpit and jet units. It skipped over several fields and came to rest and caught fire. The pilot hopped out and started to run.'

The German pilot, *Oberfeldwebel* 'Ronny' Lauer of I/KG 51, was able to scramble to safety.

So ended the first phase of the Me 262 fighter-bomber operations. The exaggerated efforts by the Luftwaffe to keep secret the new aircraft had been successful beyond any possible expectation: there is not a single mention in Allied wartime combat reports or intelligence documents of Me 262 fighter-bombers taking any part in the Battle of France. No doubt the ineffectiveness of their bombing attacks contributed to this comforting ignorance.

Meanwhile, deep in Bavaria, *Erprobungskommando* 262 had begun operational trials using the Me 262 as a fighter; the targets were the lone Allied reconnaissance aircraft venturing close to the unit's base at Lechfeld. It was during one of the early missions that the commander, *Hauptmann* Werner Thierfelder, lost his life on 18 July under circumstances that are far from clear. German records state that his aircraft was 'shot down' in combat and crashed near Landsberg with the pilot still on board. But a careful search through British and American records reveals no engagement that links with this loss (and Allied long-range reconnaissance aircraft were, in any case, unarmed). A possible cause of the crash is that Thierfelder lost control of his aircraft when he tried to follow a reconnaissance aircraft diving away to escape him.

At full throttle in a shallow dive of about 20 degrees from 26,000 feet, an Me 262 could be well beyond its compressibility threshold of Mach .83 before it had descended through about 7,000 feet. Any increase in speed thereafter resulted in a greatly increased nose-down trim change, requiring considerable backwards pressure on the control column to prevent the dive from steepening uncontrollably; cutting the throttles had no appreciable effect, for the clean-lined jet fighter continued to gather speed in the dive. 'Quax' Schnoerrer recalled an incident during which he had tried to follow down a reconnaissance aircraft and got into such trouble: 'I pulled back on the stick with all my strength, but the 262 refused to come out of its dive. It was extremely frightening. Finally, in desperation, I jettisoned my canopy; this caused a change of trim, and the aircraft came out of the dive by itself. I landed without my canopy and with the skinning of the wings rippled; the 262 was a write-off.' During the Me 262's combat career, several German pilots had similarly narrow escapes. Others, less fortunate, dived into the ground seemingly for no reason. The slender available evidence suggests that Werner Thierfelder, the world's first jet fighter unit leader, might have fallen to this cause.

There was little time to mourn the fallen commander. Soon after Thierfelder's death his successor arrived at Lechfeld: *Major* Walter Nowotny, an extremely popular young fighter pilot credited with 255 victories on the Eastern Front. The task of gaining operational experience with the new fighter continued.

The first report of an interception by an Me 262 followed one week after Thierfelder's death, on 25 July. Flight Lieutenant A. Wall, RAF, flying a reconnaissance Mosquito of No 544 Squadron, had just carried out a photographic run over Munich at about 30,000 feet when the jet fighter was first sighted some 400 yards astern. Wall opened his throttles wide and pushed down the nose of the Mosquito to build up his speed, curving steeply to port as he did so. During the next 15 minutes the Me 262 carried out three firing runs on the reconnaissance aircraft. Wall found that even when he used maximum boost the jet fighter easily overhauled him. But he found little difficulty in out-turning his assailant; at one stage, after three

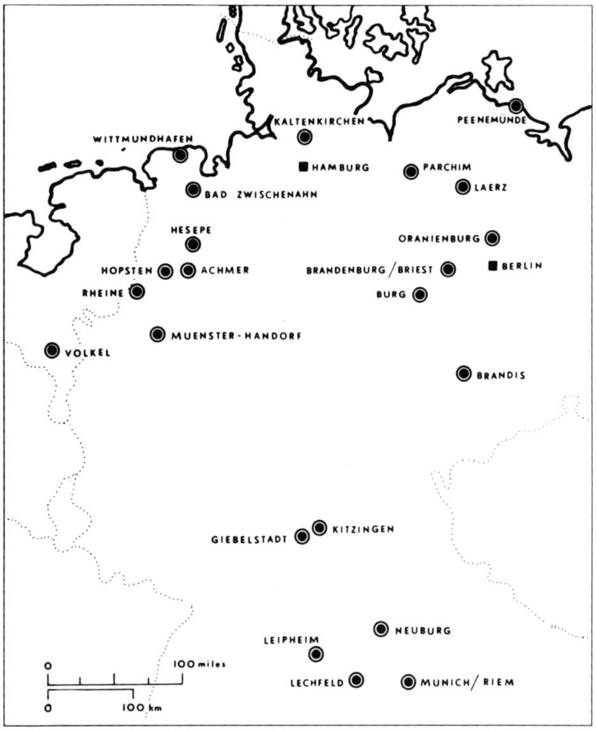


Main airfields used by jet aircraft in Germany and Holland.

complete turns, Wall found himself on the tail of the Me 262 and could have attacked had his aircraft been armed. Towards the end of the action the Mosquito crew heard two dull thuds and the navigator attempted to open the emergency exit in preparation for baling out, should this prove necessary. With great difficulty he opened the inner hatch, to find that the outer door had disappeared, having broken off near the hinges. In the meantime, however, Wall was able to escape into cloud. The Mosquito landed at Fermo near Ancona in Italy, where the crew found that it had suffered no cannon strikes; but the tip of the port tailplane was damaged, having almost certainly been struck by the outer door as it broke away. This accounted for the two dull thuds the men had heard. Although the Mosquito had escaped, the action was a clear warning to the high-flying Allied reconnaissance crews, that their long run of near-invulnerability over Germany was coming to an end.

During the following month, August, Nowotny's pilots claimed five kills: a Mosquito by *Leutnant* Weber on the 8th, a lone B-17 by *Feldwebel*

Lennartz on the 16th, a Lightning by *Oberfeldwebel* Baudach on the 24th, and on the 26th a Spitfire to *Leutnant* Schreiber and a Mosquito to *Oberfeldwebel* Recker.

During July there had been heavy air attacks on the factories producing components for the Me 262, against Leipheim on the 19th and against Regensburg on the 21st. As a result of the shortages of airframe components, and the long-running shortage of engines, the number of Me 262s delivered to the Luftwaffe slumped from 59 in July to only 20 in August.

From a document produced by the Messerschmitt Company, we know that by 10 August 1944 a total of ten prototype Me 262s and 112 production aircraft had been built. Of the former, the 1st, 2nd, 4th, 5th, 6th and 7th prototypes had either been written off or otherwise discarded from the test programme. Twenty-one Me 262s had been destroyed during Allied air raids on the factories; eleven others had been wrecked in accidents or in action. The remaining 84 aircraft were now disposed as follows:

| | |
|---|---|
| I.*Gruppe* of *Kampfgeschwader* 51 (fighter-bombers) | 33 |
| *Erprobungskommando* 262 (fighters) | 15 |
| Rechlin Test Centre | 14 |
| Retained at Messerschmitt for flight trials | 11 |
| Retained at Junkers for engine trials | 1 |
| At Blohm und Voss for conversion to two-seaters | 10 |

The Rheinmetall Borsig Mk 108 (right) carried by the Me 262, with one of its 30 mm rounds. This weapon fired 330 gr (11 oz) high explosive or incendiary rounds at a rate of 660 per minute. This cannon was extremely effective against light metal structures such as aircraft as shown by the photo below the effect of a single hit on a Spitfire during a ground firing trial. The low muzzle velocity of only 540 m (1750 ft) per second rendered the weapon unsuitable for strafing ground targets, however.

Messerschmitt 262s of *Kommando Nowotny*, photographed in the autumn of 1944. Almost certainly these pictures were taken at Lechfeld in Bavaria where the unit was working up for operations; to have lined up aircraft like this at any of the airfields in western Germany at this time would have invited their immediate destruction by Allied fighter-bombers. The half-track *Kettenkrad* vehicle was widely used by the Luftwaffe for towing aircraft. *(via Bokleman)*

With the stabilisation of the battle front in the West early in September, 1st *Gruppe* of *Kampfgeschwader* 51 was able to mount pin-prick attacks against Allied positions from its bases at Rheine and Hopsten just inside Germany. Typical of these was the attack on the forward airfield at Grave, home of No 421 (RCAF) Squadron with Spitfires, on 2 October:

'The attack on the airfield began at 11.00 hours with the dropping of anti-personnel bombs by a jet-propelled aircraft flying at 3,000 ft. In this raid three pilots were injured and one officer and six airmen suffered wounds of minor degree. Several tents were holed and the kit of several officers and airmen badly riddled. Slit trenches were dug and tin hats became fashionable. At noon the second attack came and it was wide of the mark. The third attack resulted in a number of deaths among personnel of the RAF Wing on the other side of the airfield and some Dutch civilians living in the vicinity suffered serious injuries.*

Three days later other Canadian pilots, flying Spitfire IXs of No 401 Squadron, had their revenge. The action was typical of the sort of free-for-all chase that would become common when German jet aircraft were engaged during the months that followed. Sqn Ldr Roy Smith, leading the patrol, afterwards reported:

'I was leading 401 Squadron at 13,000 ft in the Nijmegen area about 5 miles NE of the bridge. We were flying on a NE course when I sighted an Me 262 coming head on 500 ft below. He went into a port climbing turn and I turned starboard after him with several other Spitfires chasing him. He then dived down towards the bridge twisting and turning and half rolling at very high speeds. He flew across Nijmegen turning from side to side. I saw a Spitfire get some strikes on him and he streamed white smoke from the starboard wing root. He flew on at very high speed still and I managed to get behind him and fire two 3 second bursts at 200 to 300 yds approx. He zoomed very high and I saw strikes on him in the port and starboard nacelles . . .'

Flight Lieutenant Hedley Everard was one of the others attacking at the same time:

'. . . I half rolled after it and it started a slow spiral going straight down. I first opened fire from 900 yds and followed it chasing it all the time. At 5,000 ft he began to level out heading south. Throttling back, not to overshoot, I opened fire with machine-guns only from 150 yds. A streamer of white smoke came from it and it accelerated rapidly drawing away . . .'

Flying Officer John MacKay followed Everard in:

'. . . I got on the tail of the Me 262 following it down to the ground, firing whenever I could get my sight on the aircraft. Saw strikes on the after part of the fuselage and the port or starboard wing root. The aircraft was extremely manoeuvrable. The pilot was hot and put the aircraft through everything in the book . . .'

* Official History: *The RCAF Overseas, The Sixth Year.*

The 'Split-S' manoeuvre, employed by fighters wishing to pickup speed rapidly to engage an enemy below. It was frequently used by P-51 pilots trying to catch German aircraft.

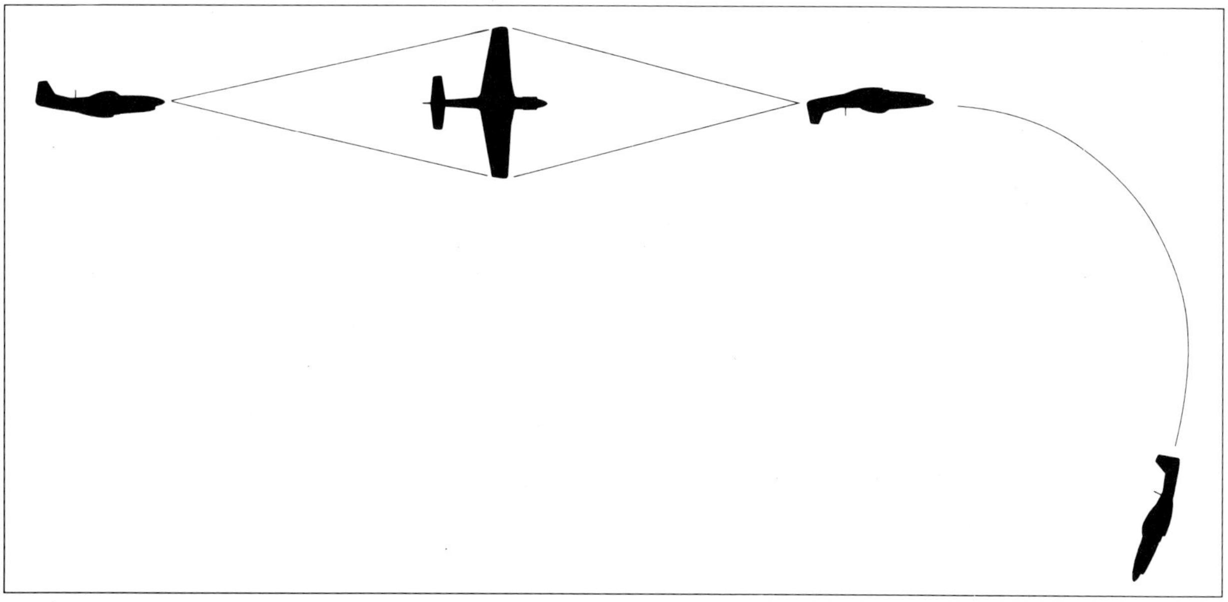

Flying Officer Gus Sinclair was able to score hits also, before he was crowded out by two other Spitfires diving from above. Then Flight Lieutenant Tex Davenport administered the *coup de grâce*:

'. . . I finally closed in to 300 yds astern and emptied the remainder of my guns approx. 10 or 12 seconds into the kite, observing strikes all in engines and fuselage. The aircraft was burning all this time. The pilot seemed to be unhurt and put up a good fight all during this, at the last realising the fight was up he attempted to ram Red 1 (Smith) on the way to the ground where he crashed and burned . . .'

The German pilot, *Hauptmann* Hans-Christoph Buttmann of I./KG 51, had indeed aquitted himself well before he was killed in the crash; and in doing so he demonstrated the measure of air superiority necessary to contain the Me 262 menace.

Although the Allied piston-engined fighters could not compete with the Me 262 in terms of maximum horizontal speed and climb, there were often so many about that some were able to attack from above, converting a height advantage into a speed which matched that of the jets. A further advantage enjoyed by the Allied fighter pilots, was the newly-introduced gyroscopic gunsight, which automatically calculated how far ahead the fighter pilot needed to aim his rounds on a turning or crossing opponent. Designated the Gyro Gunsight Mark II in the Royal Air Force, and the K-14 in the USAAF, the new sight enabled pilots to score hits on high speed crossing targets and greatly increased the overall effectiveness of air-to-air gunnery. The gunsight was used by most of the Canadian pilots during the action on 5 October, and would make a major contribution in many of the successful combats against German jet aircraft during the remainder of the war.

A report circulated round Allied anti-aircraft units in October stated that, of the meagre enemy air activity observed over forward positions in Holland, most was put up by Me 262 fighter-bombers:

'When employed for bombing the aircraft normally makes its run-up in a glide and has, so far during the day, bombed quite indiscriminately mostly with anti-personnel bombs, which though causing some casualties have done little material damage. Normal speed appears to be between 300 and 350 mph and maximum speed of about 500 mph has not normally been used until bombs have been dropped. It has not so far been reported that the aircraft has used its cannon against (ground) targets and if, as is at present believed, the armament is four 30 mm low velocity air-to-air cannon, it is unlikely that it will do so . . .'

On 13 October there was a lucky escape for one of the pilots of I./KG 51. *Unteroffizier* Edmund Delatowski had an inconclusive brush near Volkel with a Royal Air Force Tempest flown by Pilot Officer Robert Cole of No 3 Squadron. Cole ran into the Messerschmitt's slipstream and had to break away, then turned after the jet far in front of him. With the throttle wide open and his aircraft descending in a shallow dive Cole reached 480 mph, but even at this speed the Me 262 was pulling away from him slightly. The chase continued eastwards over Holland for about 40 miles then, feeling he had shaken off the pursuit, Delatowski slowed his Messerschmitt a little. This was the chance Cole had been waiting for and he closed in to firing range and loosed off a couple of short bursts with his cannon:

'The Messerschmitt appeared to explode like a flying bomb and threw off a number of pieces, including the pilot in a parachute. It went down in a shallow spin and exploded on the ground where the remains burnt out.'

Delatowski parachuted to earth near Deventer, with only minor injuries to the head and left arm.

With the end of the Battle of France, and with it the rescinding of Hitler's insistence that the Me 262 should be used operationally only as a fighter-bomber, the way was at last open for the type to go into action with a front-line fighter unit. By September the problems of mass-producing the Jumo 004 turbo-jet had at last been solved, with the result that during the month a total of 91 Me 262s were delivered to the Luftwaffe.

*Kommando Nowotny* (as *Erprobungskommando* 262 had been re-designed) began to expand to *Gruppe* strength, and by 30 September it possessed 23 Me 262s. Four days later the unit began moving to forward airfields at Achmer and Hesepe, near Osnabrück in western Germany. The primary target for the jet fighters was to be the American escort fighters covering the bomber attacks; if the former could be forced to jettison their underwing tanks, they could be prevented from covering the bombers on their deep penetration attacks. The bombers could then be engaged more effectively by the German piston-engined fighters. From the start, however, Nowotny had serious problems. Not only did the new fighters still have teething troubles, particularly with the still unreliable jet engines, but the Allies soon learnt the location of the bases operating the jets and began mounting standing patrols over them. Concealment of the airfields being used by the jet aircraft was impossible: the standard Luftwaffe airfields had asphalt runways, and the asphalt was liable to catch fire when jet aircraft operated off them. So the bases for the jets had to have concrete runways, and this made them readily evident on the photographs brought back by the omniscient Allied reconnaissance aircraft. Once their bases were known it did not take long to establish the 'Achilles heel' of the jet fighters: their vulnerability to attack from conventional fighters when they were flying slowly immediately after take-off or during their approach for landing.

On 7 October *Kommando Nowotny* put up several Me 262s for the first time, to contest a multi-pronged American assault against Poelitz, Ruhland, Magdeburg, Kassel and Zwickau. First Lieutenant Urban Drew, flying a P-51 of the 361st Fighter Group, was escorting one of the B-17 formations passing almost over Achmer when he spotted two Me 262s taxying out to take-off:

First Lieutenant Urban Drew who, flying a P-51 of the US 361st Fighter Group, destroyed two Me 262s of *Kommando Nowotny* on 7 October shortly after they had taken-off from Achmer. *(USAF via Hess)*

*Major* Walter Nowotny, the commander of the first Me 262 fighter unit to be declared fully operational, was killed in action on 8 November under circumstances that are far from clear. Probably he was shot down in error by the flak defences at Achmer. *(Schnoerrer)*

'The lead ship was in take-off position on the east-west runway and the taxying ship got into position for a formation take-off. I waited until they both were airborne and then I rolled over from 15,000 ft and headed for the attack with my Flight behind me. I caught up with the second Me 262 when he was about 1,000 ft off the ground; I was indicating 450 mph and the jet aircraft could not have been going over 200 mph. I started firing from about 400 yds, 30 degrees deflection. As I closed on him, I observed hits all over the wings and fuselage. Just as I passed him I saw a sheet of flame come out near the right wing root. As I glanced back I saw a gigantic explosion and a sheet of red-orange flame shot out over an area of about 1,000 ft. The other jet aircraft was about 500 yds ahead of me and had started a fast climbing turn to the left. I was still indicating about 400 mph and I had to haul back on the stick to stay with him. I started shooting from about 60 degrees deflection, 300 yds, and my bullets were just hitting the tail section of the enemy aircraft. I kept horsing back on the stick and my bullets crept up the fuselage to the cockpit. Just then I saw the canopy go flying off in two sections and the plane rolled over and went into a flat spin. He hit the ground on his back at about a 60 degree angle.'

One of the German pilots, *Leutnant* Gerhard Kobert, was killed in the action. The other *Oberleutnant* Paul Bley, managed to bale out and escaped without injury.

In the meantime other Me 262s of *Kommando Nowotny* were climbing to engage the bomber formations and Nowotny himself, *Oberfaehnrich* Heinz Russel and *Feldwebel* Heinz Lennartz each claimed a B-24. After his victory, however, Russel was engaged by a pair of P-47s of the 479th Fighter Group flown by Colonel Hubert Zemke and Lieutenant Norman Benolt and shot down; the German pilot baled out and landed without injury.

Thus, during its first real action, *Kommando Nowotny* had lost three Me 262s shot down and one pilot killed, for a claim of three American bombers. It was hardly an impressive ratio, but it was one that would become common as the German jet fighters were sent into action against a foe greatly superior numerically.

Between the beginning of October and the end of the first week in November 1944 *Kommando Nowotny* claimed to have shot down four American heavy bombers (all B-24s), twelve fighters (P-47s and P-51s) and three reconnaissance aircraft. During the same period the unit lost six Me 262s in combat and seven destroyed; nine others were damaged in accidents.

On 4 October *Oberleutnant* Alfred Teumer was killed attempting to land his Me 262 with one engine flamed out; and on the 28th *Oberleutnant* Paul Bley suffered fatal injuries when, shortly after take-off, he ran into a flock of birds and both engines flamed out. Two other Me 262s were wrecked during attempted single-engine landings; three were wrecked and one damaged in other take-off landing accidents; one was wrecked and four damaged following emergency landings after running short of fuel; two were damaged following a partial or total failure of the undercarriage to extend; and one suffered damage but no records appear to exist of the cause. On 29 October *Leutnant* Alfred Schreiber collided with the Spitfire reconnaissance aircraft he was intercepting; both aircraft were destroyed, but Schreiber was able to bale out.

*Oberfeldwebel* Willi Banzaff was lucky to escape with his life during the action on 1 November. As American heavy bombers were withdrawing after attacking Gelsenkirchen and Ruedesheim, he carried out a lone attack on P-51s of the 20th Fighter Group and shot down one of them. Banzaff continued towards the B-17s bent on engaging them also. But by that time the P-51s of 20th FG were diving after him in vengeful pursuit, as were others of the 352nd FG and P-47s of the 56th FG. Suddenly the sky seemed alive with American fighters scrambling to get into a firing position on the lone jet fighter. Banzaff descended rapidly to 10,000 ft then turned away at high speed towards the north, trying to outrun his pursuers. In turning, however, he gave some of the diving American fighters the chance to cut him off. The P-47s and P-51s opened fire at long range and hits were scored on the fuselage and left wing. Lieutenant Walter Groce of the 56th FG called over the radio 'Spread out and we'll get him if he turns!' Shortly afterwards Banzaff did turn, giving Groce the chance he had been waiting for. He made the most of it. Then, in the terse wording of the 56th FG report: 'After repeated hits the jet started to smoke; pilot jettisoned canopy and baled out, 8,000 ft. Two unidentified P-51s in vicinity shot at pilot on chute.' Credit for shooting down the Me 262 was shared between Groce and Lieutenant William Gerbe of the 352nd FG. In spite of the unchivalrous conduct of two of his foes, Banzaff reached the ground safely.

Three days later, on 4 November, Banzaff was in action again but this time his luck ran out. German records state that he was shot down and killed in action with enemy fighters, but a careful check through Allied records reveals no claim that links with this.

The initial complement of pilots of *Erprobungskommando* 262 had comprised experienced pilots, many of them from twin-engined fighter units, who had had a full training in instrument flying. In *Kommando Nowotny*, however, some of the pilots had come from single-engined fighter units and lacked proper training in instrument flying (the normal training programme for German single-engined fighter pilots included only a rudimentary training for this). For these men the Me 262, with its high speed, short endurance and compressibility problems if too rapid a descent was made, was not an easy machine to handle. Add to this the almost continual harassment from Allied fighters patrolling near the bases, and the fine judgement

TOP:
Me 262 fighter-bomber of KG 51 being towed out at Rheine, late in 1944. *(Goetz)*

LEFT:
Single-seat Me 262 fitted with *Neptun* radar and nose-mounted aerials, tested in action by *Oberleutnant* Kurt Welter at the end of 1944. *(via Creek)*

BELOW:
An Me 262 with collapsed nose gear at Lechfeld. This photo is of particular interest because it is one of the very few to show an aircraft in German markings with the nose bulge for the vertically mounted camera; almost certainly the aircraft belonged to *Kommando Brauegg*.

necessary for landing the aircraft because of the poor throttle response of the engines, and one can see that there were several traps awaiting the less-experienced pilot. The result was that, in spite of the high hopes entertained for the Me 262 as a fighter, its first month of operations in this role had been disappointing. Tangible success remained tantalisingly beyond the grasp of Nowotny's *Kommando*.

Then, on 8 November, disaster struck the jet fighter unit. It had sent up several Me 262s to engage a large force of American bombers returning after an attack on the Mitteland Canal, and these scored some kills: *Leutnant* Franz Schall claimed the destruction of three P-51s and *Oberleutnant* Guenther Wegmann claimed one more. But shortly after Schall's last kill Lieutenant James Kenney of the 357th Fighter Group was able to get into a firing position and he hit the Messerschmitt with an accurate burst which jammed both throttles. Schall was forced to bale out. Shortly afterwards, Nowotny himself was in trouble. Lieutenant Edward Haydon, also of the 357th was returning from a strafing attack near Hanover when he caught sight of an Me 262 descending south of Dummer Lake:

> 'I gave chase drawing maximum power, and as I was beginning to close on the 262 I was slowly over-taken by ships of the 20th Fighter Group. At this time the 262 led us across an airfield south of Dummer Lake which immediately let go with all of its flak at us. The Me 262 pulled up and rolled over on its back, crashing about 100 feet in front of me, at which time I was about 50 feet high. The pilot was not seen to bale out.'

The 'airfield south of Dummer Lake' was almost certainly Achmer. The leading P-51 of the 20th FG was that flown by Captain Ernest Fiebelkorn. Nowotny's final radio call stated *'Ich bin getroffen'* — 'I've been hit', but it is not clear whether this meant the aircraft, or Nowotny himself, had been hit. Shortly afterwards Nowotny's Me 262 dived into the ground about four miles north of Achmer; the position links with that mentioned in Haydon's report. During the action *Kommando Nowotny* lost two Me 262s — Schall's and Nowotny's — and no other Me 262 unit reported losing a pilot during the day. There is clear evidence, therefore, that the Me 262 pursued by Haydon and Fiebelkorn had been Nowotny's. But the question remains: who fired the fatal burst? Neither of the American pilots had managed to get into position to open fire on the jet fighter, and no other Allied pilot reported a combat that can be linked with it. The meagre evidence available suggests that the German fighter ace was shot down in error by the Achmer flak defences.

Two-seat Me 262 fitted with *Neptun* radar and employed in the night fighter role.

*Generalmajor* Adolf Galland had actually been at Achmer on 8 November, visiting Nowotny to assess the effectiveness of his *Kommando*. The General saw enough to realise that Nowotny had been given an almost impossible task: to bring into service a completely new fighter with several novel features, using pilots in many cases without a proper conversion training, and all of that from airfields close to the front line in an area in which the enemy enjoyed massive numerical superiority. Adolf Galland's reaction was characteristically decisive: he ordered the unit to return to Lechfeld in Bavaria, to re-form and undergo further training.

*Kommando Nowotny's* new commander was *Major* Erich Hohagen and, on 24 November, it was re-designated IIIrd *Gruppe* of *Jagdgeschwader* 7. Initially the new *Geschwader* took the honorary title 'Hindenburg', from the recently disbanded bomber unit *Kampfgeschwader* 1; but soon afterwards it was renamed *Jagdgeschwader Nowotny* after its fallen leader.

Once back in the relative safety of Bavaria, III./JG 7 was able to devote itself to the essential task of improving the level of training of the less experienced pilots. And there were the regular overflights by Allied reconnaissance aircraft, on which the German pilots could practice their skills. Typical of these actions was that on 26 November, when *Major* Rudolf Sinner took off to intercept a reconnaissance P-38 escorted by three P-38 fighters engaged in a high altitude photographic mission over Munich. The reconnaissance pilot, Lieutenant Renne, had just completed his run over the target when he spotted Sinner's Me 262 closing on him rapidly. Renne immediately called in his escorting fighters, released his drop tanks, opened his throttles wide and turned into his assailant to give the most difficult deflection shot. The two aircraft passed each other almost head-on without Sinner being able to open fire, then Renne wheeled his Lightning round in a tight turn to the right in an endeavour to meet the next attack head-on also. By now, however, the escorting P-38s were closing in on Sinner who was forced to break away sharply. In doing so the German pilot pushed down the nose of his Me 262 too steeply and then, to his horror, found himself going down out of control: in his haste to escape he had gone over the aircraft's compressibility threshold. After several hair-raising seconds wrestling with his control column, Sinner finally succeeded in extricating the Me 262 from its dive by the use of his tailplane trim control. The German pilot glanced back at his foes and caught sight of them high above and far to the north of him, leaving long condensation trials as they regained formation and headed southwards for their bases in Italy. Bravely, in view of his own recent narrow escape, Sinner resolved to go after them. He pushed open his throttles and this time the rapidly climbing jet fighter was able to move unseen into a firing position behind one of the escorting P-38s. 'The burst from my four 3 cm cannon scored hits on the tail and the right wing. It rolled over on its back and went down burning, in a turn to the left,' Sinner later recalled. 'I pulled up and turned left for home, heading for Lechfeld now short of fuel.' The American pilot, Lieutenant Julius Thomas, baled out and landed near Kitzbuehl where he was taken prisoner.

Following the difficulties experienced by *Kommando Nowotny*, as a result of the over-hasty conversion of pilots on to the Me 262, towards the end of November a formalised training programme was introduced. IIIrd *Gruppe* of *Ergaenzungs Jagdgeschwader* 2 was re-formed at Lechfeld as an operational conversion unit for new Me 262 pilots under the fighter ace *Oberstleutnant* Heinz Baer. The conversion began with 20 hours flying on conventional fighters with their throttles fixed, to accustom the pilots to the problem of flying an aircraft whose throttles could not be adjusted in flight at high altitide (if this was attempted in the Me 262 the engines were liable to flame-out). All the pilots then received three days' theoretical instruction in the operation and handling of the jet engines. Next, those pilots without experience of twin-engined aircraft were sent on a short course at Landsberg; there they received five hours flying in the Messerschmitt Bf 110 and the Siebel Si 204, concentrating on the problems of asymmetric flight. There was a further day's theoretical instruction on the Me 262, after which the embryo jet pilots received some ten hours flying and gunnery training on the Me 262. The men were then pronounced fit for combat, and were sent to the operational units. It was only a cursory training, especially as some of the pilots came straight from advanced pilot training having never flown on an operational unit. But it was certainly better than what had gone before and, given the desperate position in which Germany now found herself, the best that was possible.

One further problem that now exercised the Luftwaffe High Command was that of providing for the Me 262 fighter units pilots with an adequate training in instrument flying. The American heavy bombers, equipped with radar, were able to navigate to and attack targets even though the route from their bases was blanketed by cloud. This meant that on many occasions the German fighters would have to be able to climb and descend through cloud, if they were to provide an effective defence. As we have observed, the normal training for German single-engined fighter pilots had not included a full instruction in instrument flying (though some pilots later received it). Yet a rapid descent through cloud in the Me 262 was an operation fraught with difficulties for pilots without such training, with the fearful phenomenon of compressibility always waiting to

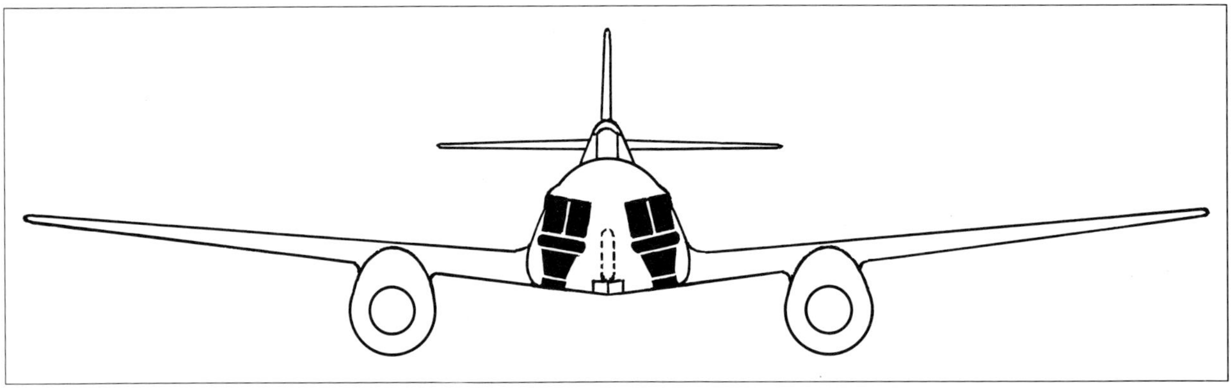

Layout of cameras in the nose of the reconnaissance version of the Me 262, positioned on either side of the retracted nose wheel.

snatch at the unwary. Obviously, given sufficient time, the newer pilots could have received the necessary additional training in instrument flying. But time was short and so was fuel.

By the end of 1944 there was, however, a large pool of instrument-trained pilots available to the Luftwaffe: those who had belonged to the bomber units, most of which had had to be disbanded in the previous summer due to the shortage of fuel. The idea now arose that many of these men could be used to fly the Me 262 in action, *as a fighter*. It was felt that the ex-bomber pilots, with considerable experience of both instrument flying and multi-engined aircraft, would be better able to handle the Me 262 on cloudy days than those from the German single-engined fighter units lacking instrument training. That the ex-bomber pilots had not been trained or given experience in aerial combat in the fighter role was accepted as a drawback but not an overriding one: these Me 262s were intended not to dog-fight with the enemy fighters, but to go straight in and knock down the enemy four-engined bombers. The idea of using the ex-bomber pilots in this way was supported by *Oberst* Gordon Gollob, *Oberst* Dietrich Peltz and, more importantly, by *General* Karl Koller who was the Chief of the Luftwaffe General Staff and also by Goering. It was bitterly opposed by *Generalmajor* Adolf Galland and several of the fighter leaders, who felt that turning over the Me 262s to pilots untrained in fighter operations was a major blunder. Several later accounts have linked this controversy with Hitler's earlier order that the Me 262 should be used only as a fighter-bomber; the two issues were, however, entirely separate. The authors have examined the evidence regarding the operation of the Me 262 by ex-bomber pilots carefully and believe that there are cogent arguments on both sides.

In the death throes of the Third Reich, with enemy forces now massing in the east, the west and the south for the final push into Germany itself, the question of which pilots were to operate the Me 262 sparked off a major clash within the operational High Command of the Luftwaffe. The upshot was that, as a result of this and other disagreements with Goering, *Generalmajor* Galland was dismissed his post as Inspector of Fighters. And the re-equipping of some of the ex-bomber units with the Me 262 went ahead: the first such unit, *Kampfgeschwader (Jaeger)* 54, began its conversion at Giebelstadt at the end of November. Three further ex-bomber units, *Kampfgeschwader* 6, 27 and 55, were scheduled to receive the jet fighter early in 1945.

During the final three months of 1944 a total of 342 Me 262s were built, which meant that sufficient were now available for other roles. In November *Kommando Welter* was formed, a night fighter unit based at Burg near Magdeburg under the command of *Oberleutnant* Kurt Welter. Initially the unit had only two Me 262s, both single-seaters, one of which was fitted with the pilot-operated FuG 218 *Neptun* radar. The primary targets for these first jet night-fighters were the fast high-flying Mosquito bombers of the Royal Air Force, which until now had been able to attack their targets with little risk of interception. Also at this time *Kommando Brauegg* was formed, a short-range reconnaissance unit under the command of *Hauptmann* Brauegg. For this role the Me 262 was

The *Deichselschlepp* (pole-tow) airborne trailer, tested with the tenth prototype Me 262, as a method of increasing the bomb load this aircraft could carry. The wing was taken from a V1 flying bomb. The towing bar was about 6 m (19 ft) long and the swivel fitted to the tail of the Me 262 allowed both horizontal and vertical movement of the trailer in flight. Electrically fired explosive bolts were fitted to enable the pilot to jettison the trailer. During the flight trials carrying a 1,000 kg (2,200 lb) bomb in this manner considerable difficulties were experienced with 'porpoising' of the trailer and the movement being transmitted to the aircraft via the towing bar. During one such trial flight test pilot Gerd Lindner lost control of his Me 262 and had to bale out. During another trial a turn by the towing aircraft imposed excessive loads on the towing swivel, which tore away from the rear fuselage. On yet another trial the explosive bolts failed to function, but Lindner skilfully landed the Me 262 with the trailer and bomb still attached. In the end the trials were abandoned, the method being described as 'hazardous and unsatisfactory'. *(via Schliephake)*

fitted with a re-designed nose section, with the guns removed and two Rb 50/30 aerial cameras mounted to look downwards and outwards. To accommodate the tops of the cameras and their film magazines, two large tear-drop fairings were fitted just ahead of the cockpit of this version; in addition a window was cut in the floor of the cockpit to enable the pilot to sight his cameras on ground features vertically underneath the aircraft.

At the close of 1944, however, the great majority of Me 262 sorties were still being flown by the fighter-bombers of *Kampfgeschwader* 51. The 1st *Gruppe* flew from Rheine and Hopsten while the IInd *Gruppe*, which had recently commenced operations after re-equipping with the Me 262, flew from Hesepe. On 16 December the German army opened its last major offensive of the war, in the Ardennes area, and the Me 262s were frequently committed against Allied troop concentrations and supply centres. As a counter to these operations, the Allied fighter forces mounted numerous standing patrols over the battle area. There is little evidence that the fleeting hit-and-run attacks by the jet fighter-bombers caused significant damage. Probably their greatest effect was that by pinning down the enemy fighters in this way *Kampfgeschwader* 51 prevented them from bombing and strafing German troops. During the grim closing months of the war, it was the nearest thing to air support the battered German army could expect.

On New Year's Day 1945 the Luftwaffe gambled almost the whole of its fighter force in the west in a massive all-out attack by nearly a thousand aircraft on Allied airfields in France, Holland and Belgium. Taking part in the attack were some twenty Me 262s of KG 51, assigned to attack the airfields at Eindhoven and Heesch in Holland. The Eindhoven attack made in concert with Messerschmitt Bf 109s and FW 190s of *Jagdgeschwader* 3, proved to be the most successful of the entire operation and caused destruction or damage to more than fifty Spitfires and Typhoons of the three Wings based on the airfield. In contrast the attack on Heesch, made in concert with *Jagdgeschwader* 6, achieved little. At least two Me 262s were lost during the action, one of which fell to ground fire near Heesch.

During the first weeks of 1945 *Kampfgeschwader* 51 mounted attacks against Allied positions whenever the weather allowed, in conjunction with the Arado Ar 234s of *Kampfgeschwader* 76. On 10 January there were 22 jet bomber sorties against Strasbourg; on the 23rd there were thirty more against the same target.

Two Me 262s were modified as high altitude horizontal bombers, with the guns removed and a specially constructed wooden and perspex nose cone to house a bomb-aimer lying on his stomach and a Lofte tachometric bombsight. The aircraft carried the same bomb load, two SC 250 bombs, as the normal fighter-bomber version. The trials with the type appear not to have been successful, however, and no further aircraft were modified in this way. *(via Heise)*

The horizontal bomber version being towed by a refuelling vehicle. *(via Creek)*

By the beginning of 1945 a total of 564 Me 262s had been accepted by the Luftwaffe and production was running at about 36 per week. Yet the Luftwaffe Quartermaster-General's records for 10 January listed only about 61 of these aircraft in service with operational units, distributed as follows:

| | |
|---|---|
| I. and II./KG 51 (fighter-bombers) | 52 |
| 10./NJG 11 (night-fighters)approx. | 4 |
| *Kommando Brauegg* (short-range recce) | 5 |

Probably three times as many more were distributed amongst the units working-up to go into action or training pilots: the three *Gruppen* of *Jagdgeschwader* 7, KG (J) 54, the conversion unit III./Erg. JG 2, and the various test centres. By then an estimated 150 Me 262s had been destroyed in the air or on the ground by enemy action, or in accidents. Taken together, this accounts for some 400 Me 262s and the figures are, if anything, on the high side. By that date, however, the Luftwaffe had accepted some 600 Me 262s from the makers and it is interesting to speculate on the whereabouts of the remaining 200 aircraft, one third of the total. Without doubt a large number of the remainder were tied up in the German rail system: surprisingly, until very late in the war, the majority of Me 262s were dismantled after their acceptance test flights and sent to the operational units *by rail*; from now until the end of the war a large proportion of the Allied bomber attacks were aimed at systematically dismantling the German rail network, with the result that many Me 262s simply got lost in transit.

It is interesting to note that on 10 January the Quartermaster-General's list recorded no Me 262 *day fighters* in service with operational units; this was *four months* after Hitler had released the Me 262 for service in this role. At this time III./JG 7 was at full strength but still working-up, with one *Staffel* each at Brandenburg-Briest, Oranienburg and Parchim, all in the Berlin area. I./JG 7 under *Major* Desdorffer was forming at Kaltenkirchen near Hamburg, as was II./JG 7 under *Major* Erich Rudorffer at Briest. At the same time, further south, I./KG (J) 54 was hastily converting on to the Me 262 at Giebelstadt near Wuerzburg.

The first of the Me 262 units declared ready for the new phase of jet fighter operations was I./KG (J) 54, which put up about ten machines on 9 February to counter a multi-pronged American attack on targets at Magdeburg, Weimar, Lutzkendorf, Bielefeld, Paderborn, Arnsberg and Dulmen involving more than 1,500 heavy bombers. The result was an utter defeat for the German unit, whose ex-bomber pilots had been sent into action with only the sketchiest training and without ever having had any gunnery practice in the Me 262. P-51 Mustangs of the 78th, 357th and 359th Fighter Groups claimed five Me 262s destroyed during the action, for one B-17 damaged. In fact I./KG (J) 54 lost six Me 262s on that day, only one of which can be linked with certainty to an American combat report. Lieutenant John Carter of the 357th FG later reported that, as he was on a bomber escort mission in the vicinity of Fulda at about 24,000 feet his squadron encountered the jet fighters:

'Cement Blue Flight leader dropped his tanks immediately and made an attack on the four Me 262s that were low and to our left. The Me 262s split, two going to the right and two to the left. Cement Blue leader took one of the Me 262s that went to the right and I took the other. I followed the jet that I was after for about ten or fifteen minutes. I got in some good bursts at him but he was out of range and gaining distance on me all the time. I was still after this jet when I spotted another Me 262 about 12,000 to 15,000 feet below me and he appeared to be in a glide. I gave up the one that I was chasing at the time, rolled over and split-essed on the one below me. I gained on him very rapidly and gave him several bursts. I was out of range, but saw a few strikes. I was still closing on him when the pilot baled out.'

Variously captioned in the past, this photograph depicts Me 262s of *Kampfgeschwader (Jaeger)* 54 at Giebelstadt early in 1945. Almost certainly the aircraft on the left had started life as a fighter-bomber version; hence the unusual camouflage scheme and only one gun port on each side of the nose, though the bomb racks have been removed. *(Baetcher)*

This claim links with the loss of the Me 262 piloted by *Major* Ottfried Sehrt, the commander of I./KG (J) 54, who baled out north of Frankfurt with a bullet through his shin; the wound was not serious, however, and less than a week later he was back with his unit. The commander of the *Geschwader*, *Oberstleutnant* Baron Volprecht von Riedesel, was less fortunate: he was still on board his Me 262 when it plunged into the ground near Limburg, following his action with the raiding force.

Just over two weeks later there was another bad day for KG (J) 54, this time for the newly-formed IInd *Gruppe*. On the morning of the 25th, as four of the unit's Me 262s were getting airborne for a training flight, they were spotted by Mustangs of the 55th Fighter Group. Captain Don Penn, leading a fighter sweep through the area, afterwards reported seeing the jets taking off from Giebelstadt:

'We were flying at 13,000 feet, and I ordered the Squadron to drop tanks and engage the enemy aircraft. I dived on one jet, using 50 inches of mercury and 3,000 rpm. He was making a slight turn to port at 1,000 feet heading back towards the drome, so I levelled off about 3,000 yards behind him and put on full power. My indicated airspeed was then about 500 mph and I expected him to use full power also and attempt to pull away from me. However I closed rapidly, firing from 1,000 yards. At 500 yards I observed the 262 to have its wheels down. I cut down on my power and at 300 yards started striking the enemy aircraft in the right power unit. Closing to 50 yards, I broke sharply over the top of the jet, watching him as he rolled over and went straight in and exploded.'

Other pilots in Penn's squadron also engaged the slow-flying jets, shooting down two others. *Leutnants* Hans Knobel and Josef Lackner, and *Feldwebel* Heinz Klausner, were killed during the brief encounter. Altogether KG (J) 54 lost 12 Me 262s on that day, six in air combat, two as a result of technical failures and four on the ground during a strafing attack.

Von Riedesel's replacement as commander of KG (J) 54 was *Major* Hans-Georg Baetcher, a distinguished bomber pilot who had previously flown Arado Ar 234 jet bombers with KG 76. When Baetcher took over the *Geschwader* its three *Gruppen* had between them about twenty Me 262s based at Giebelstadt, Kitzingen and Neuburg. 'KG (J) 54 had been declared ready for operations prematurely,' Baetcher recalled. 'The first thing I did was to order further training. The main problem was to get the ex-bomber pilots used to the much greater speed — the 262 cruised two or three times faster than the Ju 88s or He 111s the pilots had flown previously. Also we had only single-seat Me 262s, no two-seaters. On the other hand the pilots on the unit all had quite a lot of flying experience and so were able to cope with problems that might have been too much for a less

BELOW AND OPPOSITE:
R4M 55 mm high explosive rockets, mounted in twelves on wooden racks under the wings of the Me 262. The rockets had approximately the same trajectory as the rounds from the Mk 108 cannon, so both weapons could be aimed using the normal Revi sight without adjustment. The tail of the R4M had eight fins which extended after launch. *(via Schliephake)*

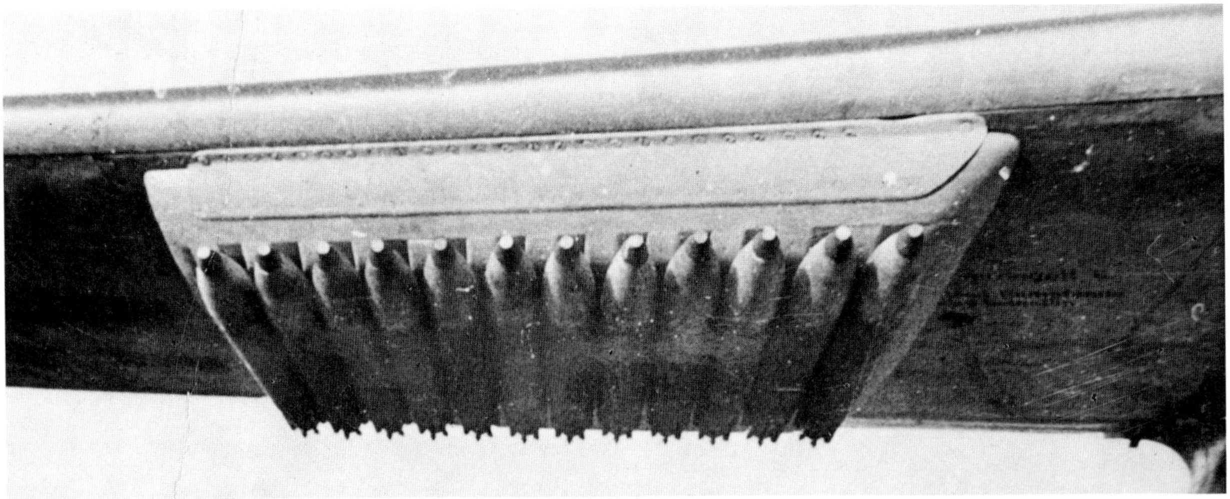

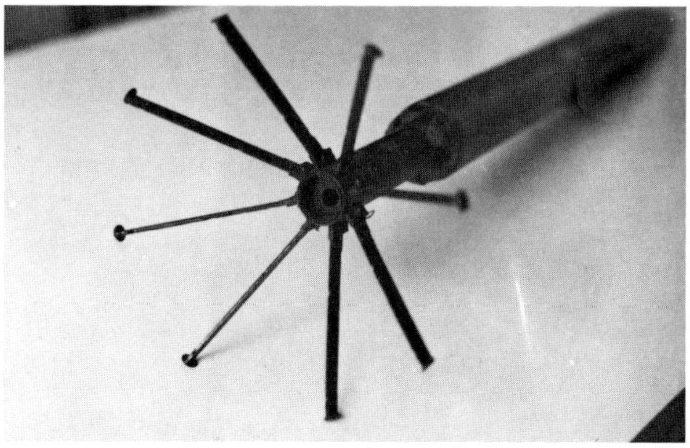

experienced man.' In spite of the difficulties experienced by the ex-bomber pilots during their early combats, Baetcher still feels that in the circumstances the decision to employ men with blind-flying training to operate the Me 262 was correct, especially during the winter when cloud prevented the other jet fighter units from operating. 'The biggest error,' he felt, 'was that the German fighter pilots had not been trained in blind flying in the first place.'

It was not until the third week in February that III./JG 7 was considered ready for action again; but now, having had time to bring its pilots up to a higher standard of training, the unit was considerably more proficient in combat. On 21 February Mustangs of the 479th Fighter Group were patrolling the Berlin area when they encountered an estimated fifteen Me 262s which behaved quite differently from those previously encountered:

'Bounce was directed at Red Flight, as squadron was making a shallow turn to the left from an easterly direction. Bounce came from 3 o'clock position at our level by four Me 262s flying the usual American combat formation, looking like P-51s with drop tanks. Our Red Flight broke into jets but they crossed in front of our flight up and away. A second flight of four Me 262s flying in American combat formation then made a bounce from the rear, 6 o'clock high. Our flight turned into this second Me 262 flight and the Me 262s broke climbing up and away. At this time the first flight of Me 262s came back on us again from above and to the rear. We broke into this flight and this kept up for three or four breaks, neither ourselves nor Jerry being able to get set or close in for a shot. Each time we would break they would climb straight ahead outdistancing us. Within the Jerry flight the number 4 man, while turning, would fall behind and slightly above, so that it was necessary to take on this number 4 man or he would slice in on our tail if our Flight would take on the rest of the Jerry flight.'

The American pilots noted that the German pilots '. . . were aggressive and experienced. They were not caught in a turn, and if they were caught in such a position would roll out and climb up and away. It was impossible to catch or climb with them.' It seemed that the German pilots' aim, during the inconclusive combat, was to force the Mustangs to drop their external fuel tanks so that they would have to leave the area; in this they were unsuccessful, however, for the American pilots were able to ward off the repeated attacks with the tanks still on their wings. The report illustrated well the sort of inconclusive action likely to result when well-handled jets confronted well-handled Mustangs; the Me 262 was no real threat to the latter. But there was no doubt that the jet fighter posed a considerable threat to the American bombers, for with its high speed it could pierce the screens of escorting Mustangs with relative ease.

During February the most successful German jet fighter pilot was *Leutnant* Rudolf Rademacher of III./JG 7. After shooting down a Spitfire reconnaissance aircraft near Brunswick on the 1st, he was credited with a B-17 on the 4th, two more on the 8th and one on the 14th, a P-51 on the 16th, a further B-17 on the 23rd and a B-24 on the 25th, making his score for the month eight kills.

Near the end of February a new and potentially very effective Me 262 fighter unit was formed under the command of *Generalmajor* Adolf Galland, following his recent removal from the post of Inspector of Fighters: *Jagdverband* 44. The official order for its formation, dated 24 February, stated:

'JV44 is established at Brandenburg-Briest with immediate effect. Ground personnel are to be drawn from 16./JG 54, Factory Protection Unit 1 and III./Erg JG 2. The commander of this unit receives the disciplinary powers of a Divisional Commander as laid down in Luftwaffe Order 3/9.17. It is subordinated to Luftflotte Reich and comes under *Luftgaukommando* III (Berlin). Operational *Verband* 'Galland' is to have a provisional strength of 16 operational Me 262s and 15 pilots.

signed *Generalleutnant* Karl Koller
Chief of the General Staff of the Luftwaffe.'

Behind this terse order was the establishment of one of the most remarkable fighter units ever formed. That it should have been commanded by a general was only one of its unique features; for now, with the German conventional fighter units able to operate only rarely due to the shortage of fuel, Galland was able to draw to JV 44 several of the most experienced and successful fighter pilots in the Luftwaffe. As he later commented, 'The *Ritterkreuz* was, so to speak, the badge of our unit.' In addition to Galland himself with this covetted decoration, there were *Oberst* Johannes Steinhoff, *Oberst* Guenther Luetzow, *Oberstleutnant* Heinz Baer, *Majors* Gerhard Barkhorn, Erich Hohagen, Karl-Heinz Schnell and Willi Herget, *Hauptmann* Walter Krupinski, *Oberleutnant* Hans Gruenberg, and *Leutnants* Klaus Neumann and Heinz Sachsenberg. But even a unit with this level of expertise took time to set up in the final chaos of the Third Reich, and not until the end of March would it be ready for action.

Meanwhile, during February, *Kampfgeschwader* 51 continued to put up more operational sorties with its fighter-bombers than all the other Me 262 units put together. One of the strongest reactions was on 14 February, when more than 55 jet bombers took part in attacks against British forces advancing near Kleve. Three of the Me 262s were caught and shot down by prowling fighters of the 2nd Tactical Air Force, two of them on the way to their target by Typhoons of No 439 Squadron RCAF; when it still had its bombs on board, the Me 262 was slowed sufficiently for it to be caught by conventional fighters. Flight Lieutenant L. Shaver later reported:

'I was leading a section of four aircraft of 439 Squadron on an armed recce of the Coesfeld-Enschede area. While flying west at 7,000 feet at approximately 20 miles from Coesfeld, I observed two Me 262s line abreast flying west at 3,000 feet. I informed the other pilots and dived to attack. I came in line astern slightly below the enemy aircraft and opened fire with a short 2-second burst at 100 yards. No strikes were observed. I raised my sights slightly, closed to 50 yards and again opened fire with a 2-second burst. The enemy aircraft exploded in mid-air. I flew through the blast of the exploded aircraft and saw the other Me 262 break off to port. I fired two 2-second bursts from the quarter position but did not observe any strikes. I then saw Red 3 (F/O Fraser) attacking from above and to the rear of the second enemy aircraft. Both the enemy aircraft and Red 3 disappeared below cloud, I observed a plume of black smoke bulging above cloud.'

Fraser followed his victim below cloud, and saw it crash into the ground. The two German pilots, *Oberleutnant* Hans-Georg Richter and *Feldwebel* Werner Witzmann, both of II./KG 51, were killed.

Early in March the Me 262 fighter units made their first determined attempt to engage the American bomber formations. On the 3rd there were 29 Me 262 sorties, mainly from III./JG 7, put up against the heavy USAAF attacks on Magdeburg, Brunswick, Hannover, Chemnitz and other targets; twenty of the German pilots reported making contact with the enemy and they claimed the destruction of six bombers and two fighters. *Hauptmann* Heinz Gutmann of III./JG 7 was shot down and killed during the action. The USAAF records list only three bombers and six fighters lost on that day, and there was no claim of a Me 262 destroyed.

Following this great exertion the Me 262 fighter units saw little action for more than two weeks. Then, on the 18th, 37 jet fighters were launched against the heavy attack on Berlin by 1,221 bombers escorted by 632 fighters. During this action the new R4M air-to-air rocket was used for the first time; twelve of these 55 mm impact-fused missiles were carried on a wooden rack under each wing of the Me 262, making 24 rockets in all, in addition to the four 30 mm cannon. *Oberleutnant* Guenther Wegmann of III./JG 7 led six Me 262s carrying R4M against one of the American formations, and the German pilots loosed off their rockets against the B-17s from a range of 1,000 yards.

The victims were the 100th Bomb Group (the Bloody Hundredth), whose B-17s had become badly strung out. Two of the heavy bombers went down right away and a third suffered serious damage. During a subsequent firing pass a third B-17 had its entire tail blown off, and the bomber damaged in the first attack was finished off. Then the jet fighters had to break away to avoid the escorting P-51s, streaking in to protect their charges.

Guenther Wegmann was on his way back to Parchim when he sighted a further formation of B-17s and, after manoeuvring into position, went in to attack with his guns. He opened up at the bomber on the right of the formation and saw hits on the starboard wing. Then accurate return fire from the bombers began to strike home and his Me 262 shuddered under the impact of several hits. He felt a severe blow against his right leg and at the same time his laminated glass windscreen starred under the impact of one of the enemy rounds and his instrument panel was wrecked by another. Wegmann accelerated away from the bombers and their escorts and took stock of his situation. He felt down at his leg and found, to his horror, that one of the .5 in rounds had passed clean through it leaving a hole large enough for him to push in his hand; strangely however, he felt no pain. His first inclination was to try to get his crippled fighter back to Parchim, though with many of his instruments shot away he had to fly the aircraft 'by the seat of his pants' and control the engines by ear. Then, as he descended past about 13,000 feet, a tongue of flame came streaming back from his right engine. Now there could be no question of reaching his base at Parchim: he had to bale out before the fire reached his fuel tanks. Wegmann jettisoned his canopy, undid the seat harness, pulled off his helmet and throat microphone and then rammed the control column forwards. The centrifugal forces lifted him out of the cockpit like a cork out of a champagne bottle. The injured pilot came down near Wittenberge, where one of the first to reach him was a Red-Cross sister who improvised a tourniquet to stop the arterial bleeding. Her move saved Wegmann's life, but there was nothing anyone could do to save his leg; a couple of hours later it was removed in the nearby hospital.

During the action on 18 March 28 German jet fighter pilots reported making contact with the enemy, and claimed the destruction of 12 bombers and one fighter (all except two of the bombers were claimed by JG 7); in fact, probably only eight of the heavy bombers fell to the Me 262s. As well as Wegmann's aircraft, one other Me 262 of III./JG 7 was lost during the action: *Oberleutnant* Karl-Heinz Seeler was seen approaching one of the bomber formations, but then disappeared without trace. Further west, the 1st *Gruppe* based at Kaltenkirchen near Hamburg also lost two Me 262s, in a collision during the scramble take-off which cost the lives of the fighter ace *Oberleutnant* Hans Waldmann and *Oberfaehnrich* Guenther Schrey.

On the following day, the 19th, the Me 262 fighter units put up 45 sorties; of these 28 made contact with the enemy and claimed six bombers shot down for the loss of two Me 262s and their pilots. On the 20th there were 29 jet fighter missions, of which 24 made contact and nine heavy bombers were claimed for the loss of four Me 262s.

On 21 March the Me 262 units put up 31 sorties against a force of more than a thousand American heavy bombers attacking the airfields at Handorf, Hesepe, Vorden, Zwischenahn, Marx, Wittmundhafen, Ahlhorn, Achmer, Hopsten, Rheine and Essen/Muelheim, most of which were used by the German jets. Twenty-five of the Me 262 pilots reported making contact with the enemy; one was *Leutnant* Fritz Mueller of III./JG 7, who afterwards wrote:

'I took off with my *Rotte* on 21-3-45 against the major enemy incursion in the area Leipzig-Dresden. On this day our radio traffic was especially heavily jammed by the enemy. At 7,500 m, while south of Dresden, I came upon a B-17 flying east at the same altitude as the main bomber force but about 10 km to one side and about 4 km behind it, with four Mustangs above it flying escort. It seemed to me that this machine was on some sort of special mission, and I resolved to attack it. The enemy radio jamming was so powerful that communication was impossible. I flew close underneath the four Mustangs, which were now following my *Rotte* trailing black smoke (which meant they were flying at full throttle); but a glance at my airspeed indicator showed that I would not have to worry about them. The Boeing was now ahead of me in a left hand turn, so that I was flying about 10 degrees to the left and about 5 degrees above it. At about 1,000 m the rear gunner opened up a harassing fire. Then it was all over in seconds. At a range of about 300 m my wing man and I opened up with our cannon and gave it short bursts allowing slight lead. We saw a dozen rounds exploding against the fuselage and between the engines. Then we were already past him. Curving round in a wide circle (with the Mustangs behind us, still training smoke but getting smaller the whole time) we observed the end of the bomber. It spun down through about 2,000 m, with several large bits falling from the fuselage and wings, then exploded. At that moment the radio jamming ceased.'

Whatever the mission of the lone B-17 on that day, it was almost certainly not radio jamming. The sole 8th Air Force unit engaged in that activity was the 36th Bombardment Squadron, which operated B-24s; it put up three aircraft to jam German fighter communications on that day and all returned safely. The most probable explanation of the sudden ending of the radio interference is that the jamming transmitters carried by the 36th B.S. had to be switched off when other American aircraft in the vicinity were using their radar for bombing, lest the transmissions interfered with the blind bombing equipment.

From an examination of the records it seems that five heavy bombers were shot down by Me 262s during this action, compared with a German claim of 13. USAAF fighters claimed the destruction of nine Me 262s, but JG 7 lost only two pilots on that day and I./KG (J) 54 lost one more. The only American combat report that can be linked with specific German losses on that day was from Lieutenant Harry Chapman of the 361st Fighter Group in P-51D, who was able to make good use of his K-14 gunsight:

'While flying Yorkshire Blue 3 on March 21st approximately 0955 in the vicinity of Dresden, Germany, escorting B-17s 20,000 feet, my box of bombers was attacked by a flight of four Me 262s. After hitting the bombers, they continued their pass into my flight. We broke into them and my flight leader confirmed their identity. The number 4 man of the enemy flight kept turning into us until he was making a head-on pass at me. With a K-14 sight set at 2,400 feet, I put the pip on his canopy and fired a 1 to 1½ second burst from 10 to 20 degrees deflection. I observed strikes on the nose part of the enemy aircraft and the left side from leading edge of the wing forward burst into flames. He passed to the left of me and was seen by other members of my squadron to be smoking and spiraling down. One member of Yorkshire Yellow flight saw him hit the ground and explode.'

The victim was almost certainly one of the two Me 262s of III./JG 7 which crashed in the Dresden area at about this time; the pilots, *Leutnant* Joachim Weber and *Unteroffizier* Kurt Kolbe, were both killed.

By this stage of the war the Luftwaffe had its own equivalent to the Allied K-14 and gyro gunsights: the EZ 42 sight produced by the Askania company. In service, however, the computing mechanism of the EZ 42 proved so unreliable that if it was fitted in the Me 262 the sight graticule was usually fixed so that it functioned in the same way as the old *Revi* sight.

Of the changes to the Me 262 fighter since its introduction into service almost a year earlier, the most important was the fitting of improved Jumo 004 B-series engines; these now had a slightly longer life (nominally 25 hours running time, though they often failed before this), and could tolerate slightly less careful throttle handling without bursting into flames. Another modification which proved popular with Me 262 pilots was a new control column with a hinged extension, which allowed greater leverage during flight at high speeds (there were, of course, no powered flying controls at this time).

After the action on 21 March there were further pitched battles between Me 262s and American formations daily until the 25th; then followed a lull of four days, before the next great exertion. On 30 March the Luftwaffe put up 31 jet fighters against the heavy attacks by the 8th Air Force against Hamburg, Bremen and Wilhelmshaven. One of the German pilots in action that day was *Leutnant* 'Quax' Schnoerrer of III./JG 7 who, with his wing man *Oberfaehnrich* Viktor Petermann, made contact with a formation of B-17s near Hamburg. Both pilots attacked the bombers and scored hits, but Schnoerrer's Me 262 was hit by return fire from the enemy gunners and had to break away with his port engine flamed out. He curved away in a descending turn to the south-east, looking for a suitable airfield on which to land his crippled aircraft. It was then, however, that a section of four Mustangs spotted him and came bearing down to attack. Unable to fight or to flee, Schnoerrer rolled his Me 262 on to its back, jettisoned the hood, released his seat straps and fell from the cockpit; but as the tail came past he suffered a severe blow against his right leg. The German pilot's parachute opened normally, but his landing was painful in the extreme: in hitting the tail his leg had been badly fractured. Picked up by civilians, he was driven to the nearby hospital at Uelzen.

Always the German jet fighters were vulnerable when they were taking off or landing. On the same day Captain Robert Sargent of the 339th Fighter Group was leading a pair of P-51s escorting the bombers running in to attack Hamburg when:

'I saw two enemy aircraft taking off from Kaltenkirchen airfield. I called them in and we split-essed down on them. Unfortunately due to their camouflage we lost them for a second and when we got down to their level I was able to pick up just one of them. From here on it was easy. My air speed was 430 mph and I estimated his as being about 230 mph. As we closed I gave him a long burst and noticed strikes immediately, the left unit began to pour white smoke and large pieces of the canopy came off. The pilot baled out. We were at 300 feet at this time and the plane dove into the ground and exploded causing a large oil-like fire which went out almost at once. The pilot's chute did not open fully and the last I saw of him was on the ground near the plane with the chute streaming out behind him. Lt Kunz did a splendid job of covering my tail and after the encounter we pulled up and looked for the second jet. But when we sighted him he was going balls out for central Germany and we couldn't overtake him.'

The pilot of the Me 262 Sargent had shot down, *Leutnant* Erich Schulte of I./JG 7, was killed.

The B-17s and B-24s of the US 8th Air Force were the main victims of the attacks by Me 262s, but they were not the only ones. During the closing months of the war Royal Air Force Bomber Command had been mounting powerful daylight attacks on targets in Germany. On 31 March 460 Lancasters and Halifaxes of Nos 1, 6 and 8 Groups set out to attack the U-boat assembly yards at Hamburg. It had been intended that the bombers should pick up their escorts — twelve squadrons of Royal Air Force Mustangs — over Holland. In the event, however, the third wave of bombers drawn from No 6 (Canadian) Group was late at the rendezvous point and missed the escorts. Over the target the Mustangs warded off several attempts by Me 262s to attack the first two waves of bombers. But there was no such protection for the third wave and during the sharp encounter that followed 19 Halifaxes and four Lancasters fell in rapid succession. Following the action the German pilots, who belonged to III./JG 7, claimed to have shot down ten Lancasters. The bombers' gunners claimed to have destroyed four of the jet fighters and probably destroyed three more, but in fact none of the Me 262s were lost during this part of the action. The very speed of the jet fighter attacks was something entirely new to most of the RAF bomber crews and the official report on the action afterwards stated:

'The usual technique of the jet-propelled fighters appears to be an approach from astern or the fine quarters, possibly with a preference for slightly above, opening fire at 800-900 yards and closing rapidly to close range. In a few cases, however, fire was not opened until 300-400 yards. Combat reports stated that the closing speed of these fighters is so great that they frequently do not have time to fire more than one burst. More than one rear gunner reports that although he had opened fire at 900-1,000 yards he had only time to fire 200 rounds before the fighter broke away 3-4 seconds later at 30-50 yards, and one stated he was unable to rotate his turret fast enough to obtain strikes on the fighter at this close range though he had opened fire at it at 900 yards . . .'

Almost certainly the reference to the jet fighters 'opening fire at 800-900 yards' related to the R4M rocket attacks, which were made from such ranges. The RAF heavy bomber crews, who flew in vics of threes in loose gaggle rather than the serried formations of the American counterparts, went into their famous 'corkscrew' evasive manoeuvre when they came under fighter attack. This countermeasure, which was something quite new to the Me 262 pilots, probably prevented the bomber losses from being considerably higher.

During a series of defensive operations against RAF and US heavy bombers on 31 March, JG 7 flew a total of 38 sorties with Me 262s and lost four aircraft. Allied records confirm that the jet fighters probably shot down 14 heavy bombers and 2 fighters, making this the most successful day ever for the Me 262.

By the end of March 1945 the Me 262 had also started to establish a reputation as a potent counter to the previously immune Mosquito bombers of the RAF attacking targets in the Berlin area at night. Soon after its formation, *Kommando Welter* was re-designated the 10th *Staffel* of *Nachjagdgeschwader* 11. Initially the unit had operated from Burg near Magdeburg; but when Allied bombing had made this airfield unusable, operations continued from a nearby stretch of straight *Autobahn*. By 24 January Welter's personal score using the Me 262 by night stood at two four-engined bombers and two Mosquitoes, thus confirming the usefulness of the jet fighter for night operations. By the end of January the first Me

An Me 262 just off the assembly line at one of the heavily camouflaged plants situated in woods in the vicinity of Augsburg. During the early months of 1945 large numbers of these jet fighters were accepted by the Luftwaffe, but only a small proportion of them went into action with front-line units. *(Selinger)*

An Me 262 carrying the 'Running Fox' emblem of JG 7 and, unusually for this aircraft, a pair of launching tubes for 210 mm rockets on the bomb racks under the nose. None of the pilots of JG 7 interviews recall having seen such an installation and it is believed it was a one-off modification which saw little use. *(Girbig)*

262B two-seat trainers had arrived at Staaken near Berlin for conversion for the specialised night fighter role. These aircraft carried FuG 218 *Neptun* radar, with the indicator and control units in the operator's position in the rear seat; the fixed radar aerials on the nose cut about 60 kph (about 38 mph) off the maximum speed of the Me 262, but it still had an ample speed margin even over the Mosquito. The first two-seat night fighter began operations in February, but the conversion of these proceeded only slowly and in fact the majority of the Me 262 night operations were flown by single-seaters without radar, their pilots depending on the assistance of searchlights to find their targets. Most, if not all, of the thirteen Mosquitoes lost at night in the Berlin area during the first three months of 1945 probably fell to Welter's Me 262s. Welter himself had been credited in some accounts with the destruction of 20 enemy aircraft while flying the Me 262 by night, but this figure is probably on the high side. Certainly other German pilots were also successful in this role. One was *Feldwebel* Karl-Heinz Becker who claimed the destruction of five Mosquitoes at night between 21 and 30 March; in each case these claims link with British losses. Becker's kills were made flying a single-seat Me 262, with no airborne radar.

April 1945 was to see the climax of the actions between the Me 262s and the American raiding forces, for by now as well as JG 7 and KG (J) 54, Adolf Galland's elite *Jagdverband* 44 had started operations from Munich/Riem. The first major action of the month was on the 4th, when just under a thousand heavy bombers struck at the airfields at Parchim, Perleberg, Wesendorf, Fassberg, Hoya, Dedelsdorf and Eggebeck, as well as the U-boat assembly yards at Kiel. By now the American fighter pilots had perfected the art of catching the German jet fighters in the act of taking off and climbing away from their bases, and as the bombers approached, Mustangs moved into position over the enemy airfields.

*Major* Rudolf Sinner of III./JG 7 was climbing away from Parchim through a hole in the cloud to engage the bombers, with seven Me 262s, when he suddenly caught sight of Mustangs diving on his force from out of the sun. Lacking the speed to escape, the Messerschmitts broke formation and dived back for the protection of the flak around the airfield. Sinner's assailants were P-51s from the 339th Fighter Group. Captain Kirke Everson afterwards reported:

'At about 0915 hrs Red Flight dropped below the broken clouds to investigate an airfield at Parchim while the remaining flights circled at 10,000 feet. Several Me 262s came up through the clouds and our squadron immediately dove into them. Lt Croker and I attacked the one nearest to us, who immediately dove into the clouds taking evasive action. When we came out of the cloud he was about 1,600 feet range and 2,000 feet altitude. We fired two more bursts and his right unit caught fire. He again went into another cloud and when he came out we were still on his tail.'

Sinner was now in an almost impossible position. The diving Mustangs were much faster than he was and, because of the proximity of the ground, he could not dive away to gain speed. He could now see eight Mustangs closing in for the kill, and as he made for cloud his fighter received its first hits. Sinner's throttles were fully forward but the jet fighter was gaining speed with almost painful slowness. In an effort to reduce drag and so increase his acceleration the German pilot pressed the firing button for his R4M rockets; but there was a fault in the mechanism and they remained firmly in place. The next thing Sinner knew was that his aircraft was hit again; this time it caught fire and the cabin began to fill with smoke. The German pilot jettisoned his canopy and jumped from the Messerschmitt, which by now was flying at about about 440 mph; he was indeed fortunate to miss the tail of the aircraft, and his parachute opened just before he hit the ground. Suffering burns to the head and hands, Sinner was rushed to hospital.

*Leutnant* Franz Schall, who had taken off with Sinner from Parchim, was also caught by the Mustangs and shot down during the action; but he managed to parachute to safety.

Messerschmitt Me 262s from other bases did succeed in getting off unmolested, however; and once it had attained fighting speed the jet fighter was as formidable as ever. At about the same time as Sinner came under attack at Parchim, *Leutnant* Fritz Mueller was leading other Me 262s off from Laerz. He easily evaded a force of Thunderbolts sweeping ahead of the bombers, then he caught sight of a formation of Liberators heading south-eastwards from the Bremen area. He closed in rapidly on his quarry, in a descending turn to the right:

'From a range of 600 m I fired off all of my R4M rockets, aiming about 50 m in front of the first Liberator to allow for deflection. They struck the fuselage and wing centre section of one of the Liberators flying in the middle of the formation. It reared up, fell back, then began to go down.'

Mueller watched his victim level out, and it seemed he would have to make a second attack to finish it off:

'But before I could get into firing range, the Liberator began to go down rapidly in a wide descending turn to the left. I saw six parachutes leaving it. Then the Liberator stood on its head and went vertically down from 2,000 m into a cloud bank, in the Bremen area.'

Almost certainly the unit Mueller's *Staffel* had attacked was the 448th Bomb Group, which lost three B-24s in rapid succession to an attack by jet fighters.

According to German records the Luftwaffe put up 47 jet fighter sorties on 4 April; of these 44 reported making contact with the enemy and they claimed the destruction of seven bombers and two fighters and the probable destruction of three bombers. Eight jet fighters were lost and five damaged; five jet pilots were killed or missing, and three wounded.

The German pilots converting on to the Me 262 during March and April 1945 found themselves pitch-forked into the chaos of the final weeks of the war with no time for any formal training course. One of these was *Leutnant* Walther Hagenah, an experienced fighter pilot with several victories flying the Messerschmitt Bf 109 and the Focke Wulf FW 190. He well remembers the cursory training on the Me 262 he received when he was sent to III./JG 7: 'Our "ground school" lasted one afternoon. We were told of the peculiarities of the jet engine, the danger of flaming out at high altitude, and their poor acceleration at low speeds. The vital importance of handling the throttles carefully was impressed upon us, lest the engines caught fire. But we were not permitted to look inside the cowling at the jet engine itself — we were told they were very secret and we did not need to know about them!' Towards the end of

*Leutnant* Walther Hagenah received a hasty conversion on to the Me 262 at the end of March 1945, and was sent into action with less than six hours on type. *(Hagenah)*

March Hagenah was given one dual flight in an Me 262B trainer, a solo flight in an Me 262, and then he was pronounced ready to fly the single-seater. Since he was undergoing his conversion at an operational unit, however, he was able to fly only when there was an aircraft not needed for combat. There were other problems: 'By the time I reached III./JG 7 there were insufficient spare parts and insufficient spare engines; there were even occasional shortages of J-2 fuel. I am sure all of these things existed and that production was sufficient, but by that stage of the war the transport system was so chaotic that things often failed to arrive at the front-line units,' he recalled. An experienced pilot with some training in instrument flying, Hagenah was able to cope with the transition to the Me 262 with little difficulty; but around him he saw less-experienced pilots trying to do the same thing, and for them the problems were far greater: 'In our unit, flying the Me 262, we had some pilots with only about a hundred hours total flying time. They were able to take-off and land the aircraft, but I had the definite impression that they were of little use in combat. It was almost a crime to send them into action with so little training. These young men did their best, but they had to pay a heavy price for their lack of experience.'

By the end of the first week in April 1945 more than 1,200 Me 262s had been accepted by the Luftwaffe. On 9 April however only about 200, or one in six, were serving on the strength of the front-line units distributed as follows:

| | |
|---|---|
| Stab/JG 7 (fighters) | 5 |
| I./JG 7 (fighters) | 41 |
| III./JG 7 (fighters) | 30 |
| *Jagdverband* 44 (fighters) | about 50 |
| I./KG (J) 54 (ex-bomber pilots flying fighters) | 37 |
| 10./NJG 11 (night fighters) | about 9 |
| I./KG 51 (fighter-bombers) | 15 |
| II./KG 51 (fighters-bombers) | 6 |
| NAGr 6 (ex-*Kdo Brauegg*, reconnaissance) | 7 |

That figure, of 200 Me 262s in service with the front-line units, was probably never exceeded. Of the thousand others that had been accepted, possibly half had been destroyed by enemy action in the air or on the ground, or in accidents. Probably about a hundred served with non-operational units. The remainder sat, unused, in railway sidings or aircraft parks. During the final months of the war the business of getting more than a small proportion of the available Me 262s into action, in the face of the debilitating Allied air attacks on German airfields and the transport system, proved beyond the Luftwaffe.

10 April saw the climax of the Me 262 operations when 55 fighter sorties, the greatest number there would ever be, were put up to counter attacks by more than 1,100 US heavy bombers with strong fighter escort on military targets around Oranienburg and the airfields at Neuruppin, Briest, Zerbst, Burg near Magdeburg, Rechlin, Laerz and Parchim.

One of those taking off to engage the raiders was Walther Hagenah, on his first operational flight in the Me 262. Hagenah took off from Laerz, with an inexperienced young *Feldwebel* pilot as wing-man; his account of the action gives a vivid insight into the problems faced by the German pilots:

'Once above cloud at about 5,000 m I could see the bomber formation clearly, at about 6,000 m. I was flying at about 340 mph in a shallow climb, and turned towards them. Then, as an experienced fighter pilot, I had that old "tingling on the back of neck" feeling that something was wrong. I scanned the sky and, ahead and high above, I caught sight of six Mustangs passing above from almost head-on. At first I thought they had not seen me, and continued towards the bombers. But to be on the safe side I glanced back and it was a good thing that I did, because the Mustangs were curving round and diving on the pair of us.'

With the Mustangs' increased speed in the dive, and Hagenah's reduced speed in the climb, the former closed in rapidly and opened fire at extreme range. Tracer rounds began to flash past the jet fighters, disconcertingly close.

'I lowered my nose slightly to increase my speed and resolved to try to outrun the Mustangs. I did not attempt any manoeuvres to throw off their aim: I knew that the moment I turned, my speed would fall and then they would have me. I told the *Feldwebel* with me to keep going, but obviously he was scared of the tracers because I saw him weaving from side to side, then he broke away to the left. That was just what the Mustang pilots wanted and in no time they were on to him. His aircraft received several hits and I saw it go down and crash.'

During all of this the Mustangs had ignored Hagenah. From a safe distance he watched the enemy fighters re-form and turn west for home. Vengefully he went after them.

'I closed on them rapidly from behind, but when I got to about 550 yds the Mustang leader started to rock his wings and I knew I had been seen. So I loosed off my 24 R4M rockets, into the middle of them.'

Hagenah felt sure that one or two of his rockets scored hits on the enemy fighters, but a detailed search of the American records has revealed no mention of this. Keeping his speed high the German pilot curved away from the Mustangs and soon left them far behind him. By now his fuel was beginning to run low so Hagenah made a quick check of his position and found he was near Koethen.

'I called the airfield and said I wanted to land there. They told me to be careful: there were "Indians" (enemy fighters) in the vicinity. When I got there I caught sight of enemy fighters making strafing attacks on the airfield, but the light flak defences were giving them a hard time and I was able to approach unnoticed. Then it seemed that I was spotted, because almost as one the Mustangs started to pull up. Perhaps their leader thought I was bringing in some fighters to engage them. Certainly he did not realise I was alone and short of fuel. I made a tight approach, chopped the throttles and hurled the Messerschmitt down on the grass. Before I could breath a sigh of relief at having got down safely, however, the Mustang leader realised what had happened and they were back again. But fortunately the airfield flak defences were able to beat them off and I was not hit.'

Meanwhile, other Me 262s had been able to get through to the bombers. In hit-and-run attacks on the force of 400-odd B-17s attacking Oranienburg, the jet fighters knocked down five bombers. The 41st Combat Wing reported: 'The formation was attacked by five jet aircraft immediately after bombs away. The planes came in high from 5.30 and 6 o'clock and shot down two aircraft, both flying the No. 2 position in the high element of the Lead and Low Squadrons respectively.' The 94th Combat Wing, part of the same attacking force, reported: ' Attacked just after the target with three to four Me 262s attacking singly in trail. Attacks were made from 5 to 7 o'clock, level and above. The enemy aircraft started their attacks from approx. 1,000 yards out, coming in as close as 50 yards before breaking away to the right of the bomber formation. Enemy pilots seemed very aggressive and daring . . .', After the action gunners on board the bombers reported 'These Me 262s had two or three guns in each wing just outside the jet units . . .', a clear reference to the use of R4M rockets which were ripple-fired off their underwing racks.

Of the 55 Me 262s which had taken off for this, the strongest-ever reaction by German jet fighters against an American attack, 48 reported making contact with the enemy. Ten heavy bombers were destroyed, against a German claim of nine certainly and three probably destroyed. The American counter-attacks against the jet fighters were both vigorous and effective, however: 27 Me 262s, almost half the number which had taken off, were destroyed; five German pilots were killed and 14 missing. Escorting fighter units claimed a total of 20 Me 262s destroyed, a number which finds general confirmation in the German loss records. Yet even for this, the most powerful jet fighter reaction to an American attack, less than a third of the Me 262s available to the front-line fighter units had gone airborne. The losses they inflicted could easily be borne by the attackers, while the German losses on that day came close to one in ten of the operational Me 262 fighter pilots.

The action on 10 April was followed by a rapid decline in the Me 262 operations, for by now the Allied ground forces were advancing deeply into Germany from both the east and west. On that day Hannover fell, while in the south the spearhead of the American advance was nearing Nuremberg. In the east the Red Army was preparing to cross the Oder, from positions within 60 miles of Berlin. This general weakening of the military situation was immediately reflected in the order of battle of the jet fighter units, as the dwindling resources were concentrated on keeping going a few selected *Gruppen*. On 11 April, the day following the climax of the Me 262 operations, I./JG 7 and I./KG (J) 54 were both disbanded; so too were the remaining units with Me 262 fighters flown by ex-bomber pilots, KG (J) 6 and II./KG (J) 54, which had never become operational. The surviving jet fighter units were squeezed into the areas not immediately threatened by the Allied advances: in Schleswig-Holstein and Denmark in the north, and Bavaria, Austria and Czechoslovakia in the south.

For the week that followed, the Me 262s saw relatively little action. Then, on the 19th, they re-asserted their presence in dramatic fashion during a sharp attack on B-17s of the 490th Bomb Group near Prague. First an Me 262 made a head-on pass on the formation and knocked down a bomber from the leading squadron; then two more jets attacked and sent down three more bombers. The attackers belonged to III./JG 7, which had withdrawn to Prague/Ruzyne from its threatened bases in the Berlin area. The jet fighters did not get off scot-free, however, and Mustangs of the 357th Fighter Group claimed seven shot down in the area.

In an effort to provide the Me 262 with the ability to destroy enemy bombers at long range, one aircraft was fitted with a single 50 mm Mk 214 high velocity cannon and tested in action. The Mk 214, a modified version of a gun designed for installation in German tanks, fired a shell weighing 3.3 pounds and had an effective firing range of about 3,300 feet. The rate of fire was 150 rounds per minute and the high explosive shells were heavy enough to destroy the largest bomber with a single hit almost anywhere on the structure. But in operational use the automatic ammunition feed system of the modified tank gun proved over-sensitive to 'G' forces, and frequently jammed. *Major* Willi Herget of *Jagdverband* 44, in charge of the trials, found that the heavy cannon functioned well enough when tested against ground targets. During his two attempts to engage enemy bombers in the Me 262 fitted with the Mk 214 however, the gun jammed on both; on the second occasion, while he was struggling to clear the jam, he ventured too close to the bombers he intended to attack and their return fire knocked out one of his engines forcing him to break away. After that the development of the Mk 214 for air-to-air use in the Me 262 was dropped, and Herget reverted to a standard version of the jet fighter.

During the final days of April there were sporadic actions by the Me 262 units, but in the face of all-pervading Allied air supremacy they achieved little. One of the few combats of note occurred on 26 April, when *Generalmajor* Adolf Galland led a force of six Me 262s of *Jagdverband* 44 off from Munich/Riem to engage enemy bombers in the area. One of the jet fighters suffered engine trouble early on and had to turn back; the remainder continued with their mission and intercepted the bombers, French-flown B-26 Marauders of the First Tactical Air Force. Meeting the American formation almost head-on, the Me 262s passed over it then wheeled round to attack from the rear. Galland lined up on one of the bombers but, in the heat of the moment, forgot to switch the R4M battery to 'live'; the rockets remained embarrassingly on their rails when he pressed the firing button. The lapse did not save the Marauder, however. Galland closed in to short range and, following an accurate burst with his 30 mm cannon, it blew up. The German pilot pulled his Me 262 round the falling debris, then engaged a second bomber and saw his rounds exploding against it. Then, as Galland banked away to observe the effect of his attack on the second bomber, his Messerschmitt came under attack from one of the P-47s escorting the Marauders. His assailant was Lieutenant James Finnegan of the 50th Fighter Group, who later wrote:

'I saw two Me 262s "come out of nowhere" and in the flick of an eye literally blow up two bombers. After a moment I saw one of the 262s below me flying in the opposite direction. I turned over on my back, pulled tight on the stick and almost immediately had the enemy aircraft in my sights. I got off two quick bursts but couldn't see if I hit anything because the nose of my aircraft was pulled high to get a good lead. However, I then dropped the nose and observed what I thought were bits and pieces coming from the cowling. In addition, I saw smoke trailing from the wing.'

Finnegan was not mistaken: his rounds had smashed into the instrument panel and engines of the Messerschmitt, and Galland himself received several splinter wounds to his right leg. The German pilot broke off the action and escaped into cloud, then returned to Riem.

The pilots of *Jagdverband* 44 claimed to have shot down four of the Marauders, and this is borne out by the American records: the 42nd Bomb Wing lost three B-26s which went down immediately, and one more was so seriously damaged that it was forced to crash-land. Captain Robert Clark, also flying a P-47 of the 50th Fighter Group, shot down one of the Me 262s but the German pilot was able to parachute to safety.

The action on 26 April marked the virtual end of the Me 262's operational career, as one by one the last of the airfields were overrun by Allied ground forces.

For all of the great hopes entertained for the Messerschmitt 262 earlier in the war, during its nine months of operations it had been able to achieve little. From a detailed study of British and American records it appears that in the fighter role it caused the destruction of no more than 150 Allied aircraft — for the loss of about 100 Me 262s in aerial combat. In the fighter-bomber role its attacks had been so ineffectual that only rarely did they merit even a mention in Allied reports.

There are many reasons for this lack of success, but overshadowing all else is the fact that only a very small proportion of the Me 262s built ever went into action. After the end of October 1944 the various Messerschmitt plants were turning out Me 262s in numbers far greater than the Luftwaffe could usefully employ; and by the end of the war more than 1,400 had been delivered. Yet there were never more than about 200 in service with operational units at any one time; and rarely, if ever, were more than 60 Me 262 sorties of all types — fighter, fighter-bomber, night-fighter and reconnaissance — mounted on any one day. The chaotic supply situation in Germany during the final six months of the war, resulting from the incessant Allied air attacks on the German transport system, imposed a severe brake on every stage of the Me 262 operations.

In spite of what many others have said, the authors feel that Hitler's insistence that the Me 262 should be used initially as a fighter-bomber, to counter the seaborne invasion of France in its initial stages, was not misplaced. Given a touch-and-go situation such as actually occurred on Omaha beach on D-day, when the invaders were held up on the beaches for several hours and suffered severe casualties, there can be little doubt that a few score of resolutely-handled jet fighter-bombers attacking the troops coming ashore might have tipped the balance and forced the landings to be abandoned. Nor did Hitler's order delay the introduction of the fighter version into action by much. Due to the difficulties experienced with getting the Jumo 004 engine into mass production, the Me 262 did not start to become available in quantity until October 1944; and by then Hitler's order for it to be used only as a fighter-bomber had been rescinded. In the event the order delayed the operational deployment of the first Me 262 fighter *Gruppe — Kommando Nowotny* — by less than six weeks.

Certainly the Messerschmitt 262 was the finest all-round fighter in service in any air force at the end of the Second World War. Yet its margin of effectiveness over the best fighters in the opposing air forces, and in particular the Mustang, was not great enough to redress the gross numerical inferiority of the Luftwaffe during the closing stages of the war.

OPPOSITE, TOP:
Line-up of nine Me 262s at Lechfeld in June 1945, prior to their move to Melun in France where German aircraft were collected before shipment to the USA.
*(Smithsonian Institution)*

OPPOSITE, BELOW:
Close-up of the Mk 214 50 mm cannon-armed Me 262 christened *Wilma Jeanne* by US forces, being readied for the flight to Melun. *(Smithsonian Institution)*

Wilma J

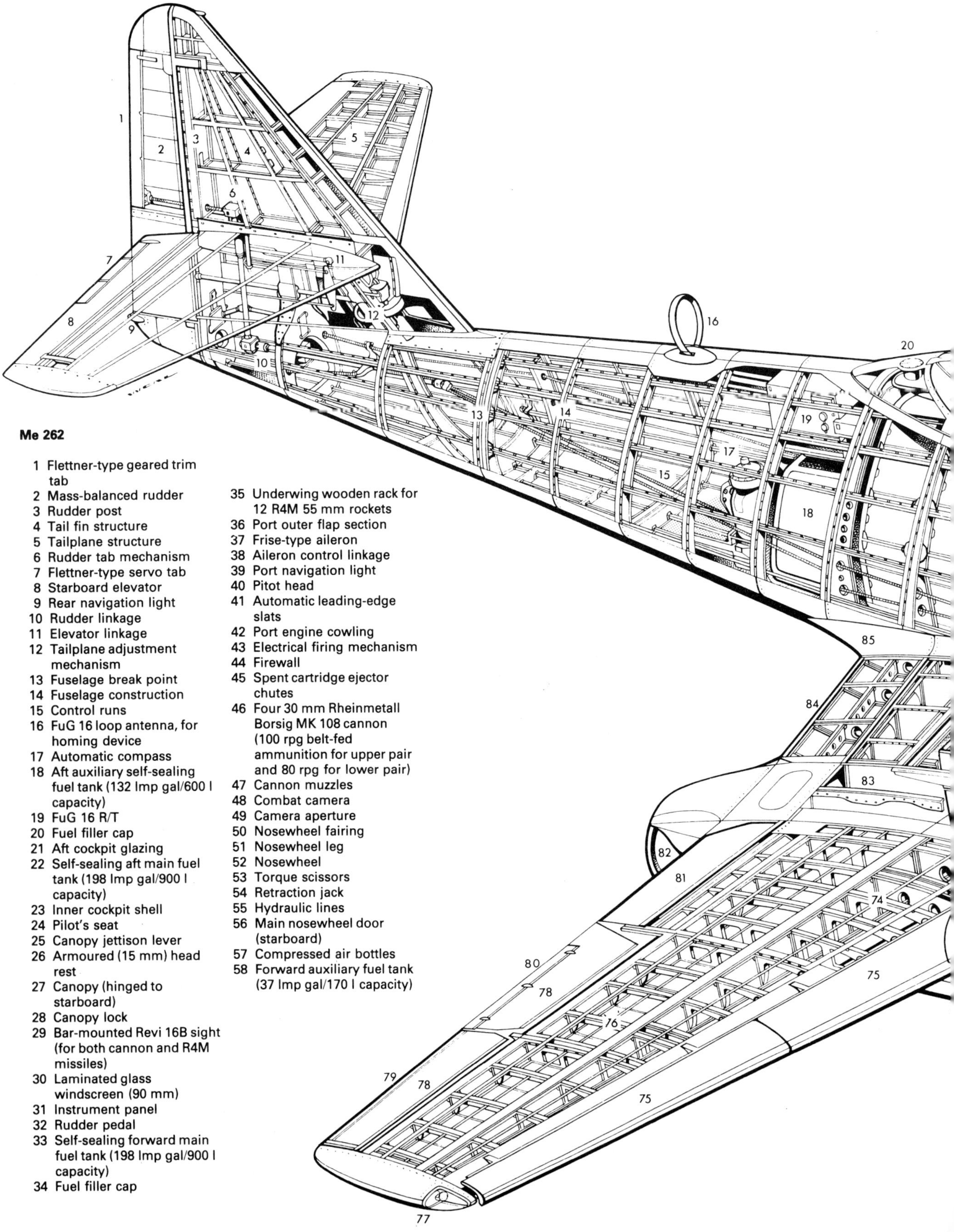


**Me 262**

1 Flettner-type geared trim tab
2 Mass-balanced rudder
3 Rudder post
4 Tail fin structure
5 Tailplane structure
6 Rudder tab mechanism
7 Flettner-type servo tab
8 Starboard elevator
9 Rear navigation light
10 Rudder linkage
11 Elevator linkage
12 Tailplane adjustment mechanism
13 Fuselage break point
14 Fuselage construction
15 Control runs
16 FuG 16 loop antenna, for homing device
17 Automatic compass
18 Aft auxiliary self-sealing fuel tank (132 Imp gal/600 l capacity)
19 FuG 16 R/T
20 Fuel filler cap
21 Aft cockpit glazing
22 Self-sealing aft main fuel tank (198 Imp gal/900 l capacity)
23 Inner cockpit shell
24 Pilot's seat
25 Canopy jettison lever
26 Armoured (15 mm) head rest
27 Canopy (hinged to starboard)
28 Canopy lock
29 Bar-mounted Revi 16B sight (for both cannon and R4M missiles)
30 Laminated glass windscreen (90 mm)
31 Instrument panel
32 Rudder pedal
33 Self-sealing forward main fuel tank (198 Imp gal/900 l capacity)
34 Fuel filler cap
35 Underwing wooden rack for 12 R4M 55 mm rockets
36 Port outer flap section
37 Frise-type aileron
38 Aileron control linkage
39 Port navigation light
40 Pitot head
41 Automatic leading-edge slats
42 Port engine cowling
43 Electrical firing mechanism
44 Firewall
45 Spent cartridge ejector chutes
46 Four 30 mm Rheinmetall Borsig MK 108 cannon (100 rpg belt-fed ammunition for upper pair and 80 rpg for lower pair)
47 Cannon muzzles
48 Combat camera
49 Camera aperture
50 Nosewheel fairing
51 Nosewheel leg
52 Nosewheel
53 Torque scissors
54 Retraction jack
55 Hydraulic lines
56 Main nosewheel door (starboard)
57 Compressed air bottles
58 Forward auxiliary fuel tank (37 Imp gal/170 l capacity)

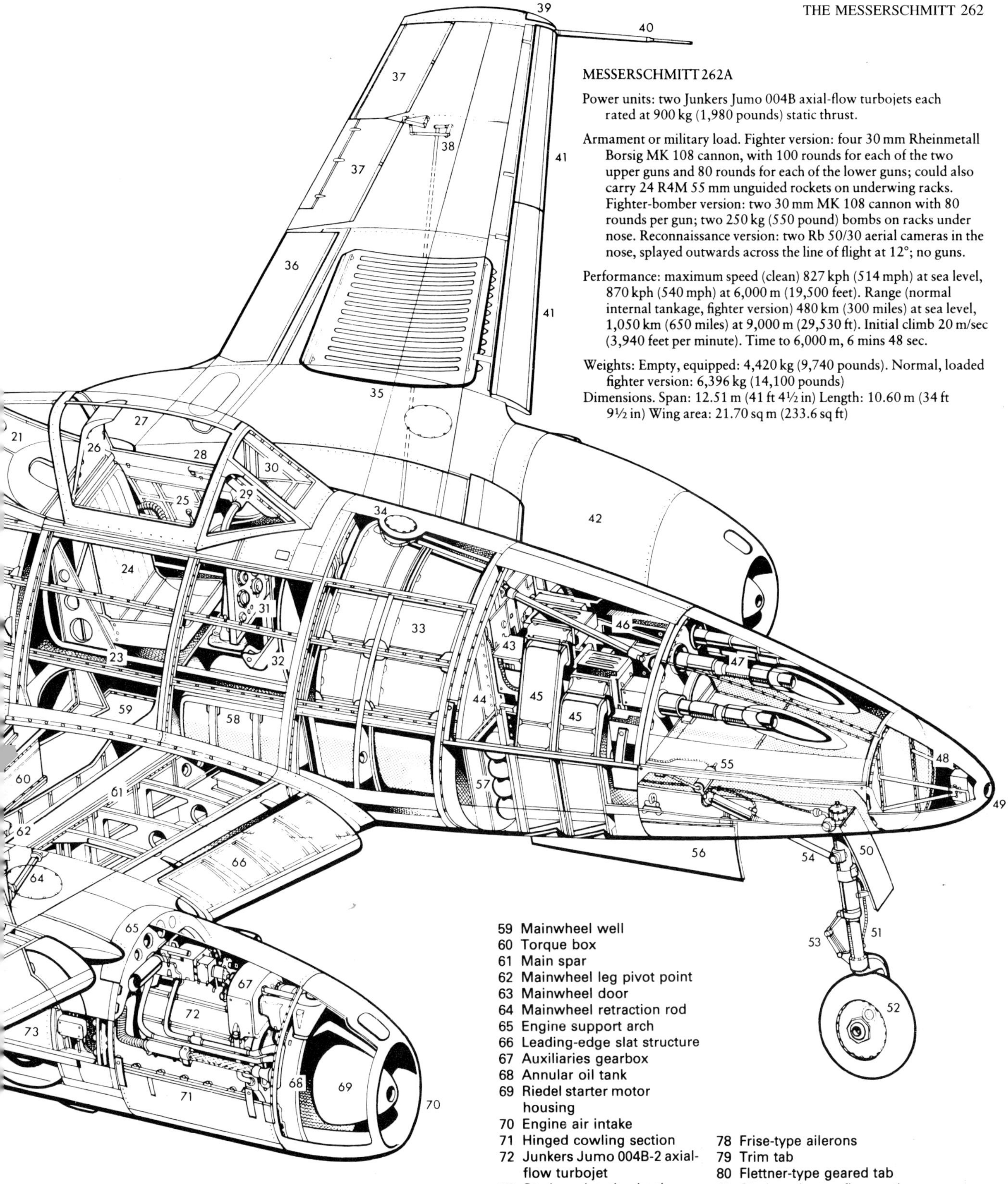

MESSERSCHMITT 262A

Power units: two Junkers Jumo 004B axial-flow turbojets each rated at 900 kg (1,980 pounds) static thrust.

Armament or military load. Fighter version: four 30 mm Rheinmetall Borsig MK 108 cannon, with 100 rounds for each of the two upper guns and 80 rounds for each of the lower guns; could also carry 24 R4M 55 mm unguided rockets on underwing racks. Fighter-bomber version: two 30 mm MK 108 cannon with 80 rounds per gun; two 250 kg (550 pound) bombs on racks under nose. Reconnaissance version: two Rb 50/30 aerial cameras in the nose, splayed outwards across the line of flight at 12°; no guns.

Performance: maximum speed (clean) 827 kph (514 mph) at sea level, 870 kph (540 mph) at 6,000 m (19,500 feet). Range (normal internal tankage, fighter version) 480 km (300 miles) at sea level, 1,050 km (650 miles) at 9,000 m (29,530 ft). Initial climb 20 m/sec (3,940 feet per minute). Time to 6,000 m, 6 mins 48 sec.

Weights: Empty, equipped: 4,420 kg (9,740 pounds). Normal, loaded fighter version: 6,396 kg (14,100 pounds)

Dimensions. Span: 12.51 m (41 ft 4½ in) Length: 10.60 m (34 ft 9½ in) Wing area: 21.70 sq m (233.6 sq ft)

59 Mainwheel well
60 Torque box
61 Main spar
62 Mainwheel leg pivot point
63 Mainwheel door
64 Mainwheel retraction rod
65 Engine support arch
66 Leading-edge slat structure
67 Auxiliaries gearbox
68 Annular oil tank
69 Riedel starter motor housing
70 Engine air intake
71 Hinged cowling section
72 Junkers Jumo 004B-2 axial-flow turbojet
73 Starboard mainwheel
74 Wing structure
75 Automatic leading-edge slats
76 Mainspar
77 Starboard navigation light
78 Frise-type ailerons
79 Trim tab
80 Flettner-type geared tab
81 Starboard outer flap section
82 Engine exhaust orifice
83 Engine support bearer
84 Starboard inner flap structure
85 Faired wing root

# Appendix

## THE ME 262 AS A COMBAT AIRCRAFT

After the war Allied Intelligence officers conducted a detailed questioning of several German pilots who had flown the Me 262 in action. The resultant report, entitled *The Me 262 as a Combat Aircraft*, gave a fascinating insight both into the technical features of the aircraft itself and the way it was used in action. The section that follows is based closely on that report.

## TECHNICAL FEATURES OF THE ME 262

### Modified Control Stick

At speeds of about 500 mph the ailerons and elevators of the Me 262 became very difficult to move with the normal control column. A new type of control column was therefore developed, to give an increased mechanical advantage to offset this difficulty; this was installed in later production aircraft. The control column itself was fitted with an extendable section, which could be locked in place to give a greater leverage.

### Gyroscopic Gunsight — EZ 42

The EZ 42 gyroscopic gunsight was fitted in several aircraft of JV 44, but faulty installation made the sight useless and it was locked so as to function in the same way as the old fixed-graticule reflector sight.

### Automatic Throttle Control

On the Me 262s in service the throttles had to be advanced slowly up to 6,000 rpm to avoid burning out the jet units. Above 6,000 rpm the throttles could be pushed all the way forward at once, because an automatic fuel flow and pressure regulator prevented a too sudden increase in the amount of fuel entering the jets and a resultant overheating. By the end of the war a new regulator had been developed to control the fuel flow, so that the throttles could be set at any point and the new regulator would ensure a safe and gradual acceleration of the engine to the rpm selected. Just before the war ended the new regulator had been tested and found satisfactory.

### Rocket-Assisted Take-off

Many experiments had been conducted into rocket-assisted take-offs with the Me 262; two 1,100 pound thrust rockets shortened the take-off run, without bombs or rocket projectiles, by between 820–980 feet. Take-offs with two 2,200 pound thrust rockets had been made in as little as 1,300 feet, without bombs or rocket projectiles.

### Performance Calculator

The endurance and speed of the Me 262 was dependent on such variables as air temperature, barometric pressure and weight. To assist pilots in calculating this a special circular slide rule was produced by the Messerschmitt Company and issued to operational units.

### New Type Parachutes

The great speed of the Me 262 made it dangerous to bale out with an ordinary parachute, because if the pilot pulled the ripcord immediately on clearing the aircraft the sudden deceleration might damage both parachute and pilot. So two new types of parachute were developed. One type was fitted with metal rings to hold the shroud lines together in pairs just below the canopy, thereby reducing the circumference of the canopy and lessening its immediate effect. Once the initial shock of opening had been absorbed, the rings slid down the shroud lines and allowed the parachute to develop normally.

The other type was the so-called 'strip parachute' (*Baenderfallschirm*), in which the canopy was made out of spaced circular strips of silk instead of continuous pieces. It opened more slowly and the rate of descent was more rapid than with the normal type of parachute. This type was soon discarded, however, because the pilots were most vulnerable during take-off and landing and therefore needed a parachute that would deploy rapidly if they had to bale out at low altitude.

### Flying Qualities

Because of the range of speeds over which the Me 262 could operate — 156 to 590 mph — the design was a compromise and it could not turn as sharply as the more conventional fighters of the period. Acceleration and deceleration in level flight were accomplished relatively more slowly in the Me 262 than in earlier fighters, but the clean airframe and the absence of an airscrew enabled the Me 262 to dive very fast.

At speeds between 590 and 621 mph the airflow around the fighter approached the speed of sound and the control surfaces no longer influenced the direction of flight; the result varied from aircraft to aircraft: some dropped a wing and went into a dive, while others went into a steadily steepening dive. Vertical dives were not performed in the Me 262, because it exceeded its limiting Mach number too rapidly.

Because of the great speed range of the aircraft and its great fuel consumption with the resultant unbalancing, constant trimming was necessary during flight as speed changed and fuel was consumed.

**Take-off and Landing Distances**

Distances for take-off varied considerably with air temperature and pressure, but the following figures were given for an Me 262 with full fuel load and 24 x R4M rockets:

| | |
|---|---|
| Grass field | 5,900–6,600 feet |
| Concrete runway | 4,900–5,900 feet |

Minimum landing distance with fuel almost expended and no rocket projectiles was 3,600 feet on either a concrete runway or a grass field.

**Service Ceiling**

Altitudes as high as about 38,500 feet had been reached by the Me 262 during test flights, but the operational ceiling for formations of Me 262s was set at about 30,000 feet because of the difficulty of holding formation at higher altitudes and the likelihood that the jet engines would flame out at altitudes much above this. Any throttle movement at altitudes above about 6000m (about 20,000 feet) was liable to cause a flame-out of the engine involved.

**Servicing**

The Jumo 004 jet unit fitted to the Me 262 was supposed to last from 25 to 35 hours, but in practice they lasted only about ten hours' flying time. The prescribed time for changing and checking a unit was three hours, but in actual practice it took eight to nine hours because of poorly fitting parts and the lack of trained staff.

Fuelling the aircraft could be accomplished in eight to 15 minutes under operational conditions, depending on the pumping speed of the refuelling vehicle.

**Operation on One Engine**

The Me 262 functioned efficiently on one jet unit, and speeds of 280 to 310 mph for as long as 2½ hours had been attained. In attempting such flights an altitude of about 25,000 feet had first to be reached before one of the engines was flamed-out, and the aircraft had to descent to below about 10,000 feet to restart it. Landing with one unit shut down was possible, but it was regarded as a hazard to be avoided if at all possible.

**Armament**

The standard armament of the Me 262 was four 30 mm Mk 108s. The close grouping of the guns in the nose was considered ballistically ideal, but some trouble was experienced in firing in the turn, when the centrifugal forces sometimes tore the ammunition belts; this fault was later cured by altering the feed mechanism. The guns were adjusted to converge their fire on a point between 1,300 and 1,650 feet ahead of the aircraft.

In combat against enemy bombers, the Me 262s of JV 44 carried 24 x R4M rocket projectiles, twelve under each wing. Each projectile contained 1.1 pound of Hexogen and had a considerable blast effect. The rockets were ripple-fired, and diverged to cover an area the diameter of the wingspan of a four-engined bomber at 600 m. Several victories were achieved with R4M and it was planned to install as many as 48 under the wings of the Me 262 for even greater effect. The trajectory of the R4M was almost the same as that of the Mk 108 cannon, so the ordinary gun sight could be used to aim it.

## TACTICAL EMPLOYMENT ON THE ME 262

The Me 262 was employed as a fighter, fighter-bomber, shallow dive bomber and for reconnaissance.

**Employment of the Me 262 by JV 44 to attack USAAF bombers**

In January 1945, by special permission of Goering, a new Me 262 fighter unit was formed at Brandenburg–Briest by *Generaleutnant* Galland, formerly chief of the Inspectorate of the Fighter

Arm. This unit, known as *Jagdverband* 44 or *Jagdverband Galland*, trained with units of JG 7 at Briest until late March, then it moved to Munich–Riem where it became operational. The 40 to 50 pilots of the unit included Galland himself, about ten holders of the *Ritterkreuz*, a dozen other highly experienced pilots and twenty–odd new pilots who had shown some promise. JV 44 was operational throughout 1945 from Riem and moved in the last days of the war to Salzburg–Maxglan, where it was overrun by American troops on 3 May.

During the short time they were operational, Galland and his more experienced pilots developed some concept of how the Me 262 should best be used in combat. They carried through a number of attacks on Allied bomber formations and achieved some success, despite heavy losses inflicted by the overpowering fighter escort that constantly harried them.

Rarely were more than 16 aircraft of JV 44 serviceable for any one mission, with the result that during any attack on USAAF bombers the German force was far outnumbered by the American fighter escort. The primary mission of the jet aircraft was to attack and destroy the bombers, and combat with Allied fighters was not accepted unless unavoidable. Hence, all the tactical employment of the Me 262 in JV 44 was hampered by numerical inferiority and strict limitation on the combat objective.

The large turning radius and poor acceleration of the Me 262 made the *Kette* (element of three aircraft) instead of the *Schwarm* (element of four aircraft) the most practical basic formation; however, JG 7 did fly missions in elements of four. The element of three was chosen by JV 44 because the lack of manoeuvrability of the jet rendered it difficult for a larger element to stay together in aerial manoeuvres. When turns were made, the formation had to be held by cutting inside or overshooting rather than by use of the throttles. When shifting position in a turn, the two rear aircraft in the element of three tried to pass below the leading aircraft to avoid losing sight of it, since downward visibility was poor in the Me 262.

The use of the element of three as the basic formation was dictated by yet another consideration: as a result of the great speeds reached by the aircraft at low altitude and because of its relatively short endurance, assembly after take-off was more difficult to effect than with piston-engined fighter aircraft. Hence it was necessary for each element to take-off simultaneously, and the standard German airfield runways were just wide enough to permit the take-off of three Me 262s side by side.

When attacking bombers formations of *Staffel* size, about nine aircraft flying in three elements of three, were used. On the approach flight the formation was made up of one element leading and the other two on the flanks slightly higher and farther back. The interval between aircraft in each element was about 330 feet in the climb and 500

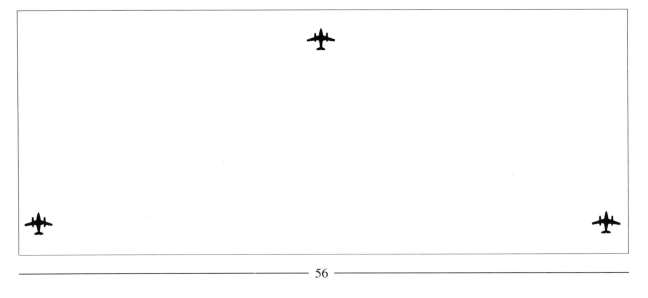

The loose *Kette* three-aircraft element used by *Jagdverband 44*, drawn to scale.

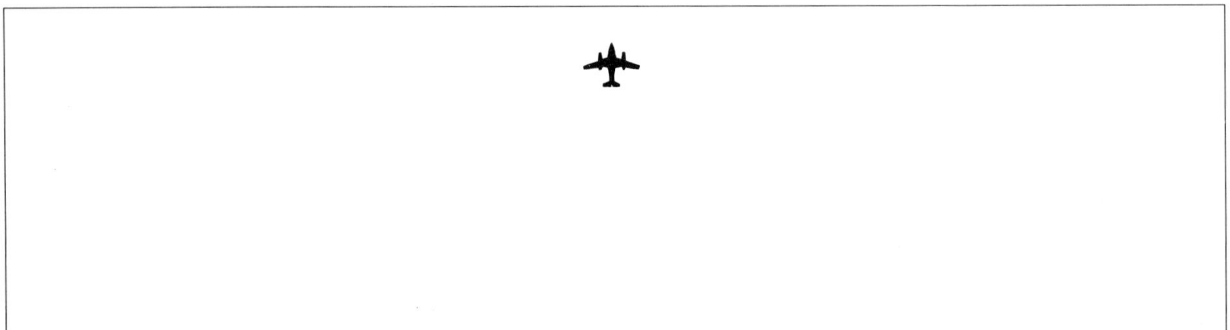

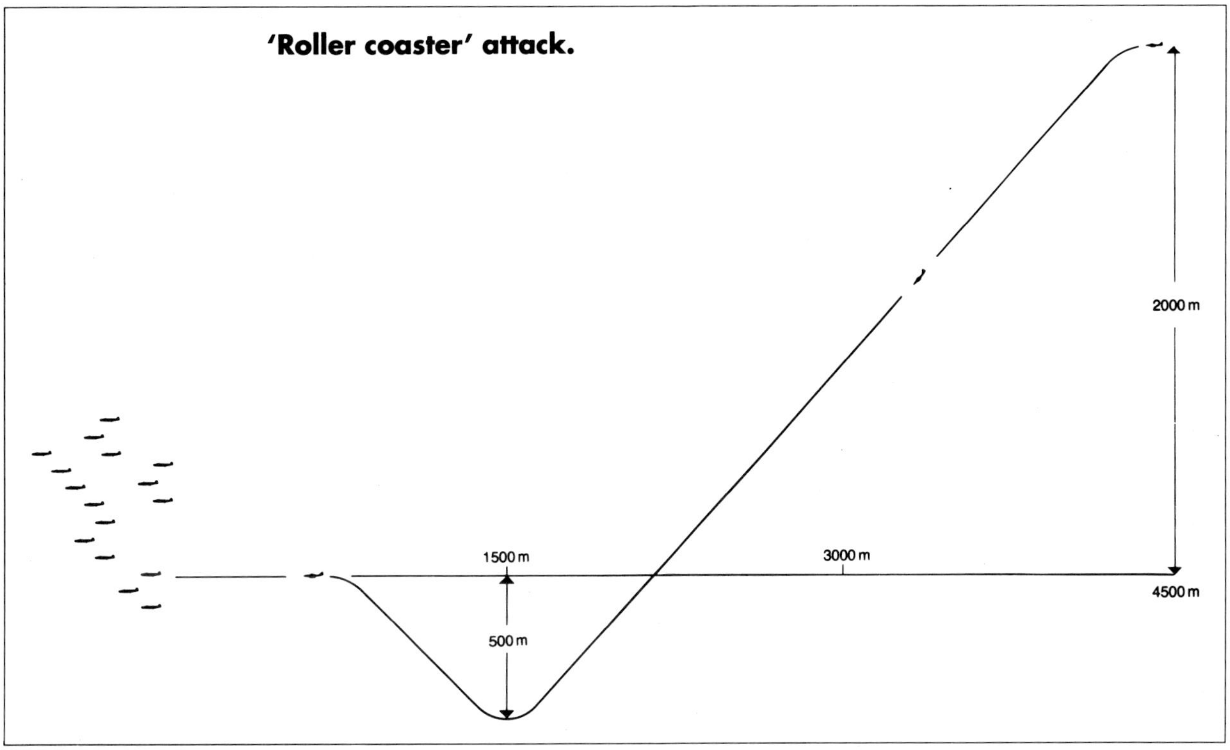


The type of attack described in the report, in which the pilot pulled up sharply at the end of his dive to 'dump' speed before going into his attacking run. This type of attack was known to American bomber crews as the 'Roller-coaster' or 'Leap frog'.

feet in level flight. The interval between elements was about 1,000 feet. If the formation was made up of more than one *Staffel*, the other *Staffeln* flew on the sides of the leader slight higher, or were strung out to one side in echelon. Because of the great speed of the Me 262 no top cover was required against Allied fighter attacks.

The jet formations were directed on to the Allied bomber formations by ground controllers using radar. Once the bomber formation had been sighted the jet fighters manoeuvred to attack one of the groups of bombers from the rear. Getting into position for this was often difficult because of the great speed and large turning radius of the jet aircraft, and decisions had to be made early while the bomber formation was some way away. The great distances involved made it difficult to judge the altitude and course of the bombers at this time, further complicating the problem.

For maximum effect it was considered advisable for one *Staffel* to attack each bomber group. In the case of a multi-*Staffel* formation, the *Staffeln* would separate and attack separate groups. The approach flight was best begun from a distance of 5,000 yds behind the bomber formation with an altitude advantage of about 2,200 yds, but entry into the bomber stream could be accomplished from as little as 2,200 yds behind the bombers.

The Me 262s formed into a column of three *Ketten* and dived to a position about 550 yds below and 1,650 yds behind the bombers to gain speed, and then pulled up and flew straight and level for the last 1,100 yds. The purpose of the dive was to increase speed to about 530 mph, necessary on account of the Allied fighter escort which was almost certain to be closing in to engage; for the best marksmanship, however, a somewhat lower speed would have been desirable. It was considered essential for the jet fighters to hold their formation and attack the whole width of the enemy bomber group, in order to split up the defensive fire from the bombers' guns.

The aircraft of JV 44 used the ordinary reflector sight, but they had painted on its screen two lines spaced so as to frame the wingspan of a B-17 at 710 yds. At this point the twenty-four R4M rocket projectiles under the wings were fired at the

An Me 262B two-seat trainer being towed to its dispersal point at Melun. *(Smithsonian Institution)*

bomber chosen as target. Fire was then opened with the four 30 mm Mk 108 cannon. The pilots aimed at the general shape of the bomber, since the range was too great to aim at any particular part of it.

In practice it was found difficult to manoeuvre into position exactly behind the bomber in the time available, and if there was any deviation the fighter pilot had to aim his rounds in front of the target.

The three *Ketten* in column would attack the bomber group, closing the range to about 160 yds, at which point they began their get-away. Because of the great speed of the Me 262 they did not have to break away behind or inside the bomber formation but could pass through or above it, thus avoiding exposing their bellies in curving away to one side. The best get-away route was found to be a flat climb passing as close as possible above the top elements of the bomber formation so as to make it difficult for the bombers gunners to score hits. Passing under the bombers was regarded as unwise because pieces of debris from damaged bombers may be sucked into the jet units and damage them.

After passing through or over the bomber formation, the Me 262s could break off their attack and fly back to their base, or repeat the attack on another formation further ahead. If they decided to break away, a shallow dive enabled them to gain enough speed to outdistance the fastest Allied fighters.

If the Me 262s had ammunition left they could pass on to the next bomber group ahead and attack it in a similar manner. But if too much speed had been lost in the first attack, the second was rendered perilous by the Allied fighter escort which by this time would usually be in position to dive to attack from above.

Reassembly of the Me 262s was not usually effected after the attack, because the elements had become too widely dispersed and fuel would be running low. The elements returned home alone, relying on their speed to outrun the Allied fighters.

Head-on attacks occurred on a few occasions by accident, and it was found that the closing speed of the jet aircraft and the bombers was too great to permit accurate sighting and firing, and there was no possibility of observing hits.

Without doubt the most unusual collection of aircraft ever parked on the deck of an aircraft carrier! When the Royal Navy escort carrier HMS *Reaper* left Cherbourg on 20 July 1945 for Newark, New Jersey, she carried an assortment of 38 captured German aircraft for testing in the USA. There were 12 Me 262s (four ordinary fighters, one fighter with a 50 mm cannon, three Me 262B trainers, one Me 262B night fighter and three photographic reconnaissance aircraft), 2 Arado Ar 234s, 3 Heinkel Me 219s, 2 Dornier Do 335s, 9 Focke Wulf FW 190s, a Tank Ta 152, 3 Messerschmitt Bf 109s, a Messerschmitt Bf 108, a Junkers Ju 88, a Junkers Ju 388, and three helicopters. All of the aircraft parked on the deck have been cocooned to protect them from the effects of salt spray during the voyage. *Smithsonian Insitution*

German pilots were of the opinion that the Me 262 would have been an effective weapon against the USAAF daylight raids over Germany if mass employment had been possible. But the gross numerical inferiority, the fuel shortage and the lack of good pilots prevented adequate combat testing of the potentialities of the Me 262.

**Use of the Me 262 to combat Allied fighters and fighter-bombers**

The use of the Me 262 as an attack fighter against Allied bombers was dictated by the impossibility of using other German fighters for this purpose and by the need to do something to stop or hinder the Allied raids. But the German pilots regarded the ideal role of the Me 262 to be that of a pure fighter, finding and destroying Allied fighters and fighter-bombers. They were sure that the employment of a few hundred jet aircraft against the Allied fighter escorts would have forced the Allied air forces to use jets themselves or drastically to curtail their operations over Germany in daytime.

The two principal advantages of the Me 262 as a fighter were its speed and climbing ability; it was admittedly inferior to Allied piston-engined fighters in turning and close manoeuvring. The two paramount qualities of speed and climb could always be used, it was felt, to gain the two basic advantages which decide aerial combat, namely surprise and superior altitude. Operating at normal altitudes for fighter combat a formation of Me 262s could, upon sighting Allied fighters, accept or refuse combat as the German formation leader chose. He could climb to gain altitude and at the same time overhaul any Allied formation. When attacked from above the Allied fighter pilots showed excellent discipline and turned into the attacking jets; but sometimes stragglers could be shot down, and the Me 262s could then pull up and repeat the attack.

Some Me 262s were lost when they attempted to 'dog fight' with Allied fighters, especially with P-51 Mustangs. In such cases the German pilots made the mistake of losing speed to gain manoeuvrability, and the P-51s proved still more manoeuvrable. If the Allied fighters were circling defensively it was considered practical to dive and fire while going through a one-third or half turn with them, then climb away. Longer turning engagements always put the Me 262 at a disadvantage.

When Me 262s were themselves attacked from above at a range too close to permit them to turn into the attacking Allied fighters, the jets had only to go into a shallow dive, put some distance between themselves and the Allied fighters, then turn round and engage. If the attack was from the same altitude and behind, instead of from above, the Me 262s could easily climb away from their assailants.

In engaging Allied fighter-bombers flying at about 16,000 feet or lower, the Me 262s enjoyed an even greater advantage than against ordinary Allied fighters. The speed advantage of the Me 262 over ordinary fighters was most marked lower down, and in addition to this the fighter-bombers were slowed by their armour and bombs. The speed of the Me 262 enabled it to fly low so as to sight the Allied fighter-bombers silhouetted against the higher clouds, then climb and attack from underneath; such tactics were not feasible for piston-engined fighters.

The Me 262s engaged Allied fighters only on rare occasions, when combat with bomber formations was not possible. But the German pilots regarded the correct use of the Me 262 to be that of attacking the Allied fighter escort and keeping it occupied, thereby leaving the bombers as easy prey for the German piston-engined fighters. In the event, however, by the time the Me 262 units were ready for combat the supplies of fuel were so short that the High Command had to order all fighters to concentrate on engaging the enemy bombers.

**Use of the Me 262 as a shallow-dive bomber and a ground strafing aircraft**

When used by KG 51 the Me 262 carried a bomb load of one 1,100 pound or two 550 pound bombs and the bombing results were as accurate as those obtained with the FW 190. The high speed of the aircraft made it possible for it to operate at low altitudes despite the Allied air superiority. When first operational, however, the Me 262s of KG 51 were forbidden to fly lower than 13,000 feet over Allied-held territory to prevent their falling into enemy hands; this resulted in very inaccurate bombing.

One of the Me 262s brought to the USA on HMS *Reaper*, given the serial number T-2-4012, was passed to Hughes Aircraft for high speed testing. The armament was removed and the gun ports covered over; the gaps in the airframe were sealed to remove all unnecessary drag, and several coats of high gloss paint were applied to give the aircraft a smooth finish. The resultant aircraft had a performance considerably better than the Lockheed P-80, the fastest US jet aircraft at that time. According to unconfirmed reports, at one stage Howard Hughes expressed the wish to pit his aquisition against the P-80 in one of the Bendix and Thompson Jet Trophy races; there is little doubt the Me 262 would have won. But, again according to unconfirmed reports, General 'Hap' Arnold got to hear of the proposal and squashed it firmly. *(Smithsonian Institution)*

Shallow-dive attacks were carried out by formations of four Me 262s, flying in line abreast at about 15,000 feet or lower with about 330 feet lateral interval between aircraft. The target was approached from a slightly oblique angle and, when it disappeared under the right or the left engine nacelle, the pilots pulled round into 30° shallow dives using the ordinary reflector sight for aiming. During the dive a speed of between 530 to 560 mph was reached; to prevent it rising further the pilot would throttle back the engines to 6,000 rpm and, if necessary, ease back on the stick. Bombs were released at altitudes around 3,250 feet. At the time of bomb release it was essential that the rear fuel tank had already been emptied, otherwise the sudden change in trim to tail heavy could cause the nose to rise up abruptly and the wings might break off. Several Me 262s and pilots had been lost in combat to this cause.

The Me 262 had been used on several occasions for ground strafing attacks against advancing Allied troops, though German pilots did not feel that it was really suitable for this purpose. The Mk 108 cannon had so low a muzzle velocity that attacks had to be carried out from 1,300 feet or below if they were to be accurate; and the ammunition load of 360 rounds was too little for this purpose. Furthermore, the Me 262 carried insufficient armour to protect the pilot from enemy ground fire.

One of a dozen Me 262s assembled and flown in Czechoslovakia after the war by the Avia company, using components left in the country after the war.

# CHAPTER 2

# The Messerschmitt 163

The Messerschmitt 163 had the distinction of being the first jet aircraft to enter operational service, and it was also the first to fly an operational sortie. Like the Me 262 this aircraft started life as a high speed test vehicle for its novel power unit and was then ordered as a fighter and went into action in the summer of 1944. At the end of the conflict the Me 163 was the fastest fighter in service anywhere in the world. Yet its effect on the conflict was minimal. Rarely were more than eight Me 163 sorties flown in any one day, and during its entire operational career it shot down probably no more than 16 enemy aircraft.

The Messerschmitt Me 163 stemmed from Alexander Lippisch's DFS 194 flying-wing rocket test aircraft, which had first flown during the summer of 1940. As a result of the success of this aircraft, which had reached a maximum speed of 341 mph on the 882-pound thrust from a Walter liquid fuel rocket motor, Lippisch received an order from the German Air Ministry to design and build three prototypes of an airframe to take Walter's projected new 1,650 pound thrust unit. The new aircraft was designated the Messerschmitt Me 163.

As in the case of the other early German jet aircraft, the airframe of the Me 163 was ready long before the power unit. So the first prototype was flown initially as a glider by test pilot Heini Dittmar, towed off from the airfield at Lechfeld by a Messerschmitt Bf 110 fighter. Like its predecessor, the new aircraft was an unconventional flying-wing design which took off from a jettisonable dolly and landed on a sprung skid. Even by the standards of the day its dimensions were minute: the wingspan was only 30 ft 7 in and the length was 18 ft 4 in; the leading edge of the wing was swept back at 27 degrees at the root, increasing to 32 degrees for the outboard sections. In the air Dittmar found that the all-wing aircraft handled well. There were some control flutter problems at the higher speeds, but these were soon cured by altering the mass balancing of the surfaces. Once this had been done he was able to reach speeds of over 525 mph during unpowered dives.

In August 1941 the new Walter R II-203 rocket motor was pronounced ready for flight, and installed in the Me 163. On the 13th Dittmar made the first powered flight in the aircraft from Peenemünde West airfield. The Me 163 demonstrated an exceptional turn of speed and, during one of the early tests, Dittmar easily exceeded the current world air speed of 469 mph.

The Walter R II-203 ran on two fuels: highly concentrated hydrogen peroxide (*T-Stoff*) and an aqueous solution of sodium or calcium permanganate (*Z-Stoff*). The latter was a benign liquid, but the same cannot be said for the former. Highly concentrated hydrogen peroxide is an unstable compound, liable to decompose on contact with copper, lead or organic material of any sort; and when it decomposes it gives out heat at about the same rate as burning gunpowder. It is highly corrosive, and not its least unendearing feature is that it will burn away human flesh if the liquid is in contact with it for more than a few seconds. The use of this fuel was to pose many problems when the Me 163 later entered service.

Soon after the maiden flight of the Me 163, Rudolf Opitz joined Dittmar in the test programme. Opitz later recounted his first flight in the Me 163 to one of the authors. Following a thorough briefing by Dittmar, Opitz switched on the motor, opened the throttle and started to accelerate across the grass at Peenemünde West. From the beginning, however, Opitz found that his thoughts were 'behind' the rapidly moving rocket

ABOVE:
Heini Dittmar preparing to take the DFS 194 experimental rocket aircraft, the predecessor of the Me 163, for a flight on 3 June 1940.

As the rocket aircraft is being pushed to take-off point, Dittmar follows carrying his flying suit. *(Willie Elias)*

ABOVE AND LEFT:
Helgo Jahnke makes a final check of the rocket motor, then helps Dittmar into his flying suit. *(Willie Elias)*

ABOVE:
One wing supported by a ground crewman, the rocket motor is started and the diminutive aircraft begins its take-off run. *(Willie Elias)*

aircraft. As a result the machine was about 30 m (100 feet) above the ground before he suddenly realised that the take-off dolly was still attached. Already he was well above the altitude to jettison it safely: if he let it go now the handbuilt dolly would almost certainly be wrecked when it smashed into the ground. Not thinking too much about it, Opitz left the dolly in place under the fuselage. He burned off the rest of his fuel, then made a gliding approach and a perfectly normal landing. As he came to a halt, however, excited spectators came running towards him. On the dolly the Me 163 had very little directional control, and they had feared that when the wheels touched the ground the aircraft would have swung violently out of control. Others who later

Rudolf Opitz joined the Me 163 test programme soon after it began, and later became chief test pilot for the project. *(Opitz)*

attempted to land the aircraft on its dolly would not be so lucky as Opitz had been.

During the initial flight trials of the Me 163, it became clear that the aircraft was capable of horizontal speeds somewhat greater than those being achieved: during each attempt to get it to its maximum speed, the fuel ran out while the aircraft was still accelerating. To overcome this problem, it was decided to use a Messerschmitt Bf 110 to tow the rocket aircraft to altitude; freed of the need to expend fuel in the take-off and climb, the Me 163 could use all of its fuel for the speed run. Exactly what the maximum speed would be, Lippisch and his design team could only speculate; but the magic figure of 1,000 kmh (621 mph) seemed to be within the grasp of the small aircraft.

The great day came on 2 October 1941, when Opitz in the Messerschmitt Bf 110 towed Dittmar in the third prototype off from Peenemünde West for the speed run. The Me 163's fuel tanks were only three-quarters full, but that was to be sufficient. Dittmar cast off the tow at 13,000 feet, started the rocket motor and accelerated rapidly. He took the aircraft to over 609 mph then, without warning, the nose suddenly pitched down violently and he lost control: the Me 163 had gone over its threshold of compressibility. As this happened the rocket motor cut out, the severe negative 'G' forces preventing the fuels from reaching the combustion chamber. The speed rapidly dropped and Dittmar was able to regain control and take the aircraft in for a normal landing.

Post flight examination of the instrumentation carried by the aircraft revealed that immediately before the rocket cut out Dittmar had in fact reached just over 623 mph, or approximately Mach. 84 at that altitude. It was a brilliant feat, exceeding the current world air speed record by more than 156 mph; and it was probably to remain the fastest manned flight until 1947, when the official world air speed record finally overtook that figure. The dictates of wartime secrecy forbade publication of the Me 163's remarkable flight, however. All that could be done by way of public recognition was the presentation of the Lilienthal Diploma, one of Germany's highest aeronautical awards, to Dittmar, Lippisch and Walter.

The dramatic success of the speed trial aroused considerable enthusiasm from *Generaloberst* Ernst Udet, in charge of Luftwaffe equipment. Less than three weeks after Dittmar's epic flight he approved a plan submitted by Messerschmitt, for the development and construction of 70 Me 163s modified as interceptor fighters. Under the plan the Luftwaffe was to receive sufficient rocket fighters to have a *Gruppe* operational with the type in the spring of 1943. Lippisch immediately began work to redesign the aircraft for a new role, carrying two 20 mm cannon, increased fuel tankage, armour protection for the pilot and full operational equipment. It was planned to power the fighter version with the Walter R II-211 motor, under development with a target thrust of over 3,300 pounds. The new motor ran on hydrogen peroxide like its predecessor, and a mixture of methyl alcohol, hydrazine hydrate and water (*C-Stoff*).

The prototype Me 163A being prepared for its maiden flight from Peenemünde on 13 August 1941. During the initial flights the take-off dolly was attached to the retracted landing skid with no shock absorber or brakes which made take-off difficult. *(Willie Elias)*

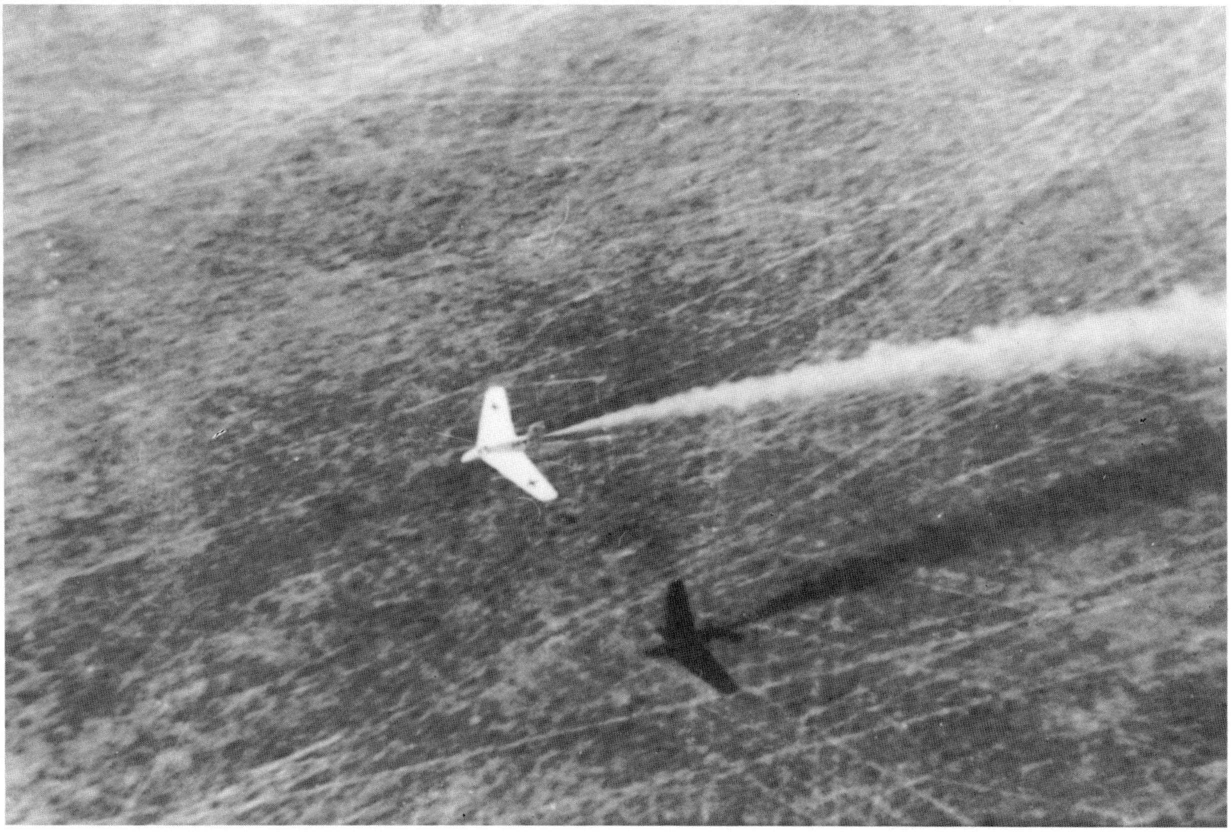

Me 163 trailing smoke from its rocket motor as it gets airborne from Peenemünde.

In the event the development of the fighter version of the Me 163 did not get very far before the death of its most powerful sponsor. In November 1941, less than a month after he had given his approval to the rocket fighter project, Ernst Udet committed suicide. Udet's term of office, in charge of the procurement of aircraft for the Luftwaffe, had been characterised by the fragmentation of the available development effort between numerous projects which were, in several cases, too innovative to be ready for service in the near future. And in the meantime the generation of combat aircraft that should have been entering service, to replace those in use since the beginning of the war — the Me 209, Me 210 and Heinkel He 177 — had all run into difficulties and were far from ready for production. The delays suffered by these projects, and the failure to meet production targets for the types already in service, caused the depression which had culminated in Udet's suicide. *Generalfeldmarschall* Erhard Milch, whose office took over Udet's responsibilities after his death, brought an air of reality to the aircraft production scene. He immediately made sweeping changes aimed at improving the production of current service types, and concentrated the development effort on those new aircraft likely to become operational in the short and the medium term. Long term projects, and those of limited operational use in the current operational stance of the Luftwaffe (and that included the Me 163 fighter), were relegated to positions well down the priority ladder or cancelled altogether. Even with increased tankage the fighter version of Me 163 would carry sufficient fuel for only four minutes' running of the rocket motor, then it would have to glide back to its base. In service, therefore, its role was limited to that of a daylight defence fighter with a radius of action of about 40 km. At the end of 1941, when the German advance into the Soviet Union was halted in front of Moscow and the sole threat to the homeland was from the ineffectual night bombers of the Royal Air Force, the Me 163 offered solutions to none of the Luftwaffe's actual or foreseen problems. Work on the rocket fighter was allowed to continue, but at a low priority.

In the spring of 1942 *Hauptmann* Wolfgang Spaete was appointed Luftwaffe project officer for the Me 163 fighter. And on 26 June the prototype of the fighter version, the Me 163B, made its first unpowered flight from Lechfeld. As usual, the development of the new motor had lagged far behind that of the airframe. Spaete formed a small trials unit, *Erprobungskommando* 16, to prepare the Me 163B for service and train pilots to fly it; but initially the new pilots were able to get rocket experience only on the Me 163A.

Not until June 1943 was the first R II-211 rocket motor, now re-designated the Walter 109-509, delivered to Peenemünde West and installed in the second prototype Me 163B. On 23rd Rudolf Opitz prepared to take the new fighter up for its first powered flight. At first everything went according to plan. The rocket started normally and, after a quick check that everything was functioning as it should, Opitz advanced the throttle through each of its three stages. With a piercing roar the aircraft accelerated across the grass but, just before it reached flying speed, the take-off dolly wrenched itself away from the fuselage. By now Opitz was too close to the airfield boundary to stop, so he gritted his teeth and held the throttle open, continuing to accelerate bumpily on his landing skid. Finally, to his great relief, the aircraft lifted off the ground. The German pilot's troubles were not yet over, however. As he eased back on the stick to begin his climb, the cockpit began to fill with stinging hydrogen peroxide fumes: in wrenching itself free, the take-off dolly had fractured one of the fuel lines. Opitz's eyes began to burn and then, even more disconcerting, the glass inside the cockpit and that of his flying goggles became covered with a thickening white film. Just when it seemed he might have to bale out, the motor devoured the last of the fuel; slowly the fumes began to clear, and with them the white film on the glass. Shaken by his two narrow escapes, Opitz returned to the airfield and made a normal landing.

On 25 August 1942 the Me 163 was demonstrated before senior officials and service officers. Standing in front of the port wing facing left, Opitz discusses flying the Me 163A with *General* Adolf Galland (in leather coat). *(Willie Elias)*

*Generalfeldmarshall* Erhard Milch, centre, congratulates Dittmar (in white flying suit) on an impressive flight. On the extreme right, wearing a trilby, is Helmuth Walter who designed the rocket motor. *(Willie Elias)*

During the weeks that followed several Walter 109-509 motors were delivered, and installed in Me 163Bs. Test-flying these as they became ready, Rudolf Opitz had further adventures. On 30 July, after a rapid climb at full throttle to 26,500 feet, he felt the rocket's thrust begin to fluctuate violently and saw the fire warning light flashing on. Opitz shut down the rocket and the light went out. During the subsequent descent he tried to re-start the rocket but it defied all of his efforts. With a large quantity of unburnt fuel still in the tanks he was in an unenviable position: the Me 163 would land faster than normal, and any accident that caused the tanks to fracture and the fuels to come together would result in a violent explosion. Opitz's only alternative was to bale out, but this would have meant the loss of one of the few available Me 163Bs; he decided to land the aircraft, and did so successfully.

On the following day Opitz had more problems. The tests called for accurate measurements of some of the rocket motor's parameters, and to allow room for the necessary additional test instrumentation Opitz agreed to the removal of the artificial horizon and the turn-and-bank indicator from his instrument panel. For this trial Opitz wore a small camera attached to a band round his head, with which he could photograph the instruments at regular intervals. In a letter to one of the authors he described the flight that followed; it was memorable, even by Me 163 standards:

'The day for the flight test was cloudless but hazy and the programme called for take-off to the north-east, establishing a maximum power climb at 320 mph indicated air speed on a straight line out over the Baltic, taking pictures of the instrument panel at 1,600 feet intervals up to an altitude of 40,000 feet. It seemed to be simple enough. However, the time schedule for taking the data was not easy to comply with when one realises that the aircraft needed only ten seconds to climb to 1,600 feet after reaching the desired airspeed and only six seconds were needed to climb through 1,600 feet at higher altitudes.

Take-off, dropping the dolly, retracting the flaps, accelerating to desired airspeed and trimming the aircraft for proper climb angle kept me very busy prior to recording my first checkpoint. The eight to ten seconds available between each of the following checkpoints were just enough to scan the instrument panel and to make necessary control adjustments to hold the aircraft within the narrow operating limits specified for the test. For a while everything went fine and I met the recording points right on the dot.

My airspeed, however, started to increase during the climb towards the 16,400 feet check point and despite corrective action I missed the required airspeed. I raised by head to look outside for a quick check of the aircraft attitude against the horizon, only to find that it was not visible because I was climbing in a heavy haze that blended perfectly with the sea below.'

Too late, Opitz realised that in trying to do too many things at once he had become dangerously disorientated; and with two of his most important flight instruments removed from the panel he had no way of discovering what the aircraft was doing. The next thing he knew was that the nose suddenly dropped and the motor cut — a sure sign that he had exceeded the compressibility threshold and was now diving out of control. Desperately he searched outside the cockpit for a reference point, and found a small island disconcertingly high on his canopy: he was in a steep diving turn to the left. Acting instinctively, Opitz was able to pull the Messerschmitt out of its dive just a few hundred metres above the flat-calm sea.

'Heading now for the coastline, which loomed out of the haze in the distance, I restarted the engine successfully and within minutes appeared over the airfield for a safe landing, much to the relief of our anxious crew who had given up hopes for my safe return after observing the aircraft arcing to the left during the steep climb and then suddenly heading down just as steeply towards the sea and disappearing below the horizon from their point of observation.

A walk-around inspection of the Me 163 after the landing quickly revealed signs attesting to the high

Heini Dittma flying one of the early Me 163Bs.
*(Transit Films)*

speeds and stresses to which I had unintentionally subjected the aircraft. The rudder had disintegrated completely; only its spar was still attached to the vertical fin. Fairing fasteners on the fuselage and wings had pulled out of their seatings.

Gradually pilots and ground crewmen became more familiar with the Me 163B and the trials programme became less of an adventure, though always one had to be careful. The pilots and those on the ground liable to come into contact with the hydrogen peroxide wore special overalls made of non-organic asbestos-based fibre. Yet although the material did give partial protection against small quantities of the rocket fuel, if there was a major spillage the liquid was able to soak through the seams of the garment and reach the man inside.

The all-up weight of the Me 163B on take-off was 8,700 pounds, just over half or 4,440 pounds was fuel for the rocket motor. And this allowed only about four minutes' running at full power, for with the throttle in the fully open position the Walter 109-509 devoured about 18.3 pounds of the two chemical fuels *each second*. Once the fuel was gone the greatly lightened Me 163B became a glider, though one with excellent handling characteristics. Rudolf Opitz remembers that the aircraft was light on the controls and the low speed handling was first class; it was, he recounted, 'absolutely spin-proof'.

ABOVE:
Refuelling an Me 163B with *C-Stoff* (mixture of methyl alcohol, hydrazine hydrate and water). When the tanks are full the aircraft will settle on the wooden stabilising posts under the wings, which prevent it rocking while it is being worked on. *(Transit Films)*

LEFT:
Ground crewman pushing the undercarriage dolly into position under the landing skid, before the aircraft was lowered into position on top of it.

LEFT:
An Me 163B photographed immediately after take-off, releasing its undercarriage dolly at a height of about 10 m (about 30 ft). *(Transit Films)*

BELOW:
This early system for recovering the Me 163 after it had landed employed inflated air bags to lift the aircraft; note the compressed air bottles attached to the top of the V-shaped towing arms. *(Transit Films)*

Me 163 drops a wing at the end of its skid landing run.

By August 1943 construction of the pre-production batch of 70 Me 163Bs was progressing well at the Messerschmitt factory at Obertraubling near Regensburg. At the same time the Klemm factory, near Stuttgart, was getting ready to build the aircraft of the main production batch, working under Messerschmitt supervision. Then, on the 17th of that month, the programme suffered a double blow. During the day USAAF heavy bombers hit the Messerschmitt plant at Regensburg, destroying 11 brand-new Me 163Bs and causing serious disruption to Messerschmitt 109 production. And that night Royal Air Force Bomber Command struck at Peenemünde, where Spaete's *Erprobungskommando* was based.

After the attack on Regensburg, and the need to concentrate everything on restoring production of the Messerschmitt 109, responsibility for producing the Me 163 became that of Klemm alone and very little help came from the parent company. And Klemm, a small firm which previously had built only light aircraft, was to prove quite unequal to the task of turning out such a high performance combat aircraft in quantity.

Following the attack on Peenemünde *Erprobungskommando* 16 moved to the nearby airfield at Anklam, where the training of pilots continued.

The training programme for new pilots began with a few flights in short-spanned gliders, to familiarise trainees with the problems of handling such aircraft. Next came towed flights in Me 163As first with empty tanks, then with progressively larger amounts of water ballast in the fuel tanks to increase the landing speed. This phase of the training culminated in three powered flights in the Me 163A, with progressively larger amounts of fuel.

Now the pilots were ready to fly the Me 163B, which was somewhat heavier than its predecessor. Starting the Walter 109-509 motor was relatively simple. The throttle had five notched positions: Off, Idle, 1st Stage, 2nd Stage and 3rd Stage. When the throttle was moved from Off to Idle, this exposed the starter button. When the button was pressed, small quantities of rocket fuels were allowed to run into the auxiliary combustion chamber; on reacting, the two chemicals drove a turbine which pumped the fuels into the main combustion chamber in the ratio of 3.25 parts of hydrogen peroxide to each part of hydrazine hydrate. The thrust of the motor built up rapidly to about 220 pounds. After a check of his two engine instruments — a fuel pump tachometer and a main combustion chamber pressure gauge — that the indications were normal, the pilot would advance his throttle through the 1st and 2nd Stages, gradually increasing the thrust. Finally, if all was still in order, he pushed the throttle to the 3rd Stage and the motor ran up to full thrust. The small fighter rode over the tiny chocks under the dolly wheels and began to pick up speed rapidly.

When it reached about 175 mph the fully-laden Me 163B would lift itself off the ground and a couple of seconds later, at about 30 feet above the ground, the pilot released the take-off dolly. Freed of the drag, the rocket fighter accelerated still faster. On reaching 435 mph in horizontal flight, still accelerating, the pilot would ease back on his stick to pull the Me 163 into a zoom climb at an angle of about 45 degrees with hardly any drop in forward speed. Held in the climb at full throttle, the rocket fighter reached just under 20,000 feet in about 2 minutes 16 seconds.

So far so good. But initially the Walter HWK 109-509 motor demonstrated a disconcerting habit of shutting down as the pilot eased forward on his stick to level out at the top of the climb. And, for technical reasons, the rocket motor could not be re-started for at least two minutes after shut-down. All in all this was a crippling tactical deficiency, since the shut-down occurred just at the time when, during a real operational mission, the Me 163 pilot would be in contact with the enemy and about to begin his attack. The task of tracking down the cause of the problem was to exercise Walter engineers for some months, for it proved impossible to reproduce the top-of-climb 'G' forces during bench running tests on the ground.

When the two rocket fuels came together they released energy at the same rate as gunpowder. This is all that remained of an Me 163B after the two fuels had come together inadvertently. *(Opitz)*

Considering the dangers inherent in the rocket fighter programme, it is remarkable that it continued as long as it did without a fatal flying accident. The first to lose his life in this way was a trainee pilot *Oberfeldwebel* Alois Woerndl, who took off under power in a Me 163A on 30 November. Gliding back with empty fuel tanks, he misjudged his approach and was killed when his aircraft flipped over on to its back after a very heavy landing. As is so often the case in flying accidents, this one had nothing to do with the really hazardous aspects of operating the aircraft.

Exactly a month later, on 30 December, *Oberleutnant* Joachim Poehs lost his life also while flying an Me 163A. Just after lift-off he released his dolly too soon; it rebounded off the airfield and struck the fuselage, causing the rocket motor to cut out. Banking his aircraft to land back on the field, Poehs hit a flak emplacement and the Me 163 smashed into the ground.

The opening of 1944 brought with it a severe deterioration of the military situation in the skies over Germany for the Luftwaffe air defence units charged with countering the American daylight raids; now the latest versions of the P-47 and P-51 escort fighters were proving able to penetrate deeper and deeper into the Reich to cover the attacks. At last there was a clear requirement for a high performance target defence fighter such as the Me 163, even if it did have only a limited endurance. The armament of two 20 mm cannon was too light to be effective against the tough American heavy bombers, so new Me 163Bs were to be fitted with a pair of 30 mm Mk 108 cannon.

Suddenly the Me 163 was back in favour again, and in an effort to speed it into operational service the Luftwaffe High Command issued orders in January for the formation of 20th *Staffel* of *Jagdgeschwader* 1, to be based at Bad Zwischenahn near Oldenburg with a strength of 12 Me 163s. The following month, under the command of *Oberleutnant* Rober Olejnik but still far short of his

complement of both aircraft and trained pilots, the unit was re-designated 1st *Staffel* of *Jagdgeschwader* 400. With one of the first operationally-equipped Me 163s to be delivered, Rudolf Opitz flew a series of interceptions against simulated enemy bomber formations at altitudes between 20,000 and 26,000 feet. But during each of them the motor cut when he levelled out the aircraft at the top of the climb; the old problem remained with the rocket fighter. Early in March the *Staffel* moved to Wittmundhafen, now with five aircraft and a dozen pilots in various stages of training.

Rudolf Opitz preparing to get airborne in an Me 163B from Bad Zwischenahn. Because of the dangers from inhaling hydrogen peroxide fumes if there was any leakage, and also because of the aircraft's very high rate of climb, the oxygen mask was worn from take-off. *(Transit Films)*

In spite of all efforts to get the Me 163 into action as soon as possible, deliveries of new aircraft from the Klemm company remained painfully slow. Not until 13 May was Wolfgang Spaete, recently promoted to Major, ready to attempt the first operational interception in a rocket fighter. After taking off from Bad Zwischenahn, Spaete was vectored on to a pair of P-47s flying near the airfield. Just as he was about to close in for the attack, however, the rocket motor cut out and he was forced to break away; fortunately for the German pilot, he had not been seen. Spaete now spent a frustrating couple of minutes before he could re-start the motor, watching his quarry getting smaller and smaller as they left him far behind. Finally the wait was up and, re-starting the rocket, he accelerated after them. Spaete overhauled the enemy fighters rapidly and swung into a firing position. Then suddenly, as he had one of the P-47s in his sight and was about to open fire, his left wing dropped violently: in concentrating on his prey, Spaete had allowed his speed to build up too far and the Me 163 had exceeded its compressibility threshold. By the time he regained control of the plunging rocket fighter, there was insufficient fuel left for a further interception. Blissfully unaware of their narrow escape, the American fighters pilots continued on their heading. Doubly frustrated, Spaete burned off the remainder of his fuel and returned to his base.

Further attempts to intercept Allied aircraft during the days that followed proved similarly unsuccessful. But on 31 May a reconnaissance Spitfire of the Royal Air Force brought back the first reliable report of a sighting of an Me 163 in the air, near Wilhelmshaven. The official report on the incident stated:

'Flying at 37,000 feet the pilot first saw a white trail about 3,000 feet below him and something over a mile distant horizontally. The trail turned into a interception course and then disappeared. The Spitfire pilot began to climb, and during the next three minutes saw the trail reappear four times, at intervals, as the unknown aircraft climbed towards him. He observed that the plane apparently covered a distance of about three times the length of the visible trail before the next emission would appear.

By the time the Spitfire had reached 41,000 feet the pilot could see the supposed enemy, but could not identify the aircraft, except that it seemed to be "nearly all wing" which possibly had a marked sweep-back. At this point the unknown aircraft was only 3,000 feet below the Spitfire, and only about 1,000 yards away horizontally. Evidently it had climbed about 8,000 feet and reduced the horizontal distance by about 1,000 yards during the time it took the Spitfire to climb about 3,500 feet. No further trails were seen, the pilot lost sight of the aircraft and soon afterwards returned to base.

The reported regularity of the appearance of vapour trails tends to bear out previous reports that the propulsion unit of the Me 163 is used only intermittently, and also suggests that it is cut in and out automatically. On the other hand this apparent regularity may have been mere coincidence.' *

The report concluded with the observation that the Me 163 may have been on a training flight, since the incident occurred only some 20 miles from Bad Zwischenahn where these aircraft had been photographed on the ground.

By now the main cause of the Me 163's motor cutting out at the top of the climb had been discovered. The two chemical fuels had to be injected into the combustion chamber in exactly the right ratio, or an uncontrolled explosion might result. As a safety measure, the Walter rocket was designed to shut itself down *automatically* if there was a break in the supply of either of the fuels. When the Me 163 was levelled out at the top of the climb, however, the change of attitude of the aircraft caused the fuels to slop about in their tanks; if a feed pipe was momentarily uncovered the safety system would detect a break in the fuel supply, and shut down the motor. The installation of additional baffle plates in the fuel tanks reduced the incidence of cut-outs, but did not prevent them altogether.

In June 1944, still without a successful engagement to its credit, the Me 163 *Staffel* was redesignated 1st *Gruppe* of JG 400, received a new commander, and was redeployed. On his promotion *Major* Wolfgang Spaete was sent to command a conventional fighter *Gruppe* on the Eastern Front; in his place as Me 163 project leader was appointed the fighter ace and leader *Oberst* Gordon Gollob. Spaete's plan for the deployment of the rocket fighter had called for a series of specially equipped airfields at approximately 62 mile intervals — ie all within Me 163 gliding range — position in an arc through northern Germany and Holland astride the American bombers' routes to their targets. But by the early part of June this plan had been overtaken by events.

Once the Allied troops had established their bridgehead in Normandy, the US Strategic Bomber commander General Carl Spaatz ordered that henceforth the *primary strategic aim* of the 8th Air

* When the Me 163 pilot throttled back to less than full thrust the visible vapour trail ceased; the rocket motor had not cut out.

Me 163B *Erprobungskommando 16* beginning a rocket take-off from Bad Zwischenahn. *(Transit Films)*

Steam gushes from the fuel pump turbine exhaust, as the ground crewman pushes the electrical trolley clear prior to starting the rocket motor.

*Oberst* Gordon Gollob, the famous fighter ace, who took over from Wolfgang Spaete as leader of the Me 163 fighter project in June 1944. *(Gollob)*

Two Me 163s (circled) of the five belonging to *Erprobungskommand 16* which were photographed at Bad Zwischenahn by an Allied reconnaissance aircraft on 11 May 1944. *(USAF)*

Force in England and the 15th Air Force in Italy was to be the destruction of the enemy fuel supplies. The effect of the resultant massed air attacks on the German synthetic oil refineries was immediate and devastating: from 175,000 tons in April, the German production of high octane aviation petrol fell to less than a third of that figure — only 55,000 tons — in June.

The few available Me 163s at bases in northern Germany could easily be avoided by the American bombers coming in from England; and they were no threat at all to the bombers coming in from Italy. So Gollob now ordered I./JG 400 to concentrate its aircraft at the airfield at Brandis near Leipzig in south-eastern Germany. The Me 163 was to be used as a target-defence fighter, to protect the vitally important oil refineries at Leuna-Merseburg, Bohlen, Zeitz and Leutzkendorf, all of which were coming under repeated attack.

The move to Brandis took about three weeks to complete, and not until the latter part of July was JG 400 ready to make any serious attempt to engage enemy aircraft. Then, on the morning of the 29th, a force of 596 American bombers set out to attack the Leuna-Merseberg complex. As the raiders began their bombing runs, six Me 163Bs scrambled off the ground at Brandis in succession and climbed steeply to intercept. Colonel Avelin Tacon, leading P-51s of the 359th Fighter Group escorting the bombers in the target area, afterwards reported:

'I encountered two Me 163s. My eight P-51s were furnishing close escort for a combat wing of B-17s, and we were flying south at 25,000 feet when one of my pilots called in two contrails at six o'clock high some five miles back at 32,000 feet. I identified them immediately as jet propelled aircraft. Their contrails could not be mistaken and looked very dense and white, somewhat like an elongated cumulus cloud some three quarters of a mile in length. My section turned 180 degrees back towards the enemy fighters, which included two with jets turned on and three in a glide without jets operating at the moment.

The two I had spotted made a diving turn to the left in close formation and feinted towards the bombers at six o'clock, cutting off their jets as they turned. Our flight turned for a head-on pass to get between them and the rear of the bomber formation. While still 3,000 yards from the bombers, they turned into us and left the bombers alone. In this turn they banked about 80 degrees but their course changed only about 20 degrees. Their turn radius was very large but their rate of roll appeared excellent. Their speed I estimated was 500 to 600 miles per hour. Both planes passed under us, 1,000 feet below, while still in a close formation glide. In an attempt to follow them, I split S'd. One continued down in a 45 degree dive, the other climbed up into the sun very steeply and I lost him. Then I looked back at the one in a dive and saw he was five miles away at 10,000 feet. Other members of my flight reported that the one which went up into the sun used his jet in short bursts as though it was blowing smoke rings. These pilots appeared very experienced but not aggressive.'

Tacon's final comment was a perceptive one, for some of the German pilots had trouble with their motors cutting out at the top of the climb — it was difficult to be aggressive if this happened. Those Me 163 pilots who were able to reach the bombers found that their closing speeds were so great that none was able to score hits. Harried by the escorting Mustangs, the rocket fighters exhausted their fuel and returned to Brandis. But there another problem awaited them. Gliding down one after the other, the Me 163s were committed to landing; and they did so in rapid succession, giving the ground crewmen no time to clear the rocket fighters from the landing ground. Fortunately for the German pilots there were no collisions between landing aircraft and those already down, but there were some near misses. It was a clear pointer to the problems that would arise in the future if several Me 163s were to operate simultaneously from one airfield.

Me 163B of 1st *Gruppe* of JG 400, at readiness at Brandis.

**Me 163**

1 Generator drive propeller
2 Generator
3 Compressed air bottle
4 Battery and electronics packs
5 Cockpit ventilation intake
6 Solid armour (15 mm) nose cone
7 Accumulator pressuriser
8 Direct cockpit air intake
9 FuG 16 radio panel
10 Rudder control assembly
11 Hydraulic and compressed air points
12 Elevon control rocker-bar
13 Control relay
14 Flying controls assembly box
15 Plastic rudder pedals
16 Radio tuning controls
17 Torque shaft
18 Port T-stoff cockpit tank (13 Imp gal/60 l capacity)
19 Control column
20 Hinged instrument panel
21 Laminated glass windscreen brace
22 Revi 16B gunsight
23 Laminated glass internal windscreen (90 mm)
24 Armament and radio switches (starboard console)
25 Pilot's seat
26 Back armour (8 mm)
27 Head and shoulder armour (13 mm)
28 Radio frequency selector pack
29 Headrest
30 Mechanically-jettisonable hinged canopy
31 Ventilation panel
32 Fixed leading-edge wing slot
33 Trim tab
34 Fabric-covered starboard elevon
35 Position of underwing landing flap
36 Inboard trim flap
37 FuG 16 receiving aerial
38 T-Stoff filler cap
39 Main unprotected T-Stoff fuselage tank (229 Imp gal/1,040 l capacity)
40 Aft cockpit glazing
41 Port cannon ammunition box (60 rounds)
42 Starboard cannon ammunition box (60 rounds)
43 Ammunition feed chute
44 T-Stoff starter tank
45 Rudder control upper bell crank
46 C-Stoff filler cap
47 HWK 509A-1 motor turbine housing
48 Main rocket motor mounting frame
49 Rudder control rod
50 Disconnect point
51 Aerial matching unit
52 Fin front spar/fuselage attachment point
53 Tailfin construction
54 Rudder horn balance
55 Rudder upper hinge
56 Rudder frame

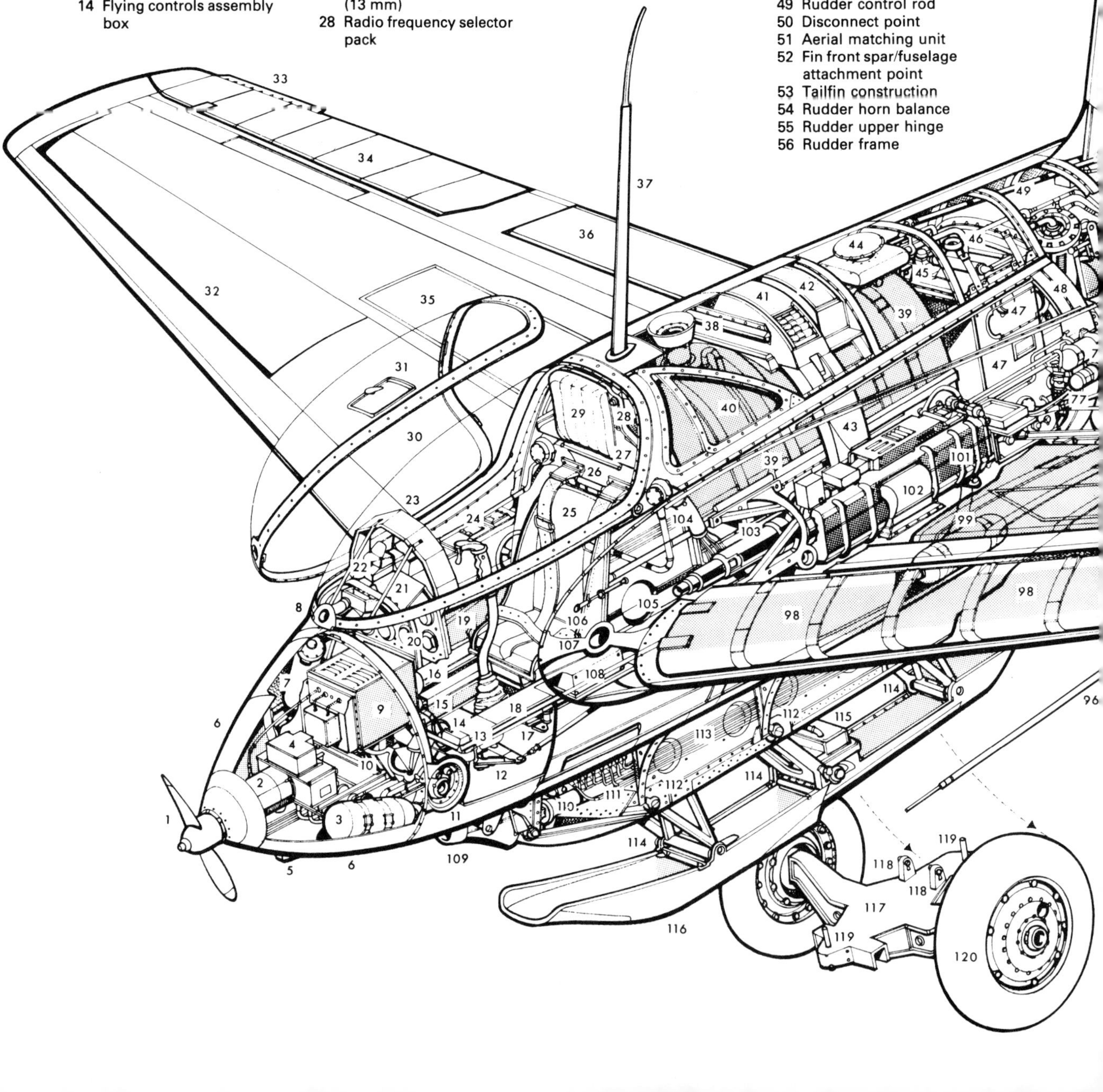

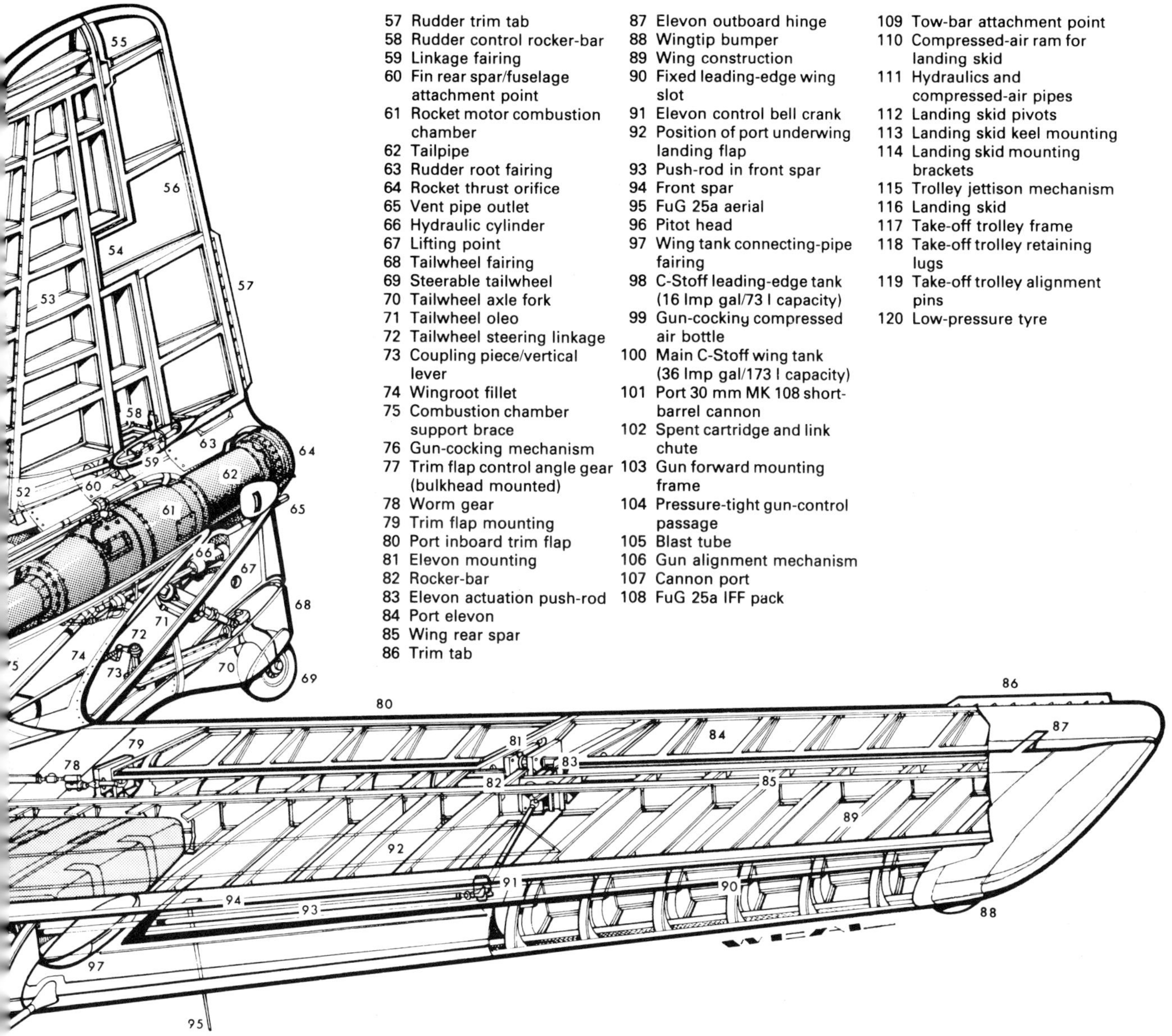

57 Rudder trim tab
58 Rudder control rocker-bar
59 Linkage fairing
60 Fin rear spar/fuselage attachment point
61 Rocket motor combustion chamber
62 Tailpipe
63 Rudder root fairing
64 Rocket thrust orifice
65 Vent pipe outlet
66 Hydraulic cylinder
67 Lifting point
68 Tailwheel fairing
69 Steerable tailwheel
70 Tailwheel axle fork
71 Tailwheel oleo
72 Tailwheel steering linkage
73 Coupling piece/vertical lever
74 Wingroot fillet
75 Combustion chamber support brace
76 Gun-cocking mechanism
77 Trim flap control angle gear (bulkhead mounted)
78 Worm gear
79 Trim flap mounting
80 Port inboard trim flap
81 Elevon mounting
82 Rocker-bar
83 Elevon actuation push-rod
84 Port elevon
85 Wing rear spar
86 Trim tab
87 Elevon outboard hinge
88 Wingtip bumper
89 Wing construction
90 Fixed leading-edge wing slot
91 Elevon control bell crank
92 Position of port underwing landing flap
93 Push-rod in front spar
94 Front spar
95 FuG 25a aerial
96 Pitot head
97 Wing tank connecting-pipe fairing
98 C-Stoff leading-edge tank (16 Imp gal/73 l capacity)
99 Gun-cocking compressed air bottle
100 Main C-Stoff wing tank (36 Imp gal/173 l capacity)
101 Port 30 mm MK 108 short-barrel cannon
102 Spent cartridge and link chute
103 Gun forward mounting frame
104 Pressure-tight gun-control passage
105 Blast tube
106 Gun alignment mechanism
107 Cannon port
108 FuG 25a IFF pack
109 Tow-bar attachment point
110 Compressed-air ram for landing skid
111 Hydraulics and compressed-air pipes
112 Landing skid pivots
113 Landing skid keel mounting
114 Landing skid mounting brackets
115 Trolley jettison mechanism
116 Landing skid
117 Take-off trolley frame
118 Take-off trolley retaining lugs
119 Take-off trolley alignment pins
120 Low-pressure tyre

MESSERSCHMITT 163B

Power unit: one Walter HWK 509 rocket motor, rated at 1,700 kg (3,750 pounds) thrust.
Armament: early versions carried two 20 mm Mauser MG 151 cannon. Later versions carried two 30 mm Rheinmetall Borsig MK 108 cannon with 60 rounds per gun.

Performance: maximum speed 955 kph (592 mph) above 3,000 m (9,750 ft). Approximate operational radius of action 40 km (25 miles). Initial climb 81 m/sec (15,900 feet per minute). Time to 6,000 m (19,500 ft), 2 min 16 secs.

Weights: Empty, equipped, 1,908 kg (4,205 pounds); normally loaded, 4,310 kg (9,500 pounds).

Dimensions: Span 9.33 m (30 ft 7½ in) Length 5.85 m (19 ft 2½ in) Wing area 18.5 sq m (199 sq ft).

The instrument panel of the Me 163B, showing the relatively sparce instrumentation required for the rocket fighter. The tanks on either side of the pilot's legs contained *T-Stoff* (highly concentrated hydrogen peroxide). *(Crown Copyright)*

After reading Tacon's report Major-General William Kepner, commanding the 8th Fighter Command, instructed his operational units:

'. . . It is believed we can expect to see more of these aircraft immediately and we can expect attacks on the bombers from the rear in formations or waves. To be able to counter and have time to turn into them, our units are going to have to be in positions relatively close to the bombers to be between them and our heavies. It is believed these tactics will keep them from making effective, repeat effective, attacks on the bombers . . .'

The fear of a massed attack by the rocket fighters was to remain with the US High Command for the remainder of the war though, for the reasons already outlined, such a move would have presented considerable tactical difficulties for I./JG 400. Kepner's order for the US escort fighters to stay closer to the bombers was a sound one: by maintaining a continual threat on the Me 163s while they were in the vicinity of the bombers, the German pilots would be forced to keep their speed high as they made their attacking runs — with a consequent reduction in the accuracy of their shooting.

On the following day, the 29th, a force of 647 US heavy bombers attacked Merseburg. This time six Me 163s attempted to intercept the raiders but, as on the first day, the results were inconclusive and neither side suffered damage.

On 31 July a reconnaissance Lightning had a brush with an Me 163 but succeeded in escaping without damage. And on 5 August no fewer than ten rocket fighters were reported in the vicinity of another American bomber formation attacking Merseburg, though yet again there appears to have been no loss on either side.

Not until 16 August was there a real fight between 1st *Gruppe* of *Jagdgeschwader* 400 and a US raiding force. On that day 1,096 B-17s and B-24s, with a powerful fighter escort, set out to attack targets at Zeitz, Rositz, Leuna, Boehlen, Halle, Dresden and Koethen. Five Me 163Bs were waiting at readiness and these scrambled into the air. One of the first to reach the bombers was *Feldwebel* Herbert Straznicky, who dived to attack a B-17 of the 305th Bomb Group. Sergeant H. Kaysen, the bomber's tail gunner, kept up an accurate fire on the rocket fighter as it ran in and when the latter broke away at short range it was streaming black smoke. Suffering from splinter wounds to his left arm and thigh, Straznicky was forced to bale out of his crippled aircraft. He reached the ground without further injury.

Shortly afterwards *Leutnant* Hartmut Ryll attacked another of the 305th BG B-17s, that piloted by 2nd Lieutenant C. Laverdiere. Closing in to short range, Ryll's accurate burst scored hits on both inboard engines and the flaps and killed one of the waist gunners and the ball gunner.

Pulling away from the bomber formation, Ryll then spotted B-17 *Outhouse Mouse* of the 91st Bomb Group straggling behind the main force of bombers after having suffered damage during an attack by FW 190s. As the Me 163 closed in for the *coup de grâce*, however, it was in its turn spotted by Lieutenant-Colonel John Murphy leading a pair of P-51s of the 359th Fighter Group. Murphy afterwards reported:

'I was escorting our bombers south-east of Leipzig at 27,000 ft when I notice a contrail climbing rapidly up towards the bombers from behind and the port side. I recognized the contrails as being produced by a jet-propelled aircraft because of its speed. Due to its speed and altitude advantage I knew I could not overtake him, but noticed a straggling B-17 to the starboard at 25,000 ft which was headed north-east of Leipzig all alone, and I headed towards him, thinking that he probably would

Me 163B of *Jagdgeschwader* 400 commencing a rocket take-off from Brandis. *(Glogner)*

be attacked. The Jettie contrail ceased about 500 yds from the bomber, and from that point on I kept him in sight as I would any other aircraft. He passed through the bombers and down to the straggling B-17 and arrived there before I could; however, I wasn't far behind and was overtaking. After he passed the B-17 he seemed to level off, and as I closed on him I opened fire from about 1,000 ft and held it until I overshot. I scored a few hits on the left side of the fuselage. I pulled up to the left as sharply as I could to prevent overshooting and getting out in front of him and lost sight of both him and my wingman. My wingman, Lt Jones, reported that the Jettie flipped over on his back in a half roll, and as he did so, he scored a sufficient number of hits on the canopy to destroy him. As Jones tried to follow him through on his dive, Jones blacked out. When I completed my sharp chandelle turn to the left, I saw another Jettie off to my left and Jones farther off and lower to my right. I started down on this one, which was making rather shallow diving turns to the left. I think I must have turned with him through two turns before overtaking him. I realized that I was going to overtake him rapidly too, but I held my fire to an estimated 750 ft and held a continuous burst, seeing continuous strikes the full length of his fuselage. Parts began falling off, followed by a big explosion and more parts falling off. I could smell the strange chemical fumes in my cockpit as I followed through the smoke of the explosion. It seemed to me that a large chunk of the fuselage from the canopy on back just popped off with the explosion.'

Murphy followed the falling aircraft some way down then, seeing another enemy aircraft about two miles off, broke off the chase. By now his P-51 was running low on fuel so he turned for home. At the end of his report he stated:

'My first impression when I saw the jet plane was that I was standing still. It seemed hopeless to try to attempt to overtake them, but my actions were prompted by a curiosity to get as close to them as possible. I believe that will be the reaction of every pilot that comes in contact with them. Another thing that is very noticeable is that their speed varies considerably, but it's hard to realize this until you find yourself rapidly overtaking them.'

From the German evidence available, it seems clear that the first Me 163 to be destroyed by Murphy and Jones was Ryll's; he was killed. The second Me 163 may possibly have been Straznicky's after he had baled out; it is known that this aircraft exploded before it struck the ground. Without having yet scored a kill, the rocket fighter unit had lost its first two aircraft in combat.

Retrieval of an Me 163B after landing, using the system employed late in the war. The *Scheuschlepper* vehicle was used, with a tracked trailer with two hydraulic arms which lifted the aircraft clear off the ground.

Eight days later, on 24 August, I./JG 400 scored its first successes. Eight Me 163Bs were launched from Brandis to engage a large force of B-17s approaching Leuna, and shortly afterwards crewmen of the 92nd, 305th 381st and 457th Bomb Groups were reporting the approach of the small rocket fighters. Badly positioned by their ground controller, *Feldwebel* Siegfried Schubert and his wingman climbed to about 32,500 feet without sighting the bombers. Both Me 163s throttled back to idling to conserve fuel and descended in the glide, searching for their prey. They were below the level of the bombers when the two German pilots finally sighted their prey: the B-17s of the 92nd Bomb Group. Both Me 163s immediately opened up to full power and swung round into the attack. Schubert singled out the leading B-17 piloted by Lieutenant Hoehler, and his short burst caused severe damage to the left wing; the bomber staggered out of the formation losing height, to crash shortly afterwards. Still with his rocket motor full on Schubert ran rapidly underneath his victim and clear of the bombers' return fire; but in his haste to get away he ran into compressibility trouble and suddenly found himself diving out of control. While Schubert wrestled with his stick his wingman made a similarly accurate firing pass on 2nd Lieutenant Steve Nagy's B-17; its No. 4 engine burst into flame, the aircraft went into a spin and it blew up at about 19,000 feet.

LEFT:
*Feldwebel* Rudolf Zimmermann's Me 163 photographed from Lieutenant Willard Erkamp's P-51, during the action on 7 October. The German pilot crash landed his damaged aircraft and was able to safely run clear, before strafing Mustangs wrecked the Messerschmitt on the ground. *(USAF)*

BELOW LEFT:
Two of the rocket pilots of JG 400 who fought during the August actions: *Feldwebeln* Manfred Eisenmann (left) and Rudolf Glogner. Eisenmann was killed when his Me 163 crashed on 24 August. *(Glogner)*

BELOW:
*Feldwebel* Rudolf Zimmermann with 'Harras', the mascot of 1st *Staffel* of *Jagdgeschwader* 400. *(Zimmermann)*

Two other Me 163s piloted by *Oberfeldwebel* Peter Husser and *Unteroffizier* Manfred Eisenmann then darted in to attack the same bomber formation; no American bombers were hit during their firing runs, however, though Eisenmann's Messerschmitt suffered tail damage from the return fire.

By now Schubert had regained control of his plunging aircraft and, having restarted his motor, accelerated back to altitude to regain the fray. This time he made contact with B-17s of the 457th Bomb Group and, throttling back to idling, attacked from almost head-on in a shallow dive. Schubert's rounds scored hits on Lieutenant Winfred Pugh's B-17, which peeled away from the formation and went into a spin, before finally blowing up at about 10,000 ft.

Also at about the same time, B-17s of the 305th Bomb Group came under attack from a pair of Me 163s and one of the bombers, piloted by 2nd Lieutenant P. Dabney, was shot down. In each case the rocket fighter pilots were able to carry out their attacking runs so rapidly that they were clear of the bombers before the escorting Mustangs could intervene.

Still there were technical problems with the Me 163, however; it seemed that as some of the problems were solved, new ones arose to replace them. Climbing out to intercept, *Feldwebel* Rudolf Zimmermann had his rocket motor prematurely cut out. Unable to restart it he pulled the handle to jettison the dangerous hydrogen peroxide, then turned through a semi-circle and headed back to Brandis.* Lacking the necessary altitude for a normal approach, he extended his skid and lined up for a straight-in approach and a down-wind landing. He later wrote:

'Coming in fast and short, I touched down early and hard. At that moment there was a tremendous explosion with flames, smoke and fragments of the aircraft lying around the cockpit. When the machine came to a halt I could see the grass landing ground through a hole in the bottom of the cockpit. Around the skid all the metal skinning had been blown away and the plywood covering on the underside of the wings had also been torn open.'

Zimmermann received a severe reprimand from his *Staffel* commander, for supposedly causing the damage by landing the Me 163 too hard. Only somewhat later, after a similar but more serious incident in which an aircraft was wrecked and its pilot badly burned, was the true cause of the explosion discovered. After being jettisoned, some of the hydrogen peroxide had run into the landing skid well and collected there. Most of it had blown away when Zimmermann had extended the skid, but when he touched down there was still a little left. As the skid's shock absorbers took the force of the landing a small quantity of hydraulic oil was sprayed on to the hydrogen peroxide; and the reaction of the two chemicals caused the explosion. Once the cause was discovered, Me 163 pilots were warned to extend their landing skid immediately after pulling the hydrogen peroxide jettison handle, to allow the airflow as long as possible to blow away any of the chemical which collected on the skid.

During the day's fighting the Me 163s had been able to destroy four enemy bombers in return for one rocket fighter, Eisenmann's, damaged in combat and another, Zimmermann's, damaged on landing. After all that had gone before, I./JG 400 had achieved its first successes; yet the rocket fighter's victory score on this day was never to be equalled in the future.

September saw operations by JG 400 on five occasions, on the 10th, 11th, 12th, 13th and 28th. The strength of the unit's reaction varied, with nine Me 163s being sent up on the last of these missions. But on all of them there were problems with ground control, and only a small proportion of the rocket fighters were able to intercept. For example, on the 28th Zimmermann was scrambled to engage an American formation flying past Brandis. Since he was to intercept at close to the limit of the Me 163's radius of action, to conserve fuel he did not use full throttle and took his aircraft up at a shallow angle of climb (for the Me 163, that is):

'Four minutes after take-off I sighted the B-17s, about 45 aircraft at about 10 o'clock at 25,000 ft. I myself was flying level at 30,000 ft at about 500 mph, in an excellent position. But about 1.5 km behind the formation my motor shut down, my fuel was exhausted. In a flat dive I curved round to the left on to the last B-17 in the box, and at 550 yds I fired one burst without visible result.'

* Later production Me 163Bs were fitted with a system for jettisoning *T-Stoff*.

Me 163 pilots of *Jagdgeschwader* 400 photographed at Brandis late in 1944: from left to right, Schorsch Neher, unidentified, Kristoph Kurz, and Jupp Muehlstroh. Note the two pilots in the background, wearing the special protective suits issued to rocket pilots. *(Glogner)*

Lacking power, Zimmermann's Messerschmitt now began to fall behind the bombers. So in a final desperate attempt he pushed down the nose of his fighter to gain a little more speed, then pulled up for a snap attack from below on the same B-17 — only to have his guns jam at the critical moment. Seething with frustration, the German pilot broke away and began his long glide back to Brandis.

On 24 September JG 400 was listed as having 19 Me 163s on strength, of which 11 were available for operations. Since well over 100 Me 163Bs had been produced by this time it is clear that, as in the case of other German jet types, only relatively few of those built were reaching the front-line units.

Also during September, the rocket fighter programme suffered a crippling setback. Following Allied bombing attacks on Leverkusen and Ludwigshaven, where the IG Farbenindustrie plants produced most of the hydrazine hydrate in Germany, there was a severe cut back in the production of this important rocket fuel. The resultant shortages were to dog the Me 163 programme for the remainder of the war (a major competitor for the limited supplies was the V1 flying bomb, which required hydrazine hydrate to power its launching catapult).'

During October there were further sporadic actions by the rocket fighters. After an unsuccessful attempt to engage American bombers on the 5th, they were more successful on the 7th. Five Me 163s took off in the first wave and, before the escorting P-51s could do anything about it, *Feldwebel* Siegfried Schubert had shot down a B-17 of the 95th Bomb Group. Landing back at Brandis, Schubert strapped into another Me 163 to have a second crack at the B-17s. Then, in the words of Rudolf Zimmermann who watched the incident:

'He started, rolling faster and faster. Near the end of the grass runway he veered towards the left; something was wrong with his take-off dolley. He hit the grass at take-off speed, flipped over as if his left wheel had come off, then there was an explosion and everything was hidden in a large mushroom cloud. Our good friend Siegfried Schubert was no more.'

Though shaken at seeing one of their comrades meet such a violent end, the Me 163 pilots continued taking off in ones and twos to engage the enemy bombers. Zimmermann continued:

'*Leutnant* Bott and I took off at 1230 pm west-bound, turning left and heading for the area 50 km south-east of Leipzig. Climbing, we opened out and began searching for targets. Looking down from an altitude of 36,000 ft, climbing at an angle of about 60 degrees at a speed of about 580 mph I saw below my right wing a lone B-17 at about 24,000 ft. Being above, I turned away circling to the left, the B-17 now being at about 1 o'clock and below, 1.5 km away. Then my motor shut down, indicating that my fuel was exhausted. I dived into a firing position, fired a burst and saw pieces flying off the bomber.'

Zimmermann's speed began to fall away, so he broke off and turned in the general direction of Brandis. A long way from base and over almost solid cloud cover, he was about to call for a homing when:

'At that moment the roof fell in. My aircraft was hit in the fuselage and on the left wing. About 80 m off my left wing a Mustang was overshooting me, his auxiliary tanks still in position. I myself was going at about 150 mph, pulling in a steep turn to the left to get behind him. At that moment his No. 2 overshot me to the right. I continued turning and, getting head-on with his No. 3, I pressed my firing button. But in the sharp turns my guns jammed.'

Leading the Mustangs was Lieutenant Elmer Taylor of the 364th Fighter Group. As he overshot,

Zimmermann pushed down the nose of his small fighter until he was diving almost vertically; his speed built up rapidly. Below him was almost complete cloud cover, except for a single hole through which he could see a reasonably sized field surrounded by trees. The German pilot continued:

'Soon out-diving the Mustangs in the opposite direction, I was ahead of the game, going down at about 550 mph and circling the meadow. Then, on approaching to land, my left wing fell as the speed dropped: the plywood skinning on the underside had been torn off by their bullets and the subsequent dive. I skimmed over the tree tops, chopping Christmas trees; my left wing dug into the ground, cutting short my landing run. I came to a halt in the middle of the field. Hearing the Mustangs approaching, I jumped out. As the first came in to attack I ran off at right angles, then dropped down. During several strafing runs my aircraft was shot up like a sieve.'

Despite the bullets flying all around him, the greatest danger to Zimmermann came from a 'friendly' Flak battery nearby; its gunners opened up enthusiastically at the low-flying Mustangs, sending several rounds which burst uncomfortably close to him.

After the Mustangs had broken off their attack and turned away for home. Zimmermann returned to his wrecked aircraft to survey the damage. It was then that he was surprised to see his friend *Feldwebel* Herbert Straznicky, who had taken off shortly before him in an Me 163, come walking towards him; how had Straznicky been able to reach the crash site so soon? Straznicky explained that he too had been pursued by Mustangs and had descended through the same hole in the clouds, but his Me 163 had come to rest almost up against the trees. While the Mustangs had strafed Zimmermann's aircraft, Straznicky had hidden in the trees and, when the attack ended, he returned to his Me 163 to find it untouched: his first thought was that the American pilots must have been lousy shots! Then he caught sight of Zimmermann's wrecked aircraft and the truth became clear. Straznicky's undamaged fighter was later collected and taken back to Brandis; Zimmermann's was a write-off.

Zimmermann and Straznicky had escaped unscathed, but in the meantime disaster had struck again at Brandis. *Unteroffizier* Manfred Eisenmann,

Captain Fred Glover, flying a P-51 of the 4th Fighter Group, shot down *Oberfeldwebel* Guenther Andreas's Me 163 during the action on 2 November. The German pilot parachuted to safety. *(Glover via Hess)*

returning to an aircraft that had probably suffered battle damage, side-slipped out of control during his landing approach. *Unteroffizier* Rudolf Glogner, sitting in a fully-tanked rocket fighter awaiting the order to scramble, watched horrified as Eisenmann's Me 163 lurched in his direction. The aircraft struck the ground hard, rebounded into the air, then dropped one wing and tumbled across the grass breaking up as it careered past Glogner's and other waiting rocket fighters. Crash crews found Eisenmann's body still strapped inside what was left of the cabin.

*Leutnant* Hans Bott had damaged one B-17, and Siegfried Schubert had destroyed another before his fatal attempt at a second mission. But these victories had been soured by the loss of three Me 163s and two pilots killed on 7 October.

For the remainder of October there was little activity by JG 400, mainly due to the poor weather and the fuel shortage that was now beginning to bite. But on 2 November there was a powerful response to a heavy attack on Leuna by B-17s of the 3rd Air Division. *Leutnant* Hans Bott,

*Oberfeldwebel* Jacob Bollenrath, *Oberfeldwebel* Guenther Andreas, Straznicky and Glogner took off and were accurately vectored into the vicinity of the enemy bombers. Andreas was first into the attack, but his Me 163 immediately came under accurate return fire and a splinter hit him above the right eye. His aircraft crippled, he tried to bale out of the falling Messerschmitt, but his canopy refused to budge at first. The German pilot undid his seat harness and pushed against the plexiglass with all of his strength until, finally and to his great relief, it came away. Meanwhile, however, the escorting Mustangs had been closing in on the gliding rocket fighter. Captain Fred Glover, who was leading the 4th Fighter Group that day, afterwards reported:

'The aircraft made a 180 degree starboard turn and headed back east in a slight dive. I dropped my tanks and headed for it on a converging course. The aircraft headed east and myself north. As the enemy aircraft crossed in front of me I recognized it to be an Me 163 rocket ship. I made a quick 90 degree turn to the east and dropped in line astern. I opened fire immediately from a range of about 400 yards. I got immediate strikes on the tail, wings and cockpit. The belly of the Me 163 caught fire and exploded. Pieces came back and I closed rapidly, after the explosion. I overshot and laid my wing down to look at him. His tail was shot off and his canopy shot up badly (in fact, Andreas had released it by this time). The Me 163 started to wallow and spin down still on fire.'

Andreas had not been aware of the presence of his assailant until the latter's rounds began striking his aircraft; throughout the attack he sat huddled in his seat not daring to move. Then, unscathed, he baled out of the stricken aircraft.

Andreas had had a very lucky escape but *Oberfeldwebel* Jacob Bollenrath, who attacked after him, was not so fortunate. Captain Louis Norley, also of the 4th Fighter Group, caught sight of Bollenrath running in to attack the bombers:

*Leutnant* Fritz Kelb of JG 400, who scored the sole victory with the *Jaegerfaust* upwards-firing weapon on 10 April 1945. He was killed just before the war ended. *(Glogner)*

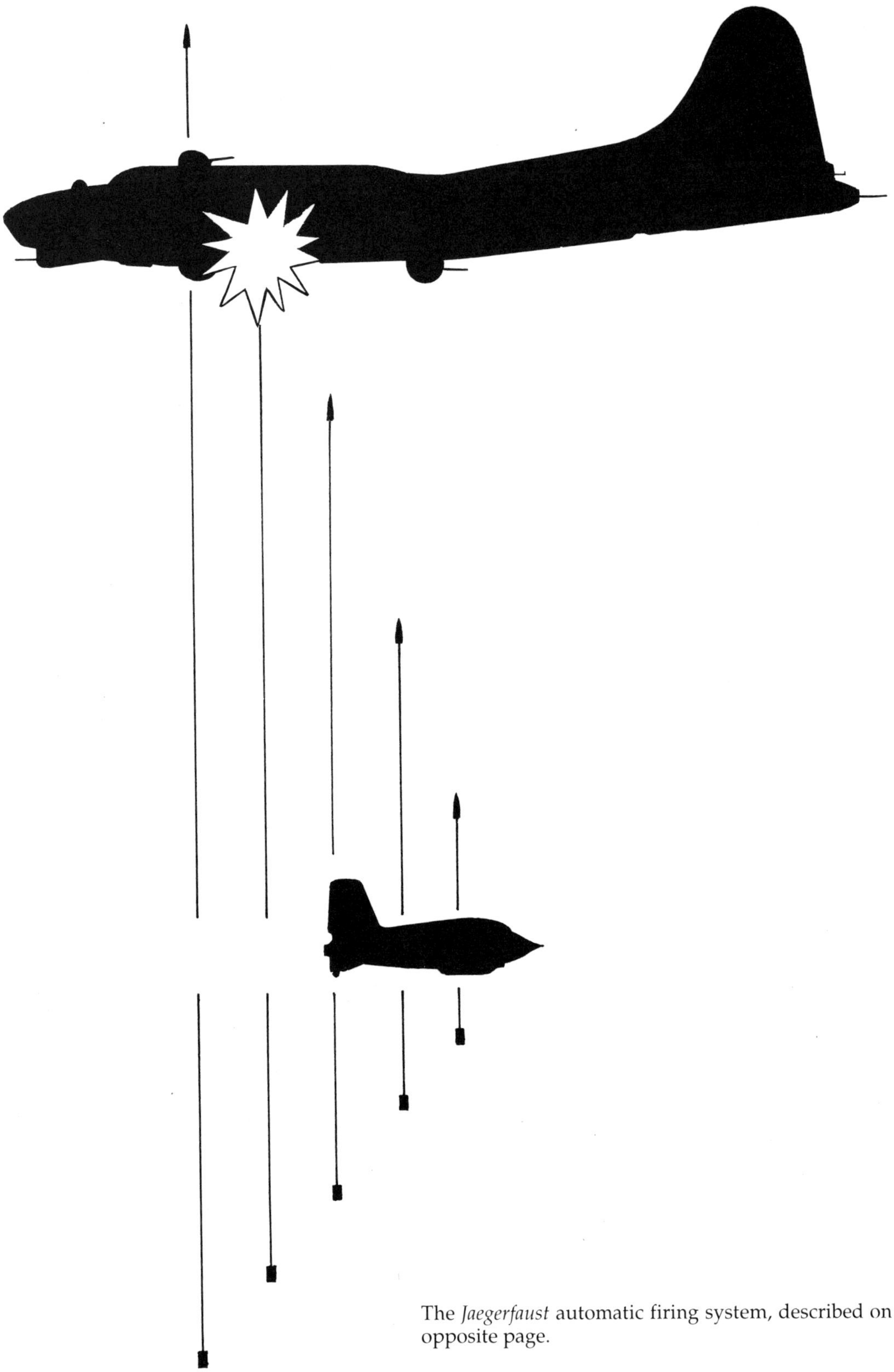

The *Jaegerfaust* automatic firing system, described on the opposite page.

'We were just completing a port orbit waiting for the jets to come down when one did pop out at 6 o'clock to me. I immediately dropped my tanks, advancing full boost and revs. I set my gyro sight for 30 feet (wingspan of enemy aircraft) and closed the graticule to maximum range. I encountered no difficulty in putting the dot on the jet; however I was quite a little out of range — about 1,000 yards. I got on the jet's tail and followed him down. The jet started pulling away from me, so I fired a few short bursts hoping to make him turn whereby I could possibly cut him off and get in range. The jet did start to level out and make a port turn — his speed dropped off considerably as his turn increased. I closed in very rapidly. I was using the K-14 sight for the first time and do not remember opening the graticule as I closed in; however I did get a couple of strikes on his tail, firing from 280 to 50 yards, 10° off. My speed was approximately 450 when I got into range. I throttled back but was unable to stay in the turn with him due to my excessive speed. I overshot him, pulled up and got on his tail again. Up to this time the jet had not been using his blower, at least he was not emitting any black smoke. As I closed on him the second time he used his blower for a couple of seconds and then cut it off again. I closed to 400 yards from 20° off, fired again and saw strikes on the tail. The jet rolled over, started straight down from 8,000 feet with fire coming intermittently from his port side and exhaust. He crashed in a small village and exploded.'

Bollenrath was still inside the cockpit when his Me 163 hit the ground.

Meanwhile other Me 163s were closing in on the B-17s and the 91st, 94th, 388th, 452nd and 493rd Bomb Groups all reported encounters with them, though the attacks were not pressed home vigorously. None of the heavy bombers was hit by the rocket fighters and, although several American gunners reported engaging the Me 163s as they came within range, nobody claimed the destruction of any of them. There is reason to believe, however, that the return fire may have caused the destruction of *Feldwebel* Herbert Straznicky's Messerschmitt which plunged into the ground with the pilot still on board. With the loss of *Oberfeldwebel* Horst Rolly, killed during the action, it had been another black day for I./JG 400: four Me 163s destroyed and three pilots killed, but no enemy aircraft shot down.

Small though it was, the engagement on 2 November was to be the last on such a scale by I./JG 400 for more than four months. The continual shortages of rocket fuel and trained pilots, together with the poor weather during the final winter of the war, combined to reduce the Me 163 operations to a negligible level. In such a climate of difficulty the formation of a second *Gruppe* of Me 163s, II./JG 400 based at Stargad in Pomerania, added little to the operational effectiveness of the type. On 10 January 1945 I./JG 400, the only unit then operational, had 46 rocket fighters on its strength of which 16 were recorded as being serviceable; II./JG 400 probably had a similar number. Production of the Me 163 came to an end in February 1945, after about 364 had been built.

In March 1945 there was a resurgence of activity by JG 400, culminating with five sorties on the 15th; none of the rocket fighters succeeded in getting through to the bombers on that day, however, and one Me 163 was claimed by an escorting Mustang.

One of the factors that had prevented the Me 163 from becoming an effective bomber-destroyer was the lack of an armament system which enabled any but the most skilful of pilots to deliver an accurate and destructive burst during the brief attacking runs. Closing in on their targets at an overtaking speed of about 160 yards per second, many pilots found that by the time they had their sight on a bomber it was time to break away to avoid colliding with it. To overcome this problem the Hasag company in Leipzig developed *Jaegerfaust* ('fighter-fist'), an automatic firing system. As applied to the Me 163, *Jaegerfaust* comprised ten vertically mounted 50 mm gun barrels built into the wing roots, five on each side. Each barrel was loaded with a single 2.2 pound high explosive shell; to balance out the recoil forces, as the shells were fired *upwards* at the enemy aircraft, counterweights weighing as much as the shells were fired *downwards* and clear of the Me 163. The barrels were fired in rapid succession, triggered by a photo-electric cell which detected the shadow of the enemy aircraft as it passed overhead. All the Me 163 pilot had to do was to prime the *Jaegerfaust* and fly his aircraft underneath the target bomber within about 325 feet either from tail-on or, if he wished, from head-on. The barrels were divided into two groups of five for firing, enabling the pilot to carry out two attacks before he had to land and reload.

*Jaegerfaust* would have enabled a poorly trained pilot to make accurate attacks on enemy bombers, and great things were expected from it. The system performed impressively during trials against a cloth target the size of a bomber's wing, stretched between two tethered balloons. Before the end of the war about a dozen Me 163s were modified to carry *Jaegerfaust*, but only once was it used in action. On 10 April 1945 *Leutnant* Fritz Kelb took off to test it out and caught a lone B-17 straggling behind its formation near Leipzig. He made a single devastating high speed attack with the new weapon and the American bomber went down shedding pieces.

Kelb's attack marked the virtual end of the Me 163's operational career. Sparkling though its speed and climb performance undoubtedly were, the aircraft operated too close to the limit of what was possible to have achieved much in war; it is doubtful whether, after almost a year in service, the rocket fighter caused the destruction of more than 16 enemy aircraft. The chemical rocket fuels were rather too exotic for general service use; and the bombing of just two key factories, coupled with the general chaos of the final six months of the war, crippled the production of one of the fuels, hydrazine hydrate. The jettisonable dolly undercarriage, which helped keep down the size and weight of the airframe, meant that the aircraft was difficult to move around prior to take-off, and after landing it was immobile until one of the specially-built lifting trolleys reached it. Once the fuel had been burnt the pilot was committed to landing the aircraft on his first attempt — the *T-Stoff* tank had to be empty prior to the landing, or there was the near-certainty of an explosion if there was a landing accident. During the Second World War, to be effective a fighting aircraft had to suffer fools gladly, for training standards in all air forces fell far below those in peace-time. The Me 163 forgave few mistakes and losses in accidents far exceeded those it inflicted on the enemy. Significantly, although each of the major Allied powers received captured Me 163s after the war, and the USA, USSR, Britain and France all later developed high performance rocket fighters of their own, nobody else introduced the type into service. In retrospect it seems clear that the rocket fighter, for all its spectacular performance, was in fact a blind alley off the main path of fighter development.

Captured Me 163 modified in the Soviet Union as a two-seat glider for training flights, with the second seat in place of the rocket motor and the *T-Stoff* tank.
*(via Geust)*

# CHAPTER 3

# The Gloster Meteor

Gloster Meteor I, EE 214, the fifth production aircraft, fitted with a 105-gallon drop tank under the fuselage.

The Gloster Meteor was the first jet aircraft to go into service with the Royal Air Force, and it was the only Allied jet aircraft to go into action during the Second World War. As in the case of the Messerschmitt Me 262, and in many cases for the same reasons, the development of the British fighter advanced in fits and starts. As with the German aircraft there was the initial and over-optimistic prospect of a high performance fighter seemingly just around the corner. Then, when engineering work began to meet that goal, there were the inevitable problems of trying to build flight-cleared turbojet engines able to achieve the predicted performance and function reliably.

By the summer of 1940 the Air Ministry in London was well aware of the potential of the new turbojets then undergoing bench testing in Great Britain. Work was well advanced on the construction of the Whittle W.1, the first lightweight British turbojet, intended for installation in the Gloster E.28/39 experimental aircraft. Also, an outline proposal had been submitted for the larger and more powerful W.2 engine that embodied many of the improvements that had become evident during the design of the earlier unit. Against this background, the Gloster Aircraft Company received a request from the Air Ministry to submit a design proposal for a fighter aircraft powered by the W.2.

When Gloster's Chief Designer, George Carter, received details of the early turbojet engine's performance, he saw that two of these units would be needed to produce the thrust necessary to propel the fighter. His design therefore centred on a near-conventional twin-jet aircraft, with the tailplane set high on the fin to keep it well clear of the jet efflux. For good manoeuvrability at high altitude the wing was a generous 374 square feet in area and, unusually for a British aircraft of this time, it featured a tricycle undercarriage. The new fighter received the Company designation G.41.

View showing the air brakes fitted to the Meteor, necessary to prevent the aircraft from exceeding its limiting Mach number in combat or during a high speed descent.

At the end of September 1940, while the Battle of Britain was being fought to a conclusion in the skies over London, Carter submitted his proposal for the G.41 to the Air Ministry. Specification F.9/40 was written around the design and early the following year Gloster received a contract to build twelve prototypes of the jet fighter as well as sufficient tooling to produce the aircraft at a rate of eighty per month. Initially the fighter was to carry an armament of six 20 mm cannon, though this requirement was later reduced to four of these weapons.

In September 1941 the G.41 was officially named the 'Thunderbolt', and the Air Ministry placed an order for twenty production machines to follow the twelve prototypes. Early in 1942, following the announcement that the new Republic P-47 fighter for the U.S. Army Air Forces had also been given that name, the British jet fighter was renamed the 'Meteor'.

By the summer of 1942 the first prototype of the Meteor was ready to begin flight testing off the 3,000 yard runway at Newmarket Heath. Like all of the early turbojets, the first Rover W.2B engines to be flight cleared were strictly limited in power; those fitted to the Meteor each produced a meagre 1,000 pounds of thrust. On 10 July Flight Lieutenant 'Gerry' Sayer, Gloster's Chief Test Pilot, lifted the prototype Meteor into the air for a brief hop. It was immediately clear that the fighter lacked sufficient power for a safe climb-away, however, and afterwards Sayer recommended that the first flight be postponed until the aircraft was fitted with engines developing greater thrust.

The problems with the W.2B engine would not be solved quickly or easily, and the Meteor programme came to a halt for want of the all-important engines to power the aircraft. Fortunately there other companies were also developing turbojet engines at this time, and by the beginning of 1943 the Halford H.1 (later re-named the de Havilland Goblin) had gained a flight clearance. The new engine developed 1,400 pounds of thrust, with 1,800 pounds available for emergencies. On the power from two H.1s, Michael Daunt lifted the fifth prototype into the air from Cranwell on 5 March to make the Meteor's true maiden flight.

Only eight of the originally planned twelve Meteor prototypes were built and flown, the other four were cancelled. The prototypes flew with various types of engine, including the Halford H.1, the Metrovic F.2. and the Whittle W.2/500, W.2B/23 and W.2B/37 engines originally been built by the Rover company but taken over by Rolls-Royce at the beginning of 1943. Apart from the Metrovic engine, which had an axial flow compressor, all of the engines were fitted with centrifugal flow compressors.

Early in 1943 the Ministry of Aircraft Production produced a set of comparative performance curves for the best two versions of the Meteor planned to appear in 1944, powered by the H.1 and the W.2/500 engine respectively, and the newest version of the Spitfire scheduled to appear at the same time. The curves showed that although the jet fighter possessed a marked advantage in terms of its maximum speed at low altitude and high altitude, to a large extent the latter was off-set by its inferior rate of climb. Moreover the rate of fuel

Air-to-air views of the Meteor I, showing the heavy framed canopy fitted to this version, and the long-span wing fitted to the Mark I and the Mark III. (NASM)

consumption of the early jet engines was considerably higher than that of the equivalent piston engines, which meant that the jet fighter's radius of action would be relatively short. The only operational role for which the Meteor was seen to be superior to the best piston-engined fighters was that of short-range daylight home defence interceptor at very low or very high altitudes.

Between the end of the Battle of Britain and the middle of 1943, the RAF had no clear-cut operational requirement for an aircraft with those capabilities. In Britain the arguments for and against putting the Meteor into mass production parallelled those that had taken place in Germany during the previous year. During the spring of 1943 the much-weakened Luftwaffe bomber force appeared rarely over Britain, and never by day. If the enemy resumed daylight attacks in strength, the RAF was confident that it could deal harshly with these using the fighters it already had. For the future the need was for fighters able to reach far into enemy territory, with more range than the current types rather than less.

As in Germany, nobody doubted that the jet fighter had enormous potential for the future. But for the time being it was decided to continue developing the Meteor, so that it would be ready to go into mass production if the war took an unexpected turn. With limited aircraft production resources and many claims being made on them, the Air Staff was reluctant to order a large scale production of the Meteor until it was seen to function reasonably well and meet a defined combat requirement.

That mood changed abruptly during the summer of 1943, following the receipt of disturbing intelligence reports of novel types of air weapon being developed in Germany, some powered by jet engines. Following a directive from the Prime Minister, the Meteor was ordered into production to meet a requirement for 120 aircraft; later the Air Ministry increased the order to 300.

At the end of 1943 the first production Meteors began coming off the assembly line. These aircraft were powered by the W.2B/23 engine, by then renamed the Rolls-Royce Welland and developing 1,700 pounds of thrust. Following flight testing, the first production machine was shipped to the U.S.A., in exchange for an example of the Bell XP-59A jet fighter for use in comparative trials at Farnborough.

No 616 Squadron, a Spitfire unit, was selected to be the first to receive the new fighter. One of its pilots, Flight Lieutenant D. Barry, was among those sent to Farnborough in June to convert to the Meteor. Later he described the cursory pre-flight briefing he received:

'We clustered round the Meteor, peering into the cockpit whilst the Group Captain went through the cockpit drill, explaining the instruments, and its flying characteristics. Next we were told we could take-off on our first familiarisation flights. This conversion briefing seemed rather sparse, especially as there were very few Meteors available and so any written-off would be disastrous — and fatal to the pilot as we did not have ejector seats. There were no Pilots' Notes available, but we felt confident, if a little over-awed at the prospect of being chosen to fly such a novel aircraft.'

Barry went on to describe his initial jet flight, in the fifth production Meteor I:

'I positioned the aircraft ready for take-off. Throttles forward, maximum power whilst holding on the brakes, then brakes released and slowly accelerate down the runway. No swing; no drag, and hold the stick level until 80 mph indicated, then ease stick back and lift off the runway at 120 mph. Wheels up and climb away, retracting the flaps. The rate of climb is initially poor, 500 feet a minute, but as the power builds up the rate increases. Local flying now, the aircraft is quiet with no noise from the engines, only a "whooshing" sound from the air passing the cockpit, like a glider . . . The Meteor feels heavy on the controls when compared with the Spitfire and especially when full of fuel. Aerobatics are forbidden in the Mark I due to its being underpowered. After a 45 minute flight, down for the landing remembering that one has to land straight off. Just one chance with no overshooting, as the power drops off when the airspeed is reduced. On landing the Meteor decelerates slowly, being heavy.'

Overall, the Meteor I was no great performer. It was distinctly underpowered, and its maximum speed of 410 mph at medium and high altitudes was no better than other fighter types already in service; also, due to the restriction on aerobatics, the jet fighter was limited in the manoeuvres it was allowed to perform.

It will be remembered that the Meteor had been pushed into production as a possible counter to the German secret bombardment weapons. On 13 June the first of these, the V.1 flying bomb, went into action. Between then and the end of the month more than 2,400 of these weapons were launched at London; about a third of them reached the capital causing widespread destruction. The Meteor's otherwise unimpressive performance envelope did however have one significant area of advantage over its piston-engined counterparts: its

Meteor III wearing the YQ identification letters of No. 616 Squadron, the only unit to operate the type in action. *(NASM)*

maximum speed did not fall away at low altitude. At sea level the Meteor I had a top speed of 385 mph and at altitudes below 4,000 feet, the band of sky inhabited by the flying bombs, the jet fighter was between 20 and 30 mph faster than its piston-engined counterparts. That margin could spell the difference between success and failure for an interception, and the formation of an operational squadron of Meteors assumed a new urgency.

No 616 Squadron moved to Manston in Kent to await the arrival its new aircraft and early in July Wing Commander Andrew McDowell, an ex-Battle of Britain pilot with 14 victories to his credit, assumed command of the unit. On the 21st the first two non-operational Meteors arrived, and pilot training began. A couple of days later five fully operational jet fighters were delivered, sufficient to equip one Flight with Meteors. The squadron's other two Flights continued to operate Spitfires.

The Meteor Flight was allowed little time to get used to its new aircraft before it was sent into action. Six days after the arrival of the first jet fighters at Manston, on 27 July Flying Officer McKenzie took-off for the first operational sortie in the Meteor: an anti-V.1 patrol over Kent. From then on the squadron maintained two aircraft on standing patrol continually throughout the daylight hours, each patrol lasting 30 minutes. While one pair of jet fighters was airborne, the pair scheduled to relieve them waited on the ground with pilots at cockpit readiness.

Great things were expected from the Meteors, but during their first week of operations they had no success against the flying bombs. The pilots of the jet fighters saw incoming V.1s on several occasions, but each time they attempted an interception something always went wrong and they came home empty handed.

A common cause of failure was the fighter's Hispano cannon armament. In the rush to get it into operational service, there had been no time for the Meteor to complete the full programme of air firing trials. Now it was discovered that under some conditions of flight the used ammunition links did not fall away cleanly, leading to a build-up in the link jettison chute that eventually caused the weapons to jam. The squadron's engineers devised a modification to overcome the problem, but it took a few days to incorporate this into all aircraft.

On 4 August Flying Officer 'Dixie' Dean manoeuvred himself into position behind a flying bomb and opened fire, only to have his guns jam after firing a few rounds. Nonplussed by the failure, the pilot continued to overhaul the V.1 and moved into position alongside it. Dean carefully placed his port wing beneath that of the flying bomb, then banked sharply and knocked the flying bomb spinning out of control. At the price of a damaged wing-tip, the Meteor had claimed its first victim. That seemed to remove the apparent jinx from the jet fighter, and later that day Flying Officer J. Roger shot down a flying bomb using his cannon.

By 15 August the whole of No 616 Squadron had converted to Meteors. That evening, however, the unit suffered its first loss. Sergeant D. Gregg took off on an anti-V.1 patrol but for reasons that are not clear he attempted an emergency landing at Great Chart airfield near Ashford and crashed on the approach. The aircraft was wrecked and the pilot killed.

During August the jet fighters accounted for a total of thirteen flying bombs, In the course of these operations one Meteor came under attack from a 'friendly' Spitfire which dived on it over English Channel. Before it could speed clear the Meteor took hits on the fuselage and tail, and its pilot just made it back to Manston using the elevator trimmer for pitch control. On 28 August Flying Officer Miller shot down a V.1, the 13th and last to fall to the jet fighter. On that same day Wing Commander McDowall suffered an engine failure and made a crash landing near Manston; the fighter was wrecked but the pilot sustained only minor injuries. Soon afterwards Allied ground forces overran the V.1 launching sites in northern France and the initial bombardment of London came to an end.

Apart from the lack of engine power and the restricted manoeuvrability, service pilots found that a serious weaknesses of the Meteor I was the poor visibility to the sides and rear of the cockpit. An official report on one of the early production machines stated:

'The view ahead was good, but in other directions left much to be desired due to the thickness of the frame and the discoloration of the transparent plastic sandwich of the canopy. This is particularly disadvantageous as

Meteor IIIs of No 124 Squadron, which began to re-equip with the fighter in August 1945. In the following spring the unit was re-numbered No. 56 Squadron, which flew later marks of the fighter, the 4 and 8, until 1954. *(Charles Brown/RAF Museum)*

regards upward view in steep turns. The view to the rear and downwards is badly obstructed by the fuselage, wings and the frames of the canopy.'

Following the end of the initial V.1 bombardment on London and the capture of the launching sites in France, small numbers of flying bombs were launched at the capital from specially modified bombers flying off the east coast of England. These attacks took place only at night, however, and although No 616 Squadron continued in the home air defence role for the remainder of the year its Meteors played no part in countering them.

In October No 616 Squadron detached four Meteors to the American base at Debden in Essex, for a large scale combat trial for the U.S. Army Air Forces. The Meteors were to deliver mock attacks against a formation of more than a hundred B-24 Liberators escorted by two dozen P-51s, imitating the hit-and-run tactics being used by the German jet fighters. The purpose of the exercise was to assist American fighter pilots to devise tactics to counter the threat, and to give the bombers' gunners practice in tracking high speed targets. The U.S. report on the exercise, flown on 10 October, stated:

'The jet aircraft made determined head-on, stern and beam attacks several times and on one occasion engaged in combat with the defending fighters. With the exception of that one engagement, the jet aircraft ignored attempts by the fighters to engage them and made attacks solely on the bombers.'

The report on the trial produced the following conclusions regarding jet fighter attacks and how best to combat them:

a. Supporting fighters must have sufficient altitude above the bombers to allow them to build up their speed in a dive in order to head off the jets.
b. Early warning of jet attacks is necessary. Attempts by fighters to head off jet attacks after the jet had started its dive were largely ineffectual.
c. The jets could very effectively use cloud cover to dive on the bombers and made their attacks and using their superior zoom-climb, pull back into the clouds.
d. The jet aircraft, in all probability, would not stay and fight with the supporting fighters. They could not compete in a tight turning circle and would probably dive, hit the bombers, continue their dive to hold their speed, and pull up a great distance from the bombers to get set for another attack.
e. The jet, because of the speed differential would be able to pick its own time and place of attack. It would be easy for the jet to find a hole in the fighter support, hit and get away.

In retrospect it is clear that the report painted an over-pessimistic picture of the effectiveness of the jet fighters, and when the defensive tactics were tested in action over Germany they proved highly effective.

In September 1944 the Meteor III flew for first time, and production aircraft followed two months later. This version was fitted with a revised sliding hood giving far better all-round visibility, as well as other refinements compared with the Mark I (the Meteor II, to be powered by Halford H.1 engines, did not go into production). The first fifteen Mark IIIs were powered by Welland I engines, the sixteenth and subsequent machines were fitted with the new Rolls-Royce Derwent I engine developing 2,000 pounds of thrust.

In December 1944 No 616 Squadron received its first Derwent-powered Meteor IIIs. Comparing the latter with the Mark I, Flight Lieutenant Barry commented that the newer machine:

'. . . was more powerful , with a higher ceiling, better acceleration and a much higher top speed of 495 mph. It was fully aerobatic too, and had an ordinary sliding hood, also it had increased fuel capacity.'

RAF test pilots found the Meteor III easy to fly, though they were critical of two aspects of its handling. One concerned the ailerons, which had deliberately been made 'heavy' by the use of relatively high gearing of the control wires. During the design of the fighter there had been concern regarding the torsional strength of the wing outboard of the engine nacelles, and the ailerons had been deliberately made 'heavy' was to prevent pilots overstressing that part of the structure. Service pilots had not encountered this problem with the Meteor I, because the earlier version was not cleared for aerobatics. The Mark III was cleared for such manoeuvres, and pilots expected to operate it in the same way as other fighter types. A Fighter Command report on the new version stated:

'The great disadvantage of the Meteor III from a tactical and general flying viewpoint is the heaviness of the ailerons throughout the speed range. At medium and high speeds evasive action and even moderate turns are very tiring . . . The Meteor III would be an excellent aircraft for all aerobatic manoeuvres if the ailerons were not so heavy.'

Another problem suffered by the Meteor III was its tendency to 'snake' at high speeds and this, combined with the heaviness of the ailerons, made it a poor gun platform during high speed combat. The same report stated:

'The failure of the Meteor to come within an acceptable standard [as a gun platform] is due to the directional snaking which occurs in operational conditions of flight so far experienced, and the heaviness and consequently slow operation of the ailerons to bring the sight back on to the target. This snaking tends to increase with increase in speed and, once it has commenced, it is impossible to correct it within the limits of time available during an attack.'

Quite apart from these problems, like all of the early jet fighters the Meteor III became increasingly difficult to control as speed was increased above its compressibility threshold of Mach .67. It was easy enough for a pilot to exceed that speed inadvertently: at full throttle below 10,000 feet, a descent of only 15 degrees gave sufficient acceleration to nudge the fighter into the area of compressibility where its behaviour deteriorated rapidly. At 500 mph (indicated) at 4,500 feet, Mach .68, there was severe snaking combined with lateral oscillation although the controls continued to be effective. If speed was increased to 510 mph at 5,500 feet, Mach .72, there was violent snaking and lateral oscillation and it required considerable force to move the stick. With a further slight increase, to 528 mph indicated at 6,000 feet, Mach .73, the test-pilot's report noted:

'Violent "juddering" (vibration up and down), stick also vibrating badly and entirely ineffective and solid. On throttling back controls became effective again after a short pause.'

The critical Mach number of the Meteor III, the point beyond which the aircraft was difficult to control, was Mach .74; the aircraft's normal maximum permissible speed, imposed by structural considerations, was 500 mph indicated at altitudes below 6,500 feet.

A comparative air-to-air combat trial against the Tempest V, one of the best contemporary piston-engined fighters, put the performance of the Meteor III into context. At all altitudes the Meteor was considerably faster than the Tempest, its advantage ranging from 75 mph at 30,000 feet, to 84 mph at 1,000 feet. During comparative acceleration tests at various altitudes, commencing with the aircraft flying side-by-side at 190 mph indicated, the Tempest showed a slight initial advantage; but once the Meteor reached 300 mph indicated it drew ahead rapidly. A comparison of climbing ability, carried out in the same way, revealed that the Tempest had the advantage; but if the Meteor accelerated to maximum speed in a slight descent and then pulled into a zoom climb, it rapidly overtook the piston-engined fighter.

The low wing loading of the Meteor (34 pounds per square foot) enabled it to out-turn the Tempest (38 p.s.f.) at all speeds. On the other hand, due to the jet fighter's poor aileron control, the Tempest had a better rate of roll and this gave it the advantage when initiating combat manoeuvres. The report on the comparative trial concluded:

'The Meteor III is superior to the Tempest V in almost all departments. If it were not for the heaviness of its ailerons and its consequent poor manoeuvrability in the rolling plane, and the adverse effect of snaking on it as a gun platform, it would be a comparable all-round fighter with a greatly increased performance.'

Development of the Meteor continued throughout this period, and one area of investigation involved the search for ways to delay the onset of compressibility and thus raise its critical Mach number. Wind tunnel tests, later confirmed by flight tests with a Meteor I fitted with wool tufts on the engine nacelles, revealed that the buffeting was caused by a sharp break-away of the airflow at the junctions between the outboard engine nacelles and the wings. A pair of longer nacelles, extended fore and aft of the originals, appeared to cure the problem and these were fitted to a Meteor I and test flown. The modification raised the aircraft's critical Mach number from .74 to .84, and at a stroke it raised the fighter's limiting speed at medium and high altitude by about 75 mph (the limiting speed of 500 mph indicated at altitudes below 6,500 feet, imposed by forces the plane's structure was designed to withstand, remained in force).

Early in 1945 No 616 Squadron started to convert to Meteor IIIs with early-type engine nacelles. In February the unit sent four aircraft, three Mark IIIs and a Mark I, on detachment to Melsbroek near Brussels to serve in the air defence role. The Meteors were painted white overall, as an identification measure to prevent the jets being engaged by Allied fighters and ground gunners. In the case of the latter this measure was only partially successful, but fortunately for the jet fighter pilots the gunners' shooting was as poor as their skill at aircraft recognition.

Initially the Meteor pilots operating over Belgium had strict orders to remain over Allied-held territory, to prevent the enemy capturing one of these aircraft. Since the Luftwaffe rarely ventured over Allied-held areas the Meteors had few opportunities to go into action, and none did so during this period.

The Meteor III pictured with the RAF fighter types in service in 1946: the de Havilland Vampire I, the Spitfire IX and the Tempest 2. *(Charles Brown/RAF Museum).*

**Gloster Meteor Mk III Cutaway Drawing Key**

1 Starboard detachable wingtip
2 Starboard navigation light
3 Starboard recognition light
4 Starboard aileron
5 Aileron balance tab
6 Aileron mass balance weights
7 Aileron control coupling
8 Aileron torque shaft
9 Chain sprocket
10 Cross-over control runs
11 Front spar
12 Rear spar
13 Aileron (inboard) mass balance
14 Nacelle detachable tail section
15 Jet pipe exhaust
16 Internal stabilising struts
17 Rear spar "spectacle" frame
18 Fire extinguishing spray ring
19 Main engine mounting frame
20 Engine access panel(s)
29 RPM indicators (left and right of gunsight)
30 Pilot's seat
31 Forward fuselage top deflector skin
32 Gun wobble button
33 Control column grip
34 Main instrument panel
35 Nosewheel armoured bulkhead
36 Nose release catches (10)
37 Nosewheel jack bulkhead housing/attachment
38 Nose ballast weight location
39 Nosewheel mounting frames
40 Radius rod (link and jack omitted)
41 Nosewheel pivot bearings
42 Shimmy-damper/self-centring strut
43 Gun camera
44 Camera access
45 Aperture
46 Nose cone
47 Cabin cold-air intake
48 Nosewheel leg door
49 Picketing rings
50 Tension shock absorber
51 Pivot bracket
52 Mudguard
53 Torque strut
54 Door hoop
55 Wheel fork
56 Retractable nosewheel
57 Nosewheel doors
58 Port cannon trough fairings
59 Nosewheel cover
60 Intermediate diaphragm
61 Blast tubes
62 Gun front mounting rails
63 Pilot's seat pan
64 Emergency crowbar
65 Canopy de-misting silica gel cylinder
66 Bullet-proof glass rear-view cut-outs
67 Canopy track
68 Seat bulkhead
69 Entry step
70 Link ejection chutes
71 Case ejection chutes
72 20-mm Hispano Mk III cannon
73 Belt feed mechanism
74 Ammunition feed necks
75 Ammunition tanks
76 Aft glazing (magazine bay top door)
77 Loading ramp
78 Front spar bulkhead

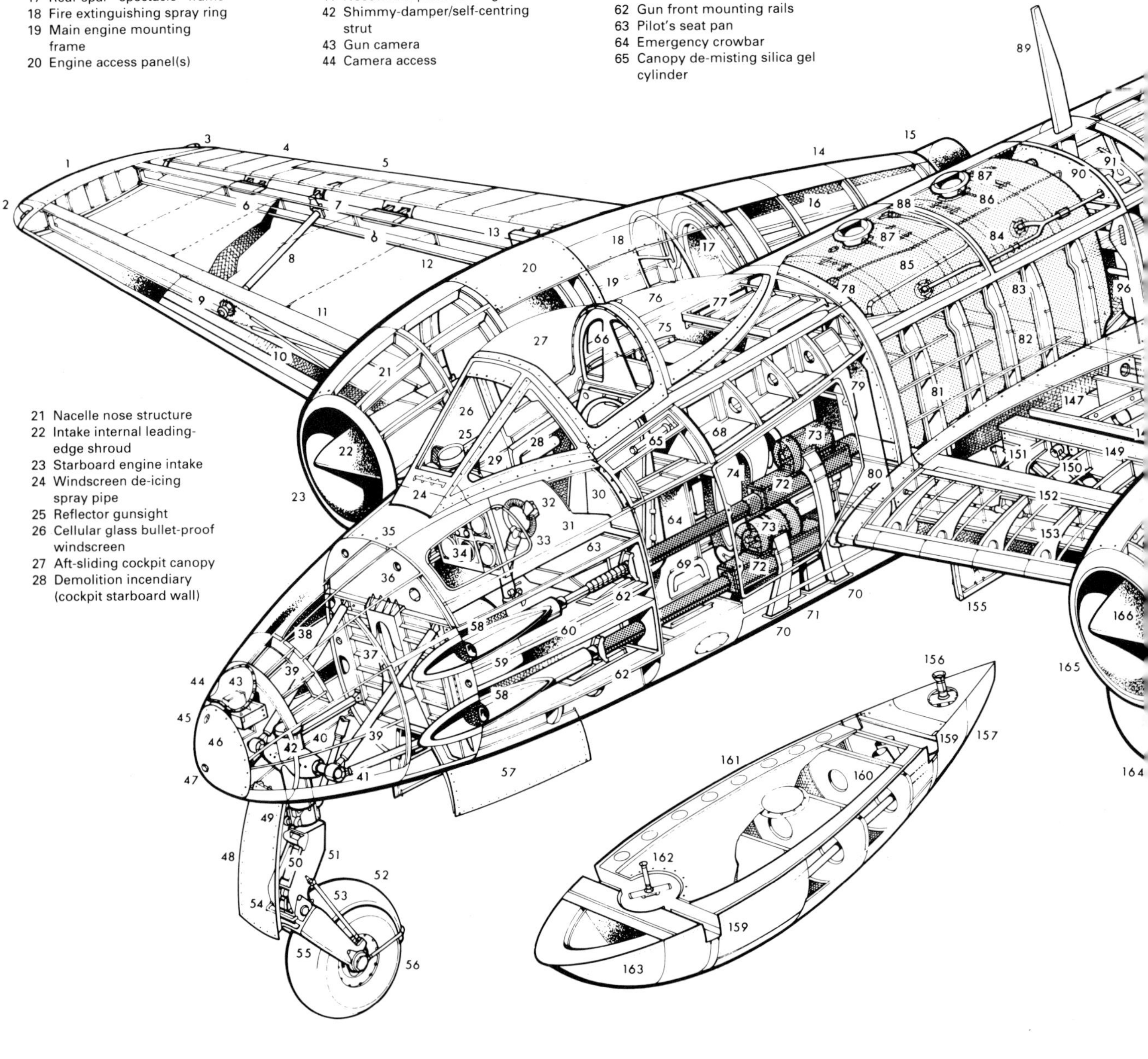

21 Nacelle nose structure
22 Intake internal leading-edge shroud
23 Starboard engine intake
24 Windscreen de-icing spray pipe
25 Reflector gunsight
26 Cellular glass bullet-proof windscreen
27 Aft-sliding cockpit canopy
28 Demolition incendiary (cockpit starboard wall)

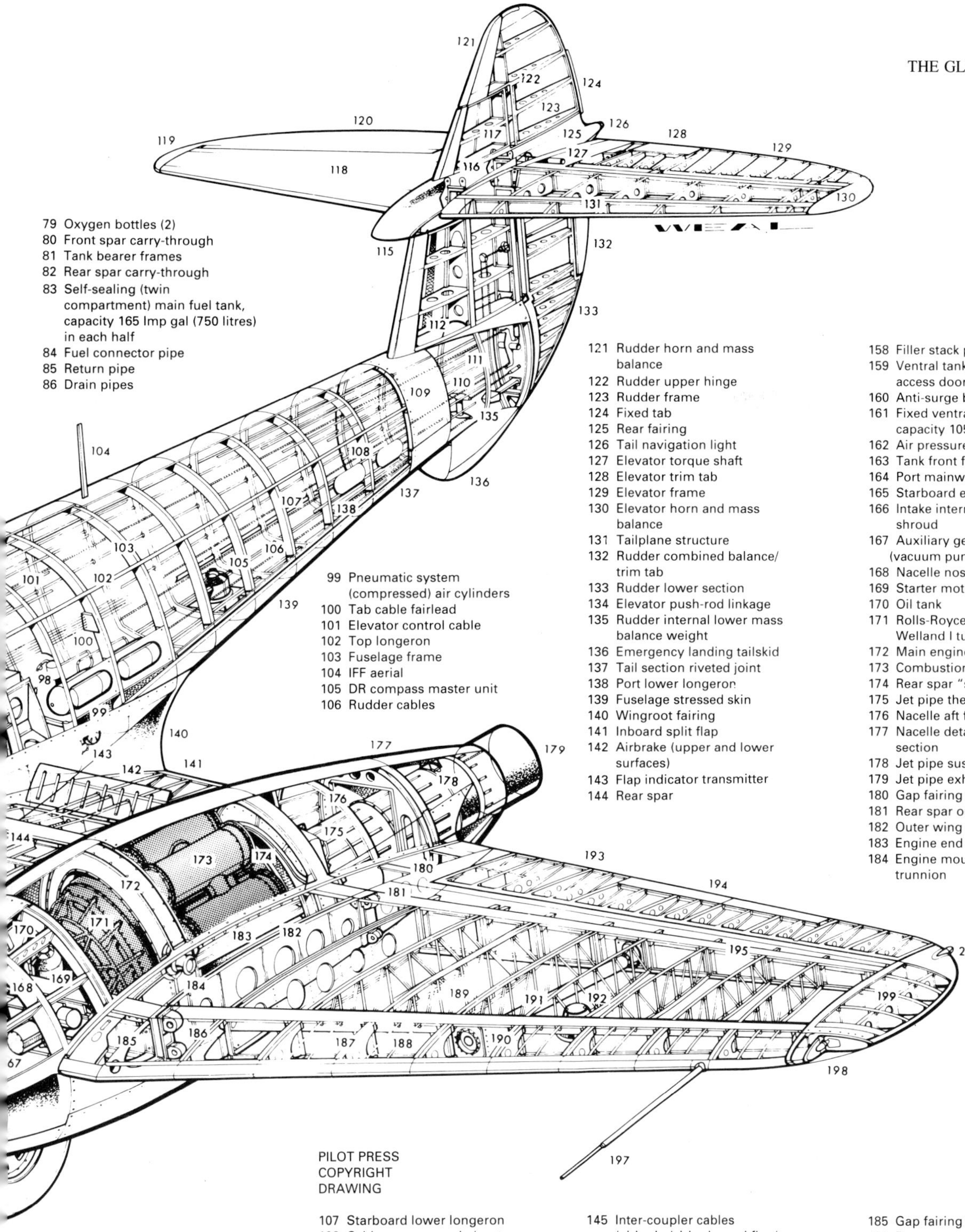


79 Oxygen bottles (2)
80 Front spar carry-through
81 Tank bearer frames
82 Rear spar carry-through
83 Self-sealing (twin compartment) main fuel tank, capacity 165 Imp gal (750 litres) in each half
84 Fuel connector pipe
85 Return pipe
86 Drain pipes

99 Pneumatic system (compressed) air cylinders
100 Tab cable fairlead
101 Elevator control cable
102 Top longeron
103 Fuselage frame
104 IFF aerial
105 DR compass master unit
106 Rudder cables

121 Rudder horn and mass balance
122 Rudder upper hinge
123 Rudder frame
124 Fixed tab
125 Rear fairing
126 Tail navigation light
127 Elevator torque shaft
128 Elevator trim tab
129 Elevator frame
130 Elevator horn and mass balance
131 Tailplane structure
132 Rudder combined balance/trim tab
133 Rudder lower section
134 Elevator push-rod linkage
135 Rudder internal lower mass balance weight
136 Emergency landing tailskid
137 Tail section riveted joint
138 Port lower longeron
139 Fuselage stressed skin
140 Wingroot fairing
141 Inboard split flap
142 Airbrake (upper and lower surfaces)
143 Flap indicator transmitter
144 Rear spar

158 Filler stack pipes
159 Ventral tank attachment strap access doors
160 Anti-surge baffles
161 Fixed ventral fuel tank, capacity 105 Imp gal (477 litres)
162 Air pressure inlet
163 Tank front fairing
164 Port mainwheel
165 Starboard engine intake
166 Intake internal leading-edge shroud
167 Auxiliary gearbox drives (vacuum pump/generator)
168 Nacelle nose structure
169 Starter motor
170 Oil tank
171 Rolls-Royce W.2B/23C Welland I turbojet
172 Main engine mounting frame
173 Combustion chambers
174 Rear spar "spectacle" frame
175 Jet pipe thermo-coupling
176 Nacelle aft frames
177 Nacelle detachable tail section
178 Jet pipe suspension link
179 Jet pipe exhaust
180 Gap fairing tail section
181 Rear spar outer wing fixing
182 Outer wing rib No.1
183 Engine end rib
184 Engine mounting/removal trunnion



87 Fuel filler caps
88 Tank doors (2)
89 T.R.1143 aerial mast
90 Rear spar bulkhead (plywood face)
91 Aerial support frame
92 R.3121 (or B.C.966A) IFF installation
93 Tab control cables
94 Amplifier
95 Fire extinguisher bottles (2)
96 Elevator torque shaft
97 T.R.1143 transmitter/receiver radio installation
98 Pneumatic system filter

107 Starboard lower longeron
108 Cable access panels (port and starboard)
109 Tail section joint
110 Rudder linkage
111 Tail ballast weight location
112 Fin spar/fuselage frame
113 Rudder tab control
114 Fin structure
115 Torpedo fairing
116 Tailplane spar/upper fin attachment plates
117 Upper fin section
118 Starboard tailplane
119 Elevator horn and mass balance
120 Starboard elevator

145 Inter-coupler cables (airbrake/airbrake and flap/flap)
146 Port mainwheel well
147 Root rib station
148 Front diaphragm
149 Undercarriage beam
150 Undercarriage retraction jack
151 Undercarriage sidestay/downlock
152 Front spar
153 Nose ribs
154 Aileron control runs
155 Mainwheel door inner section
156 Ventral tank transfer pipe
157 Tank rear fairing

185 Gap fairing nose section
186 Front spar outer wing fixing
187 Nose ribs
188 Intermediate riblets
189 Wing ribs
190 Aileron drive chain sprocket
191 Aileron torque shaft
192 Retractable landing lamp
193 Port aileron
194 Aileron balance tab
195 Rear spar
196 Front spar
197 Pitot head
198 Port navigation light
199 Outer wing rib No.10/wingtip attachment
200 Port recognition light

Meteor III wearing the markings of the Photographic Reconnaissance Development Unit, which carried out an evaluation of the type in the reconnaissance role with No 541 Squadron. The jet aircraft showed little improvement in performance over over the Spitfire PR 19 and it was not adopted for this role.

On 1 April the Meteors moved from Melsbroek to Gilze Rijen in Holland, where they were joined by the rest of the Squadron. Two days later the jet fighters made their first combat scramble, but failed to make contact with the enemy. On the 13th the unit moved again, this time to Kluis near Nijmegen. Three days later the Meteor pilots received clearance to commence operations over enemy territory. The jet fighter began flying armed reconnaissance missions over Holland, in the course of which it carried out strafing attacks on enemy vehicles whenever these could be found.

By now Allied forces were advancing rapidly into Germany, and resistance had collapsed at several points on the Western Front. No 616 Squadron had to move frequently to keep up with the changing situation on the ground. On 20 April the Meteors moved to Quakenbruck near Bremen; five days later they moved again, to Fassburg.

On 29 April the unit suffered its first losses since it re-equipped with the jet fighter. Squadron Leader Watts and Flight Sergeant Cartmell took off from Fassburg for a patrol and the last radio call heard was Watts telling his wing man to close formation as they were about enter cloud. Shortly afterwards the machines collided and both pilots were killed.

Throughout this period the Meteors carried out strafing attacks on airfields and other ground targets, and their pilots claimed seven enemy planes destroyed on the ground. The Meteors had no opportunities to engage in air-to-air combat, however. On 3 May the unit moved to Lüneburg and was still there two days later when it received orders to cease further offensive action. The war in Europe would continue for a few more days but the Meteors would play no part in it.

During May a second RAF unit re-equipped with Meteor IIIs, No 504 Squadron based at Colerne. Although this unit did not complete its conversion in time to take part in the conflict, it would certainly have seen action had the war gone on a little longer.

In July 1945 a long range reconnaissance unit, No 541 Squadron equipped with Spitfires PR 19s, received three Meteor IIIs to carry out an evaluation of the jet in this role. The jet aircraft showed little improvement in performance over the Spitfire and in several respects — notably range and high altitude operating capability — it was somewhat worse. The Meteor III did not go into service in the reconnaissance role (five years later, in 1950, the squadron would re-equip with the considerably more capable Meteor PR 10).

Had the war in Europe continued into the winter of 1945, the Luftwaffe would probably have had to contend with the Mark 4 version of the Meteor (by then the RAF had changed to arabic numbers for new aircraft marks). The prototype of the new variant was a standard Mark III off the production line, fitted with two Rolls-Royce Derwent 5 engines each developing 3,500 pounds thrust — a 75 per cent increase over the earlier fighter — and the lengthened engine nacelles that raised the critical Mach number to .84. The Meteor 4 flew for the first time in July 1945.

So long as the war lasted the world absolute speed record was an irrelevance, but with the coming of peace that changed. The prestigious record was still held by Germany, with a speed of 469 mph achieved in 1939 by a Messerschmitt 209. The defeated nation could not be allowed to retain the record and the Air Ministry ordered that two Meteor 4s be prepared to make an attempt on it as soon as possible. The aircraft were modified Mark IIIs, with the guns removed and gun ports faired over. The Derwent 5 engines were up-rated to

EE 454, the Meteor 4 which broke the World Absolute Speed Record in September 1945 with an average speed of 616 mph over the course at Herne Bay.

deliver 3,600 pounds thrust for the three minute period required to accelerate the aircraft to maximum speed and take it over the 3 kilometre course. On 7 November 1945 Group Captain H. Wilson achieved an average of 606 mph during four low altitude runs over the measured course at Herne Bay, to capture the world absolute speed record for Great Britain.

Soon afterwards the Air Ministry learned of preparations in the U.S.A. for an attempt on the Meteor's record using the Lockheed Shooting Star (see Chapter 7). Accordingly the RAF began preparations to raise its own record, again using a couple of Meteor 4s with more extensive modifications. The Derwent V engines were uprated to give 4,200 pounds thrust for short periods, clipped wings reduced the span by 4 feet 10 ins, the joints in the airframes were filled in and the aircraft were painted in high gloss finish. Extra fuel tanks in place of the guns and ammunition magazines provided an additional 69 gallons of fuel for the record attempt. Flying one of these aircraft on 7 September 1946, Group Captain 'Teddy' Donaldson raised the world record to 616 mph.

The end of the war removed the urgency to get the Meteor 4 into service quickly, and the Mark III remained in production until 1947. Altogether 210 examples were built, the last fifteen being fitted with the lengthened engine nacelles.

During this period Gloster spent a lot of time and effort in refining the Mark 4 before it went into large-scale production. The structure was strengthened and the new fighter was fitted with a pressurized cabin. Other changes made the aircraft a considerably more effective gun platform at high speeds. The clipped wings of the record-breaking Meteor were fitted as standard, the outer wing sections were stiffened and the ailerons were much lighter and crisper than those of the Mark III. Also, a modification to the rudder trim tab gearing delayed the onset of 'snaking' at high speeds.

Production Mark 4s did not enter service in the RAF until the end of 1947. In the years that followed the type became a mainstay of Fighter Command, which received 465 of these aircraft. The type was also exported widely: the Argentine government bought 100, Belgium took 48, Holland 65, Denmark took 20 and the Egyptian government bought 12.

The Meteor 8 replaced the Mark 4 in service, with a lengthened fuselage and re-designed tail services to raise the critical Mach number, with uprated Derwent engines and an ejector seat fitted as standard. Produced in large numbers by Gloster and Armstrong Whitworth in Britain, the Mark 8 was also built under licence in Holland and Belgium. Two squadrons of the Royal Australian Air Force flew Meteor 8s on operations during the Korean War. The type remained in service in front-line day fighter squadrons in the RAF until 1955.

Variants of the Meteor were developed to fill a range of roles, in addition to that of day fighter. The Mark 7 was a two-seat trainer, the Mark 9 was an armed reconnaissance fighter with cameras in the nose and the Mark 10 was an unarmed long range reconnaissance version.

Marks 11, 12, 13 and 14 were two-seat night and all weather fighters fitted with radar. In addition to the RAF these served with the French, Belgian, Danish, Egyptian, Syrian and Israeli air forces. The Mark 14 remained in front-line service in the RAF until 1961.

All told, production of the Meteor in all of its versions ran to 3,875 aircraft and the type saw front line service with ten air forces. Although it began its life as a huge leap into the unknown, and for want of anything better it continued in production and in service rather longer than it should have, there is no doubt that the Meteor secured for itself a firm and justified place in the history of aviation.

**Gloster Meteor III**
**(figures for Mark I, where different, given in parentheses)**
**Power Units**: two Rolls-Royce Derwent I developing 2,000 pounds thrust
(two R.-R. Welland I developing 1,700 pound thrust).
**Armament**: four Hispano Mark III 20 mm cannon.
**Performance**: maximum speed 458 mph (385 mph) at sea level, 493 mph (410 mph) at 30,000 ft. Range with 180 Imp gal drop tank, 1,340 miles (not known). Initial climb rate 3,980 feet per minute (2,155 fpm). Service Ceiling 44,000 feet (40,000 feet)
**Weight empty, equipped** 8,810 pounds (8,140 pounds). Weight normally loaded 13,300 pounds (11,800 pounds).
**Dimensions**: span 43 feet 0 inches; length 41 feet 3 inches; wing area 374 sq ft.

# CHAPTER 4

# The Arado 234

The Arado Ar 234, the world's first true jet bomber, was one of the great white hopes of the Luftwaffe during the final year of the war. Here at last was a machine able to outrun the fastest enemy interceptor and penetrate the strongest defences. Had the war continued past the summer of 1945 it was planned to equip the major part of the German bomber force with this type. But it was not to be. When the end came only 210 of these aircraft had been built; and such was the general chaos in Germany during the opening months of 1945 that less than half of these ever reached operational units.

Yet although the Arado Ar 234 is remembered principally for being the world's first true jet bomber to go into action, the type was conceived initially as a reconnaissance aircraft; it was in this role that it first went into operation and it was in this role that it achieved complete success.

Work on the new jet reconnaissance aircraft for the Luftwaffe began early in 1941 under Professor Walter Blume, the director of the Arado company, at the firm's Brandenburg plant. The project, initially designated the E 370, took shape as a clean high-winged monoplane with two Jumo 004 turbojets slung under the wings in pods; the projected all-up weight of the aircraft was about 17,640 pounds. Apart from the new type of

The first prototype Arado 234. *(Transit Films)*

propulsion, the only unconventional feature of the E 370 was the method of taking-off and landing: it was to take-off from a wheeled trolley which was then released, and land on retractable skids. The German Air Ministry wanted its new reconnaissance aircraft to have a range of 2,150 km (1,340 miles) and, by deleting from the structure the weight and bulk of a conventional wheeled undercarriage the necessary fuel could be carried without resort to a large airframe. Calculated performance figures for the new aircraft were: maximum speed 485 mph at 20,000 feet, an operating altitude of over 35,750 feet and a maximum range excluding reserves, of about 1,250 miles. Already the range was slightly down on the original Luftwaffe specification, but the design was accepted and two prototypes were ordered under the designation Arado 234.

By the end of 1941 the airframes of the two prototypes were virtually complete — but then began the wait for the engines for, like BMW, Junkers had run into difficulties with its new turbojet. Not until February 1943 did Arado receive a pair of 004s, and even then they were pre-production models suitable only for static ground running and taxying trials.

In the late spring of 1943 a pair of flight-cleared Jumo 004s finally became available and the Arado 234 made its maiden flight on 30 July from Rheine near Münster, with Flight Captain Selle at the controls. The flight passed off without incident for the aircraft, though there was a problem with the take-off trolley: after its release from about 200 feet the retarding parachutes failed to deploy properly, with the result that the trolley smashed into the ground and was wrecked. A replacement trolley was rushed to Rheine for the second flight, but it too was destroyed when the parachutes again failed to open after its release. Thereafter the trolley was released immediately the aircraft reached flying speed, and seldom left the ground.

By the end of September 1943 three further prototypes of the Ar 234 had flown and testing was being pushed forwards at the highest priority. Already the new aircraft had aroused considerable interest, not only for the reconnaissance role but also as a bomber. The aircraft had been discussed for this role even before its first flight, during a conference at the German Air Ministry on 9 July presided over by Erhard Milch. *Oberst* Peltz, the Inspector of Bombers, had expressed misgivings about the heavy losses suffered by his units at the hands of the continually strengthening Allied defences.

MILCH (jokingly): Now we come to the matter of jet bombers. Peltz is always modest, now he has issued a small demand for a couple of hundred, and he wishes to have them by November at the latest!
PELTZ: December!
OBERST PASEWALDT (a member of Milch's staff):
Here we have the Arado 234, on which work is now in progress on the first twenty in the initial production batch of a hundred. The type has not yet flown. When is it going to?
FRIEBEL (representing the Arado company): In one week.
PASEWALDT: The Arado 234 has made a good impression. We await (the flight trials of) this machine, to see if our hopes will be realised. It should be remembered, however, that the Arado 234 has been developed as a reconnaissance aircraft. Its consideration for use as a bomber has been a recent development.

Because it was such a small aircraft, there could be no question of the Ar 234 carrying its bomb load internally; and the use of the trolley for take-off precluded the carriage of bombs under the engines or the fuselage. Accordingly, the Air Ministry placed an order for two prototypes of a new version, the Arado Ar 234B, fitted with a more conventional tricyle undercarriage retracting into the fuselage.

The test programme gradually gained in momentum, though there was a set-back on 2 October when Flight Captain Selle was killed when the second prototype crashed during a test flight. Engineer Hoffmann of the Arado company explained the circumstances of the crash to Milch at a production conference in Berlin three days later:

'The purpose of the test flight was to make an ascent to determine the rate of climb. This ascent was completed at 29,000 feet. At every 1,000 m Flight Captain Selle reported the temperature and pressure. Then the port engine failed. He went into a glide from 8,950 m to 4,500 m (14,600 feet) at an indicated airspeed of about 190 mph and experienced elevator vibration at this speed. He noted that the skids, which he now wished to extend, failed to operate at 4,400 m. Then the airspeed indicator failed. He reported all of this by radio, so that it could be written down. He then extended the skids manually and asked to be informed if they were out: he could not tell this from the cockpit, as the indicator had failed. At 4,900 feet he reported that the port engine had

flamed out; he tried to restart it. One and a half minutes later he reported shuddering and vibration from the elevators and ailerons. Through binoculars it was then possible to see that the port engine was on fire . . .'

With one wing down, the aircraft slid straight into the ground from about 4,000 feet. From a subsequent examination of the wreckage Arado engineers found that there had been a fire inside the wing from the time Selle had first reported the engine failure. The pitot tube to the airspeed indicator ran past the engine, as did the push rods to the ailerons and the landing skids; the fire had caused the partial or complete failure of these systems. The burning engine had broken away from the wing shortly before the aircraft struck the ground, with Selle still on board.

Arado 234 trolley take-off. Following the wrecking of the take-off trolleys during the first two flights, when they were released from too high an altitude, during subsequent flights the trolley was released as the aircraft was about to get airborne and so hardly left the ground. Immediately the aircraft had lifted clear, the braking parachute started to deploy. *(Transit Films)*

While work proceeded on the wheeled Arados, four further trolley-mounted aircraft flew during December 1943 and the early months of 1944: the 5th and 7th prototypes, similar to the earlier machines; the 6th prototype, fitted with four 1,760 pound thrust BMW 003 turbojets in separate pods under the wing; and the 8th prototype with four BMW 003s paired in underwing pods.

To enable the aircraft to take off fully loaded from short runways when there was little or no

As the aircraft lifted off the ground the braking parachute is half deployed, pulling the trolley rapidly clear of the aircraft.

wind, the third prototype and subsequent twin-engined aircraft had provision for the installation of a Walter 109-500 liquid fuelled rocket booster pod under each outer wing section. Each pod developed 1,100 pounds of additional thrust for take-off and, complete with sufficient hydrogen peroxide and sodium permanganate for about 30 seconds' running, weighed 616 pounds. Once the aircraft was airborne and the rockets' fuel exhausted, the pods were released and parachuted to earth and could be re-used. A system of interconnected electrical pressure switches ensured that if one of the pods failed to deliver thrust, that on the opposite side shut down also thereby preventing a dangerous asymetric thrust condition.

In March 1944 the ninth prototype Ar 234 took the air, the first B version with a built-in undercarriage. Even before it had flown, however, the factory at Alt Loennewitz in Saxony was tooling-up for the mass production of this version. Intended for either the bomber or the reconnaissance role, the Ar 234B was powered by two 1,980 pounds thrust Jumo 004B engines and weighed 11,464 pounds empty and 18,580 pounds loaded. It had a maximum speed, clean, of 461 mph at 20,000 feet.

The maximum bomb load was 3,300 pounds carried externally. When it carried bombs or drop tanks, the maximum speed of the Arado was reduced by 35 to 50 mph. Range depended on altitude since, speed for speed, the jet engines consumed roughly three times as much fuel at sea level as at 32,500 feet; at 10,000 m the aircraft, clean, had a range of about 1,000 miles, reducing to about 340 miles if it remained at low altitude. In practice this meant that the bomber version had an effective operating radius of action, carrying a 1,100 pound bomb one way and allowing reasonable fuel reserves, of about 300 miles for high altitude attacks and about 120 miles if the aircraft remained at low altitude. Operating in the reconnaissance role at high altitude with two 66 Imp gal drop tanks, it had a radius of action of about 450 miles.

Three modes of bombing attack were possible with the Ar 234B: the shallow dive attack, the horizontal attack from low altitude and the horizontal attack from high altitude. The shallow dive attack was the most used method and typically it involved a nose-down throttled-back descent from 16,250 feet to 4,500 feet, during which the pilot sighted his bombs using the periscopic sight protruding from the top of his cabin. The low

Skid landing by one of the early Arado 234s. *(Transit Films)*

The eighth prototype Ar 234, with four BMW 003 engines in two paired pods. *(via Heise)*

altitude horizontal attack was a rather inaccurate method, employed only when poor visibility or low cloud at the target precluded any other method. the pilot simply ran over his target and released the bombs by eye.

Technically the most interesting mode of attack performed by the Arado was that from high altitude flying horizontally. Using normal map-reading or radio navigational methods, the pilot would take his aircraft to a point about 20 miles short of the target. He would then engage the Patin three-axis autopilot and swing his control column out of the way to his right. This done, he loosened his shoulder straps and leaned forward to the bomb aiming position, over the eyepiece of the Lotfe bombsight. The bombsight's controls were connected to the aircraft's automatic pilot via a simple form of computer. All the pilot had to do was hold the graticule of the bombsight over the target; the bombsight then fed the appropriate signals via the computer to the autopilot and thus it 'flew' the aircraft through its bombing run. When the aircraft reached the bomb release position, the bombs were released automatically. The pilot then straightened himself up in his seat, tightened his shoulder straps, retrieved the control column, switched out the autopilot and turned the aircraft round for home. All in all, it was a remarkably advanced system for an aircraft of 1944 vintage.

A further innovation with the Ar 234B was the braking parachute to shorten the landing run; it was the first aircraft in the world to have this as a standard fitting.

Early in June 1944, less than a year after the Arado 234A had made its maiden flight, the first of the twenty pre-production Ar 234Bs was completed.

Also in June 1944, the 5th and 7th prototypes were fitted with cameras and issued to the 1st *Staffel* of the Luftwaffe High Command Trials Detachment* at Oranienburg, a special reconnaissance unit which operated under the direct control of the High Command. *Oberleutnant* Horst Goetz took charge of the aircraft and he and another pilot, *Leutnant* Erich Sommer, began training with the new aircraft in readiness for operations. Sommer remembers having little trouble with the trolley method of take-off; it was important to line up accurately on the runway before starting the run, however, because at the lower speeds the lateral control was poor. When it reached about 100 mph the aircraft's nose began to lift by itself and he pulled the lever to release the trolley; relieved of its 1,325 pounds weight, the Arado would lift cleanly into the air. After the aircraft had landed on its skids, jacking up and refitting the trolley took about 20 minutes, then the Arado could be towed away. During one of the early flights Goetz got airborne but found he was unable to release the trolley. After orbiting the airfield to burn off fuel, he skilfully put the Arado down on the runway at Oranienburg, using almost its full length before he brought the aircraft to a halt.

Goetz's Ar 234s were each fitted with a pair of Rb 50/30 cameras in the rear fuselage. Fitted with

*Oberleutnant* Horst Goetz commanded the special trials detachment at Oranienburg, which was to carry out the world's first jet reconnaissance missions using the Ar 234. *(Goetz)*

* *Versuchstaffel der Oberkommando der Luftwaffe*

50 cm long focus lenses, the cameras pointed downwards and were splayed sidewards away from each other at 12 degrees to the vertical across the line of flight. From an altitude of 32,500 feet this split-pair camera arrangement took in a swathe of ground just over 6 miles wide along the aircraft's track.

While Goetz and Sommer learned to handle the two Arados in an operational role, the Allied troops had established themselves ashore in Normandy. Luftwaffe reconnaissance units attempting to photograph the landing areas suffered heavy losses from the screens of enemy fighters, and frequently failed to get through to their targets. German army commanders were left in almost complete ignorance of what was going on behind the front line, and often the first indication of an impending attack was the preparatory bombardment.

*Leutnant* Erich Sommer, who flew the Ar 234A during the world's first jet reconnaissance mission on 2 August 1944 described in the text. *(Sommer)*

To overcome this deficiency, Goetz received orders to move his detachment to Juvincourt near Reims in France for reconnaissance operations. From the start, however, there were problems. On 25 July the two Arados took off from Oranienburg, but Goetz's aircraft suffered an engine failure and he had to turn back. Sommer continued on and landed at Juvincourt without incident. After he landed, his aircraft was hoisted on to a low-loading trailer and towed into a hangar. There the world's most advanced reconnaissance aircraft had to remain, unusable, until its take-off trolley arrived from Oranienburg by rail. It was over a week before the trucks carrying the trolley, the special jacks and other ground equipment, spares and rocket pods, were shunted into the railway siding at Juvincourt.

Finally, on the morning of 2 August, everything was ready for Sommer to take-off for the world's first jet reconnaissance mission. The Ar 234, with its rocket pods fitted, was towed out to the main east-west runway. Sommer boarded it, strapped it, completed his pre-take-off checks and started the jet engines. Satisfied that everything was functioning as it should, he released the brakes and pushed open his throttles. Slowly the Arado gathered speed. After a run of about 200 yards he pressed the button to fire the booster rockets and Sommer felt a reassuring push against his back as the acceleration increased. Gradually the aircraft became lighter on the ground and, when the pilot released the trolley, the Arado leapt into the air trailing smoke from its boosters. A quarter of a minute after lift-off the rockets, their fuel exhausted, ceased giving thrust. Sommer pushed the button to release them and they tumbled away, then their parachutes opened to lower them gently to the ground.

Sommer established his aircraft in the climb at 2,500 feet per minute with an initial forward speed of 256 mph. Since he had taken off in a westerly direction, he needed only a slight change in heading to point the aircraft for the target area. As the Arado climbed higher and entered the thinner air, its speed gradually increased.

It took Sommer about 20 minutes to climb to 34,000 feet, by which time the Arado was almost over the battle area. From time to time he jinked the aircraft and glanced behind to see whether there were any condensation trails which might give away his position to enemy fighters; there were none. High over the Cherbourg Peninsula he turned the aircraft on to an easterly heading, easing down the nose and descending about 1,700 feet to build up his speed to about 460 mph. Then he levelled off and concentrated on flying exactly straight and level for his photographic run. Already the doors protecting the camera lenses were open; now the German pilot flicked the switch to set the cameras running, the automatic mechanism taking one picture with every 11 seconds.

It was a beautifully clear summer day, with scarcely a cloud in the sky. From Sommer's vantage point there was hardly a sign of the life-and-death struggle going on far below. If any enemy fighters did attempt to catch the high-flying Arado, he never noticed them. He was too busy holding his aircraft on a ruler-straight track, so that his cameras could take in the greatest possible area on the limited amount of film in the aircraft's magazines. The first photographic run, taking in the coastal strip, lasted about ten minutes. Sommer then turned through a semi-circle and levelled out, heading westwards for the second run parallel to the first and about 6 miles inland. The second run completed, he turned back on to an easterly heading and flew a third run 6 miles further inland and parallel to the previous two. Almost at the end of the third run the counters on his camera panel clicked to zero, indicating that he had run out of film.

His mission complete, Sommer continued heading east; now his sole aim was to get back to base with the precious film. Keeping a wary eye open for Allied fighters, he returned to Juvincourt in a high speed descent and set the aircraft down on the grass. Even before the Arado had slid to a standstill on the airfield, men were converging on it from all directions. As Sommer was clambering out, the camera hatch above the rear fuselage had been opened and the magazines of exposed film were being unclipped; then they were rushed away for developing.

During this single sortie, Erich Sommer had been able to achieve more than all of the German reconnaissance units in the west, put together, had done during the past two months: in a flight lasting less than an hour and half he had photographed almost the entire lodgement area

Close up of the rear fuselage with the upper camera hatches removed, showing the two Rb 50/30 aerial cameras.

held by the Allies in Normandy. The 380 photographs taken from the Arado caused a considerable stir. By that time the Allies had landed more than 1½ million men, 1½ million tons of supplies and nearly a third of a million vehicles in France. It took a twelve-man team of photographic interpreters more than two days working flat out to produce an initial report on what the prints showed. The detailed examination of the photographs took weeks. 'After that first sortie, lots of senior officers came to Juvincourt wanting to look over the plane,' Sommer recalled, 'but the whole thing was kept very secret and they were not allowed near it.'

Also on 2 August, Horst Goetz finally arrived at Juvincourt with the other Ar 234. During the three weeks that followed the two aircraft flew thirteen further missions. At last the German field commanders received the regular photographic coverage of the enemy positions which they had craved so long. But the time when such information might have played a decisive part in the land battle was long past. Even as Sommer's initial set of photographs were being scanned by the interpreters, American forces were breaking out of their initial lodgement area and were fanning out into Brittany: the Battle of Normandy was over and the great advance into France was about to begin. The Ar 234s brought back thousands of photographs of the Allied advance, but they did little more than present the German High Command with a minutely detailed picture of a battle already lost.

Like Schenk's Messerschmitt 262s, Goetz's Ar 234s appear to have escaped the notice of the Allied Intelligence services during the Battle of France. It is probably the highest compliment that could have been paid to the high speed reconnaissance machines and their pilots, for their task was to slip in and photograph their targets with a minimum of fuss, then return to base with the previous film.

On 28 August, as the American tanks were nearing Reims, Goetz received orders to move his two Ar 234s from Juvincourt to Chievres. It was then that 'friendly' forces achieved what the Allied

Aerial view of the 'Mulberry' artificial harbour off Asnelles sur Mer in Normandy, taken during Erich Sommer's flight on 2 August 1944.

B
A
VOLKEL
A/F
K.3111.

fighter pilots could not. As Goetz circled Chievres before landing, the ground defences, who had come to treat almost any aircraft approaching the airfield as hostile, opened fire at him. An accurate shell struck the Ar 234 just beneath the cockpit, knocking out the aircraft's electrical and hydraulic systems. Goetz broke off his approach and found that his flaps and landing skids would not extend. The aircraft was still flyable, however, so he resolved to take it back to Oranienburg where it could receive proper repairs. There Goetz made a skilful flapless belly landing, touching down at about 190 mph. A few loose stones smashed through the glazed nose and Goetz received some cuts, but otherwise the valuable aircraft came to a halt with remarkably little damage. Goetz had just climbed out of the cockpit, however, when the battered Ar 234 received its *coup de grâce*: a young fighter pilot taking off from the airfield, not expecting such an obstacle to be in his path, ran straight into the rear of the reconnaissance machine and severed the complete tail with his propeller. Goetz received further injuries from stones and flying glass and was unable to see for a couple of weeks; his Ar 234 was a wreck.

Sommer landed his Ar 234 at Chievres without difficulty, then had to move to Volkel in Holland a few days later as Allied tanks approached the area. Sommer was at Volkel on 3 September, when over 100 Lancaster bombers of the Royal Air Force carried out a heavy daylight attack on the airfield. Although Volkel's landing ground and camp areas were pot-marked with craters, Sommer's Ar 234 was not damaged in its hangar.

OPPOSITE:
The airfield at Volkel in Holland taken from a Spitfire reconnaissance aircraft of the RAF, after the attack by more than a hundred Lancaster bombers on 3 September 1944. In spite of its pock-marked appearance, the airfield continued in limited use by the Luftwaffe and Erich Sommer took off from there on the day after the attack. His Ar 234 had been in the hangar (circled, A) and was unharmed. He was towed along the taxiway marked with the dotted line and took off down the taxiway shown with the dashed line. The bomb craters along this route had been filled in, then painted so as to appear to the casual aerial observer as though they were still there. This photograph was taken on 6 September; note the aircraft in the process of taking off (circled B). The authors have found no evidence that the Allies discovered the subterfuge.

The airfield was judged unusable for normal operations so on the following day, 4 September, he made a trolley take-off from one of the taxi-tracks after some of the craters had been filled in. Sommer landed the Ar 234 at Rheine near Osnabrück, the new base for the jet reconnaissance operations.

The withdrawal to Germany coincided with an end of the missions by the trolley-mounted Ar 234s, for by September the improved 'B' version of the aircraft was becoming available with its fitted undercarriage. The slightly wider fuselage necessary to accommodate the undercarriage reduced its speed by about 20 mph; but still the aircraft was fast enough to avoid fighter interception. There was also some reduction in the radius of action of the aircraft, so two 66 Imp gal drop tanks were carried under the engines for the longer missions. In return for these limitations, of minor tactical importance considering the defensive posture in which Germany now found herself, the Ar 234B was a considerably more flexible machine able to operate from airfields without special ground equipment.

At Rheine Goetz's unit, now code-named *Kommando Sperling*, gradually built up to a strength of nine Ar 234Bs. Jet reconnaissance missions became a regular feature. Allied fighter patrols over the airfield posed an almost continual problem since, as in the case of the Me 262s, the only time the Ar 234s were vulnerable to fighter attack was when they were flying relatively slowly after take-off and when approaching to land. Goetz had his own system of look-outs posted round the airfield when the Ar 234Bs were operating, to provide warning of enemy aircraft. The jets were towed to the take-off point only when the sky around was clear, then the engines were started and they took off immediately. Goetz's pilots were ordered to keep up their speed as they approached the airfield on their return, and land only on confirmation that there were no enemy fighters about. If there was any danger, the pilots would land at an alternative airfield nearby. There were strong flak defences positioned to cover the take-off and landing lanes at Rheine, though Goetz felt that these were never strong enough to deter a really determined enemy.

Photographs of Ar 234s of *Kommando Sperling* engaged in reconnaissance missions from Rheine, in the autumn of 1944.

ABOVE:
Towing the aircraft to the take-off point using a refuelling vehicle. *(Goetz)*

---

LEFT, BELOW, TOP RIGHT:
At the take-off point the pilot boarded the aircraft, strapped in and went through the pre take-off checks. Note the 'Jet-propelled Sparrow with a Camera' emblem on the nose of the Arado, the badge of the *Kommando Sperling*. *(Goetz)*

BELOW;
Groundcrewmen pushing out the rocket pod on is special trolley. *(Goetz)*

LEFT:
After the mission, the camera magazines were removed from the aircraft for processing. *(Goetz)*

**Ar 234B**

1 Port elevator hinge
2 Tailplane skinning
3 Port elevator
4 Tab actuating rod
5 Elevator trim tab
6 Geared rudder tab (upper)
7 Rudder hinges
8 Tail navigation light
9 Plywood fin leading edge
10 T-aerial for VHF R/T set
11 Aerial for CBI 3 blind approach receiver
12 Aerial matching unit
13 Tailfin structure
14 Rudder construction
15 Rudder post
16 Rudder tab (lower)
17 Lower rudder hinge
18 Rudder actuating rods
19 Parachute cable
20 Cable anchor point/tailskid
21 Starboard elevator tab
22 Elevator construction
23 Tailplane construction
24 Elevator control linkage
25 Tailplane attachment points
26 Elevator rod
27 Port side control runs
28 Internal mass balance
29 Parachute release mechanism
30 Main FuG 16 panel
31 Brake parachute container
32 Starboard MG 151 cannon muzzle
33 Brake chute door (open)
34 Mauser MG 151/20 cannon (rearward firing)
35 Cannon support yoke
36 Spent cartridge chute
37 Access panel (lowered)
38 Ammunition feed chute
39 Tail surface control rods (starboard)
40 Ammunition box
41 Bulkhead
42 Fuel vent pipe
43 Fuel pumps
44 Fuel level gauge
45 Rear fuel cell (440 Imp gal — 2,000 l capacity)
46 Fuselage frames
47 Fuel filler point
48 Fuel lines
49 Inner flap construction
50 Exhaust cone
51 Nacelle support fairing
52 RATO exhaust

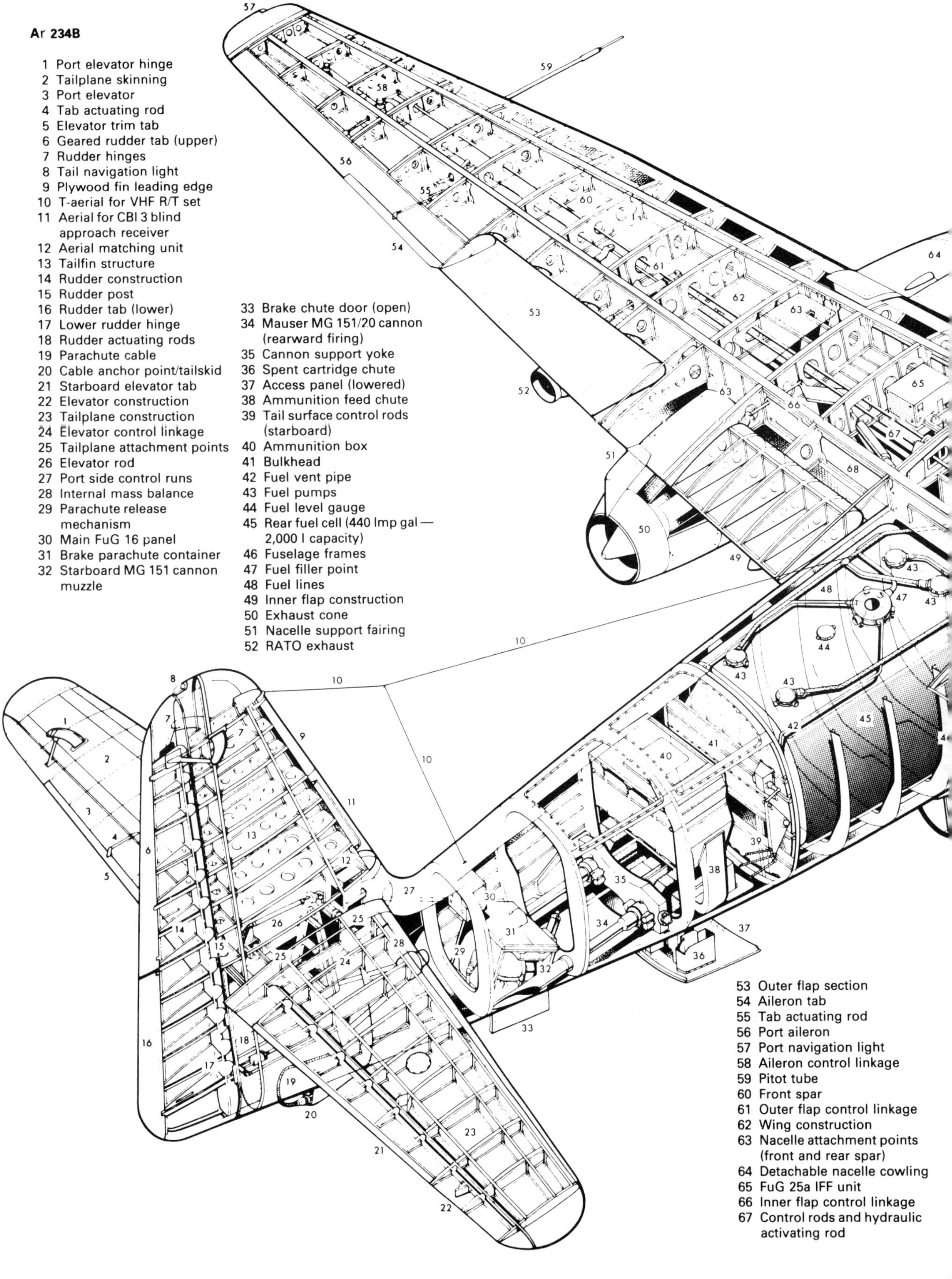

53 Outer flap section
54 Aileron tab
55 Tab actuating rod
56 Port aileron
57 Port navigation light
58 Aileron control linkage
59 Pitot tube
60 Front spar
61 Outer flap control linkage
62 Wing construction
63 Nacelle attachment points (front and rear spar)
64 Detachable nacelle cowling
65 FuG 25a IFF unit
66 Inner flap control linkage
67 Control rods and hydraulic activating rod

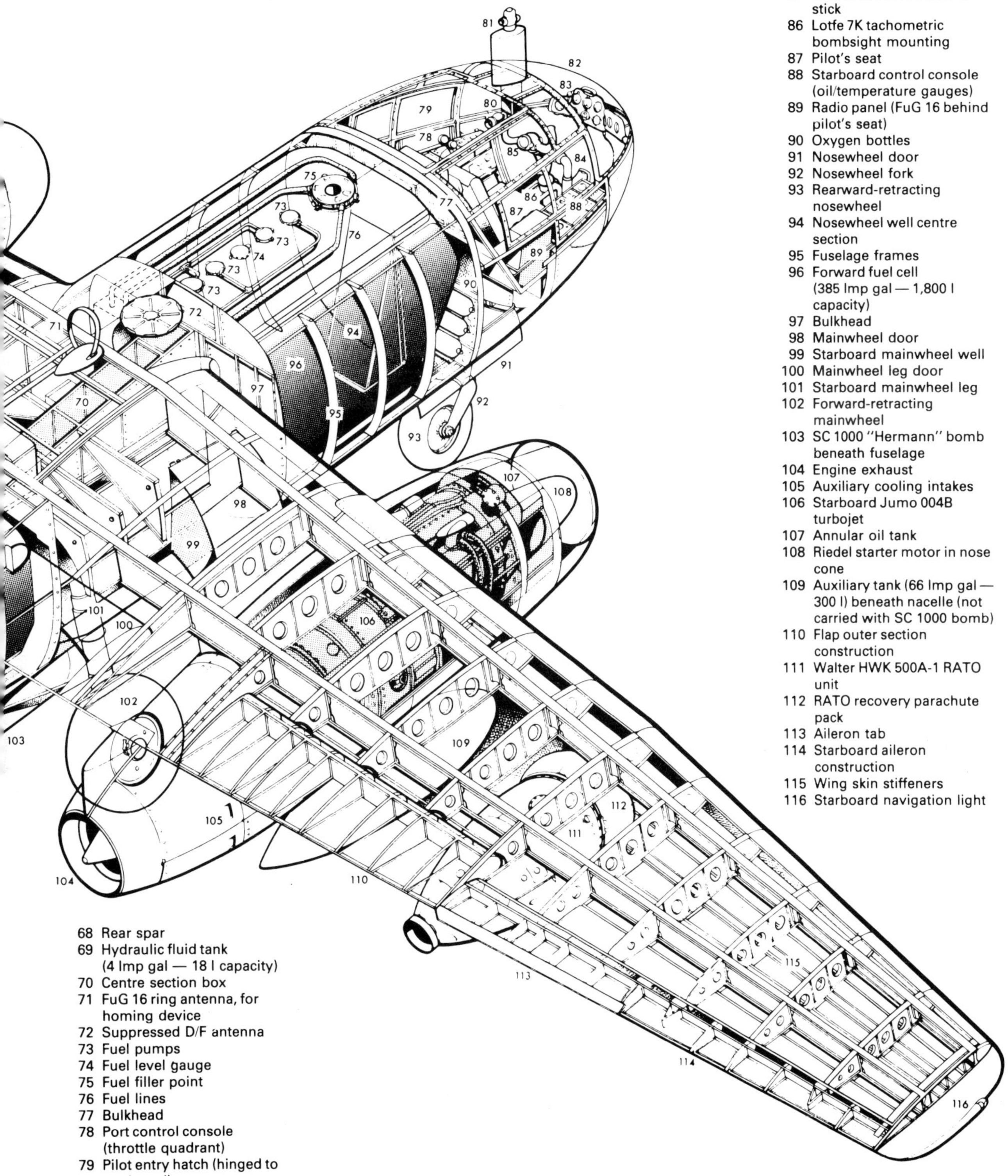


68 Rear spar
69 Hydraulic fluid tank (4 Imp gal — 18 l capacity)
70 Centre section box
71 FuG 16 ring antenna, for homing device
72 Suppressed D/F antenna
73 Fuel pumps
74 Fuel level gauge
75 Fuel filler point
76 Fuel lines
77 Bulkhead
78 Port control console (throttle quadrant)
79 Pilot entry hatch (hinged to starboard)
80 Periscopic sight
81 Periscopic head (rearview mirror/gunsight)
82 Clear vision cockpit glazing
83 Instrument panel
84 Rudder pedal
85 Swivel-mounted control stick
86 Lotfe 7K tachometric bombsight mounting
87 Pilot's seat
88 Starboard control console (oil/temperature gauges)
89 Radio panel (FuG 16 behind pilot's seat)
90 Oxygen bottles
91 Nosewheel door
92 Nosewheel fork
93 Rearward-retracting nosewheel
94 Nosewheel well centre section
95 Fuselage frames
96 Forward fuel cell (385 Imp gal — 1,800 l capacity)
97 Bulkhead
98 Mainwheel door
99 Starboard mainwheel well
100 Mainwheel leg door
101 Starboard mainwheel leg
102 Forward-retracting mainwheel
103 SC 1000 "Hermann" bomb beneath fuselage
104 Engine exhaust
105 Auxiliary cooling intakes
106 Starboard Jumo 004B turbojet
107 Annular oil tank
108 Riedel starter motor in nose cone
109 Auxiliary tank (66 Imp gal — 300 l) beneath nacelle (not carried with SC 1000 bomb)
110 Flap outer section construction
111 Walter HWK 500A-1 RATO unit
112 RATO recovery parachute pack
113 Aileron tab
114 Starboard aileron construction
115 Wing skin stiffeners
116 Starboard navigation light

As well as missions over France, Belgium and Holland, *Kommando Sperling* also flew a few sorties over England. On 5 October, for example, Goetz flew a two-hour mission to photograph shipping off the coasts of Norfolk and Lincolnshire. On the following day he took off for a reconnaissance of southern England, only to have a close shave from half a dozen P-47s which arrived over Rheine just after he completed his take-off and released his rocket pods. Fortunately for Goetz, however, the radioed warning of the fighters' approach reached him from the ground observers just in time. The German pilot jettisoned his drop tanks, put down the nose of the Ar 234B to gain speed rapidly, then easily out-distanced the enemy fighters before resuming his climb to altitude. Deprived of the fuel in the drop tanks Goetz had to cut short this time on reconnaissance, though he was still able to bring back some useful photographs.

Compared with the jet fighter units, *Kommando Sperling* had relatively little trouble with its Jumo 004 engines. The key to extending the life of the early jet engines was careful throttle handling, and the lone reconnaissance aircraft did not require the almost continual speed changes necessary when, for example, fighters flew in formation. Goetz suffered a rare instance of engine failure on 15 November over the North Sea at 32,500 feet on his way home after photographing airfields in East Anglia. The Ar 234B suddenly began to vibrate uncomfortably. Obviously one of the engines was beginning to play up, but which one? The instruments for both were giving normal indications. Goetz tossed a mental coin and throttled back the starboard engine — wrong! The good engine immediately flamed out, then refused to re-start. The vibration continued, forcing Goetz to shut down the port engine as well. Now he was sitting at the controls of a high speed glider, with an uncomfortably high rate of sink. The aircraft descended to about 6,500 feet before he was finally able to re-start the starboard engine and returned to Rheine on that one. Afterwards it was discovered that one of the turbine blades had come adrift from the port engine, throwing the whole rotating assembly out of balance.

In spite of the fact that Goetz's reconnaissance Ar 234s had been operating for nearly four months, and he himself had had a brush with enemy fighters six weeks earlier, it was not until 21 November 1944 that Allied fighters first reported seeing an Ar 234 in the air. On that day, as P-51s of the 339th Fighter Group were escorting bombers passing over Holland on their way to targets in Germany, when the Ar 234 hove into view:

'The jet aircraft approached the fighter and bomber formations from the north at an altitude of 27,000 feet which was approximately 1,000 feet above the bomber formation. Jet aircraft passed directly over the formation apparently with power off, indicated airspeed apparently 300 mph. When in 3 o'clock position to our fighter and bomber formation the jet aircraft emitted smoke from each jet nacelle for approximately 10 seconds, increasing the speed of the aircraft as it disappeared into the sun.'

Mock combats carried out at about this time, between an Ar 234B and a FW 190, highlighted the strong and weak points of the unarmed jet; a report from the Arado company stated:

'The greatest weapon the Ar 234B has over propeller-driven fighters is its speed. In a tight turning flight the FW 190 could easily get into a firing position. But if the Ar 234B flew straight ahead, or climbed or descended keeping its wings horizontal, it soon outran the FW 190. If turns have to be made they should be of great radius, that is to say wide turns. One problem is that the vision below and to the rear is restricted, and nothing can be seen rearwards on 30° on either side of the centre line. Due to this limitation of vision it is not possible to detect an attacker coming from directly behind . . .'

For the longer-ranging reconnaissance missions, for example those over England, the Ar 234 carried one 300 litre (66 Imp gal) drop tank under each engine.

OPPOSITE PAGE, TOP:
The airfield at Horsham St Faith, immediately to the north of Norwich and home of the B-24s of the US 458th Bomb Group, photographed from one of the *Kommando Sperling's* Ar 234s on 11 September 1944.

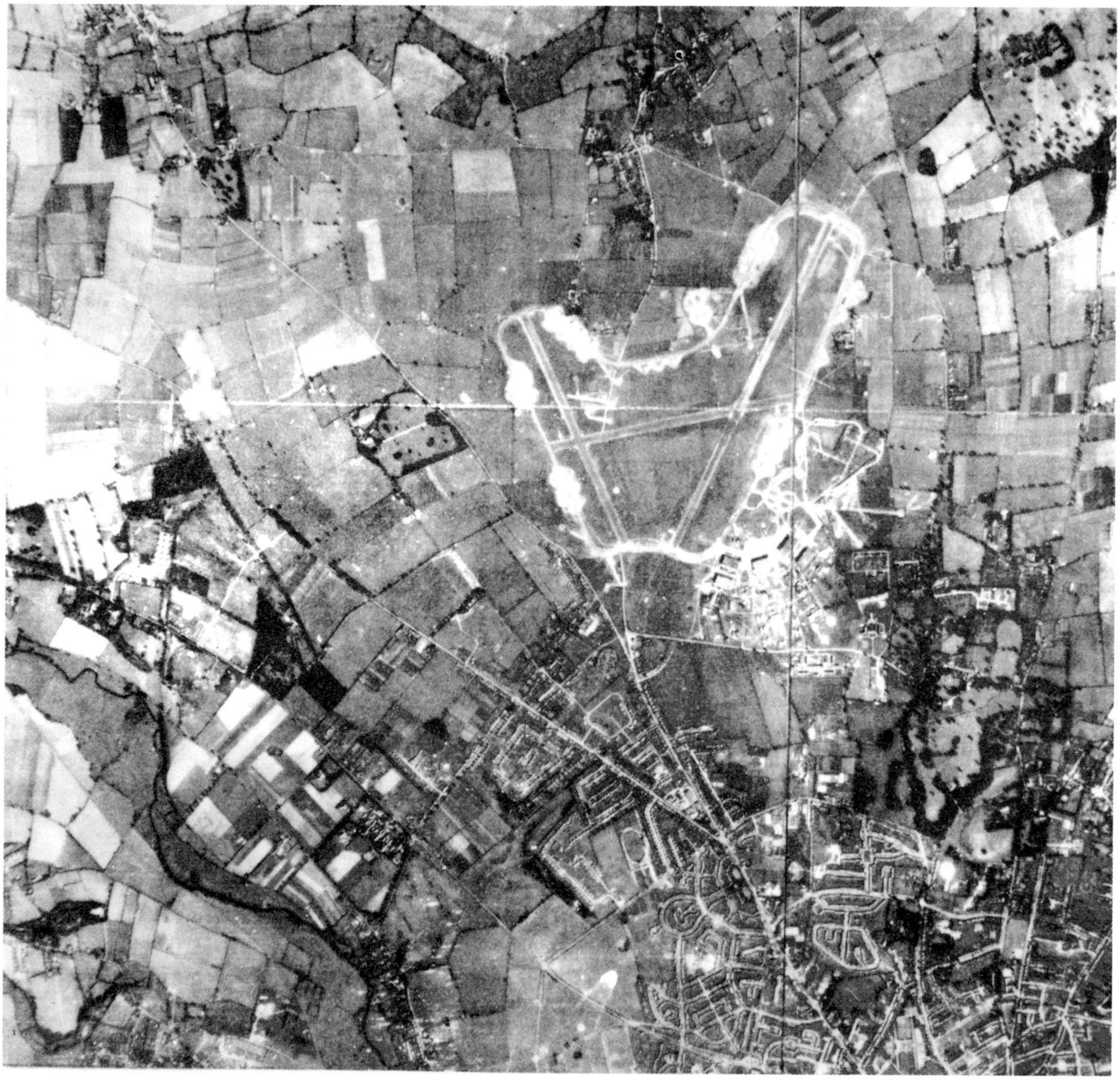

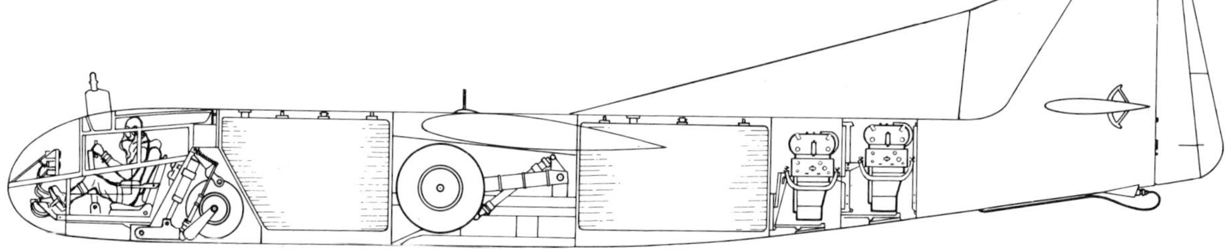

Reconnaissance version of the Ar 234B, showing the layout of the Rb 50/30 cameras in the rear fuselage.

The report concluded that the FW 190 stood a chance of engaging a correctly-flown Ar 234B only if it could achieve surprise; otherwise the jet aircraft easily evaded it by using its high speed.

Meanwhile, during the closing months of 1944, the IIIrd *Gruppe* of *Kampfgeschwader* 76 had been working-up with the bomber version of the Ar 234B, at Burg near Magdeburg. On 17 December *Hauptmann* Diether Lukesch, the commander of the 9th *Staffel*, received orders to move forwards a detachment of sixteen aircraft to Münster-Handorf, and begin operations in support of the German offensive in the Ardennes which had opened the previous day. By the 21st the move was complete. But the bad weather which prevented Allied air operations at this time also prevented those of the Luftwaffe, and the Ar 234Bs had to remain on the ground for the next two days.

Not until Christmas Eve were the Ar 234B bombers able to go into action for the first time. At 10.14 that morning Lukesch took off from Münster-Handorf, followed in rapid succession by the remaining eight bombers of the force, bound for Liege. Each Ar 234B carried a single 1,100 pound bomb under the fuselage. The jet bombers, with little to fear from enemy fighters so long as they kept their speed up, flew in a loose trail. After take-off the bombers headed north-eastwards for a few miles to conceal their base airfield in case they ran into enemy aircraft, then turned on to a south-westerly heading for their target and began their climb to a cruising altitude of 13,000 feet. Thirty-five minutes after take-off, Lukesch led the Ar 234Bs in to bomb in a shallow dive attack which took them down to 6,500 feet. The leader released his bomb on a factory complex, the others bombed railway yards in the city; the pilots reported only weak flak defences in the target area. After attacking, the Ar 234Bs remained at 6,500 feet and headed straight for their base at high speed. On his way home Lukesch flew close past a Spitfire which chanced to be in his path. The British pilot, who had no way of knowing that the only gun on board the German jet was the pilot's pistol, banked away sharply and dived to avoid the 'attacker' coming in from behind. All of the Ar 234Bs returned safely to Münster-Handorf, though one suffered an undercarriage failure on landing and incurred slight damage to the wing; the pilot, *Unterfeldwebel* Winguth, escaped without injury.

*Hauptmann* Diether Lukesch, the commander of the 9th *Staffel* of *Kampfgeschwader* 76, led the first attack by Arado Ar 234 bombers on 24 December 1944. A week later he led the world's first night attack by jet bombers. *(Lukesch)*

During a similar operation against the same target that afternoon, Lukesch led eight Ar 234Bs into the attack and again all returned safely.

On the following day, Christmas, there were two more operations against Liege, both with eight Ar 234Bs. During the morning mission the jet bombers came under attack from Royal Air Force Tempests of No 80 Squadron. Pilot Officer R. Verran managed to close in on one of the Ar 234Bs and claimed strikes on the port engine before he ran out of ammunition. The jet bomber he hit was that flown by *Leutnant* Alfred Frank, which was afterwards wrecked in a crash landing in Holland; the pilot escaping without injury. During the same mission *Oberfeldwebel* Dierks returned with a failed engine and his aircraft was damaged on landing; once again, the pilot escaped without injury. Returning from the second mission that day *Oberleutnant* Friedrich Fendrich suffered a burst tyre on landing, causing slight damage to the nose of his aircraft.

ABOVE:
Arado Ar 234Bs of 9./KG 76, photographed at Burg near Magdeburg late in 1944 when the unit was working up.
*(KG 76 Archiv)*

BELOW:
Diether Lukesch standing in the cockpit of his Ar 234 as it is towed out for a training flight at Burg.
*(KG 76 Archiv)*

The *Staffel* suffered its first pilot casualty during an operational mission on the 27th. As he was taking off to attack Allied positions near Neufchâteau, *Leutnant* Erich Dick ran into the blast wall of a flak position on the airfield. The aircraft was burnt out in the subsequent fire and Dick was severely wounded.

Operations continued at this rate during the days that followed, whenever the weather permitted. For all of these early missions the Ar 234Bs employed the shallow dive attack tactics similar to those on their initial operation. Lukesch did not favour the high altitude horizontal mode of attack, and never used it during any operational mission that he led. 'During such an attack the pilot could not see behind, and there was a continual worry about being surprised by an enemy fighter; a fighter diving from 1,000 m or 2,000 m above could easily reach our speed, especially if we were carrying bombs. Also, flying a straight course for so long would have made things easy for the enemy flak', he recalled. 'The only justification for the high altitude attack would have been to get the extra range; but the targets we bombed were all close enough to our base for us to reach them flying at medium altitudes.'

During the early morning darkness of 1 January 1945, Lukesch led four Ar 234Bs for the world's first night jet bombing mission — though in fact the bombing was intended to deceive the enemy rather than cause damage. The aircraft flew from Münster-Handorf along a circular route which took them over Rotterdam, Antwerp, Brussels, Liege and Cologne, then back to their base. The primary aim of the mission was to report on the weather over Belgium and Holland in preparation for Operation *Bodenplatte*, the massed attack on Allied airfields by the Luftwaffe planned to open soon after first light. The Ar 234Bs dropped their bombs on Brussels and Liege, to conceal the real object of their mission.

Later that morning Lukesch's deputy, *Oberleutnant* Artur Stark, led six Ar 234Bs to attack the British airfield at Gilze Rijen in Holland. For this operation each of the jet bombers carried a single AB 500 bomb container, loaded with twenty-five 33-pound anti-personnel bombs.

For the rest of January the weather restricted operations severely, and after the first of the month the Ar 234Bs were able to mount attacks on only four other days: on the 2nd, against Liege; on the 14th, against Bastogne; and on the 20th and 24th against Antwerp.

A mechanic, straddling the engine nacelle as he checks the oil level during the pre-flight inspection, gives scale to the compact Jumo 004 installation. *(KG 76 Archiv)*

On 10 January 1945 the Luftwaffe Quartermaster General's list recorded only 17 Ar 234Bs in service with operational units, distributed as follows:

| | |
|---|---|
| 9th *Staffel* of *Kampfgeschwader* 76 | 12 |
| *Kommando Sperling* (reconnaissance) | 4 |
| *Kommando Hecht* (reconnaissance) | 1 |

By this time the 1st *Gruppe* and the rest of the IIIrd *Gruppe* of KG 76 were re-equipping with the type, though neither unit was to go into action at anything approaching *Gruppe* strength. Even allowing for the aircraft allocated to these units, it is clear that only a relatively small proportion of the 148 Ar 234s delivered to the Luftwaffe by the end of 1944 had in fact been put into service. As in the case of the Me 262s, the rising crescendo of Allied air attacks on the German transport system greatly hindered the formation of operational units with the Ar 234B.

Like the other types of jet aircraft, the Ar 234s were at their most vulnerable during their take-offs and landings. The commander of III./KG 76, *Major* Hans-Georg Baetcher, recalled one occasion when he was returning to his airfield at Achmer to find Allied and German fighters dogfighting overhead '. . . and the flak gunners, being neutral, firing at everybody!' Short of fuel, Baetcher had no alternative but to run in very fast and make a 'hot' landing. At 250 mph he extended his undercarriage; as soon as his speed fell to 220 mph he lowered his flaps; at 175 mph he forced the unwilling aircraft down on the runway and immediately streamed his brake parachute. The harsh treatment proved to be to much for the synthetic rubber tyre of the port wheel, which promptly blew out. The aircraft lurched off the runway and Baetcher was treated to a high speed run across the grass before man and machine came to rest shaken, but otherwise little the worse for the experience.

By the third week in January the whole of III./KG 76 had converted to the Ar 234 and the *Gruppe* was at full strength. On 23 January eighteen Arados from the 7th and 8th *Staffeln* flew to Achmer, their new operational base. But as the jet bombers arrived over the airfield the Spitfires of No 401 (Canadian) Squadron pounced on them. During the hectic action that followed the Spitfires shot down three Arados and damaged two. Two German pilots were killed.

February was a better month for the jet bombers, and when fuel became available they were at last able to exploit their new-found operational strength. On the 8th the Arados mounted a 7-aircraft attack on targets near Brussels. During the next attack, on the 16th, III./KG 76 operated in much greater force: the unit mounted two attacks on British troops near Cleve, each with sixteen jet bombers. On 21 February the *Gruppe* flew what was to be its largest number of sorties in a single day, 37, against British troop positions near Aachen. Operations in similar strength continued throughout the rest of February and into March.

*Major* Hans-Georg Baetcher (left, in flying jacket) commanded IIIrd *Gruppe* of KG 76 early in 1945. *(KG 76 Archiv)*

Ar 234B of KG 76 undergoing servicing at Burg.
*(KG 76 Archiv)*

Following the conversion of IIIrd *Gruppe*, IInd *Gruppe* of KG 76 was the next unit to re-equip with the jet bomber. At the end of February the 6th *Staffel* (part of IInd *Gruppe*) was declared ready for operations and moved to Hesepe.

On 7 March the entire German defensive strategy in the west was plunged into crisis, when a *coup de main* operation by American troops seized the Ludendorf Bridge over the Rhine at Remargen. The bridge had suffered severe damage from demolition charges set by Germany army engineers, but was still usable. The capture of the bridge breached the last natural defensive obstacle in the west and Goering designated it a target of the highest importance. For most of the week following its capture, the bridge at Remargen was shielded by low cloud which made it difficult for Luftwaffe bombers and fighter-bombers to deliver accurate low altitude attacks. On the 9th three Ar 234s attacked the bridge, which was by then protected by a large and growing number of anti-aircraft guns; one of the jet bombers was shot down. That attack failed to inflict significant damage, as did another by a pair of Arados two days later.

On the 12th the jet bombers tried a different tactic. Throughout the day these aircraft flew 18 sorties against the bridge, flying singly and carrying out horizontal attacks from altitudes between 16,000 and 26,000 feet using the Egon radio blind bombing system. This attack, and a similar one by nineteen aircraft on the following day, also failed to dislodge the bridge.

On the next day, the 14th, the cloud cleared to reveal clear skies over Remargen. And immediately those skies were filled with large numbers of British and American fighters flying standing patrols at all levels. Eleven Arados took off to attack the bridge but as they ran in to deliver their shallow dive attacks the Allied fighters dived after them. A series of high speed engagements followed, in the course of which four Arados were shot down. And still the bridge remained standing.

By now the defenders had lost the battle to prevent the American troops establishing a strong bridgehead on the east bank of the Rhine. On 17 March the Ludendorf bridge finally succumbed to the cumulative damage from the demolition charges and the air attacks, and collapsed into the river. But by then U.S. Army engineers had erected pontoon bridges alongside it and the flow of troops eastward continued unhindered.

Following the end of the action around Remargen, the jet bombers resumed their attacks on enemy troop positions, vehicles and other military objectives. On 19 March four Arados set out to hit targets in the area around Brussels. In what was to be the nearest thing to a confrontation between opposing manned jet aircraft during the conflict, *Leutnant* Croissant attacked Melsbroek airfield with ABB 500 cluster bombs and inflicted minor damage to one of No 616 Squadron's Meteor fighters on the ground. Following the attack several Allied fighters attempted to engage the Arado but the jet bomber rapidly outdistanced them.

Not until 11 February 1945, after the type had been operating for more than six months, was a reconnaissance Ar 234 shot down by an enemy fighter. On that day Squadron Leader David Fairbanks was leading an armed reconnaissance of eight Tempests of No 274 Squadron RAF when he spotted a lone jet aircraft which he took to be an Me 262. After a lengthy chase the machine was caught and shot down, as it slowed to make its landing approach at Rheine. In fact it was an Ar 234B of Goetz's unit piloted by *Hauptmann* Hans Felden, who was returning after a photographic mission over the port of Hull; Felden was killed when his aircraft smashed into the ground.

Ar 234 taking off from Burg, trailing smoke from the booster rockets. *(KG 76 Archiv)*

From September 1944 the reconnaissance Ar 234Bs had operated regularly, photographing Allied positions usually without interference. Early in 1945 Goetz's *Kommando Sperling* had been expanded into a *Staffel*; it became the 1st *Staffel* of *Fernaufklaerungsgruppe* (long range reconnaissance *Gruppe*) 123. Two other reconnaissance *Staffeln* re-equipped with the Ar 234B, and were attached to FAGr 100 and FAGr 33. In addition, Erich Sommer had formed his own unit, *Kommando Sommer*, equipped with the Ar 234B and covering the Italian front.

Erich Sommer's *Kommando* based at Udine in Italy suffered its only pilot loss on 11 April. *Leutnant* Guenther Gniesmer was engaged in a lone reconnaissance mission when, near Bologna, he had the bad luck to run into a force of bombers escorted by P-51s of the 52nd Fighter Group. Lieutenants Hall and Cooper succeeded in getting into firing positions, and shot him down. Gniesmer baled out of the Ar 234B, but was hit by the

Ar 234 on the landing approach at Burg. *(KG 76 Archiv)*

tailplane and severely injured. He parachuted into no-man's land and was picked up by German troops, but died in hospital a couple of days later.

In addition to the bombing and reconnaissance missions, early in 1945 a few Ar 234Bs were modified for use as night fighters. These aircraft carried the FuG 218 *Neptun* radar, with nose-mounted aerials; the radar operator sat in an improvised position, inside the rear fuselage aft of the wing. The Ar 234B night fighter carried an armament of two 20 mm MG 151 cannon, housed in a pack mounted under the fuselage. Initially, this *ad hoc* night fighter unit was commanded by *Hauptmann* Bisping, who lost his life in a crash, and then taken over by *Hauptmann* Kurt Bonow. Late in March 1945, a couple of these provisional Ar 234B night fighters were operated by *Kommando Bonow*. The Ar 234B was clearly under-armed for the bomber-destroyer role, however, and there appears to be no record of it achieving any victories as a night fighter.

On 10 April 1945, the last date for which figures exist, a mere 38 Ar 234Bs were listed as being in service with operational units, distributed as follows:

| | |
|---|---|
| BOMBER UNITS | |
| *Stab Kampfgeschwader* 76 | 2 |
| 6th *Staffel* | 5 |
| IIIrd *Gruppe* | 5 |
| RECONNAISSANCE | |
| 1st *Staffel Fernaufklaerungsgruppe* 33 | 7 |
| 1st *Staffel Fernaufklaerungsgruppe* 100 | 6 |
| 1st *Staffel Fernaufklaerungsgruppe* 123 | 8 |
| *Kommando Sommer* | 3 |
| NIGHT FIGHTING | |
| *Kommando Bonow* | 2 |

During the closing stages of the war the Arado 234C, powered by four 1,760 pounds thrust BMW 003 engines, was on the point of entering large scale production. With its extra thrust, this version could take-off fully laden from the shorter airfields without the assistance of rockets. Peter Kappus, a civilian test pilot with BMW who flew the Ar 234C, recalled 'The four-engined Ar 234C had a very high performance in the take-off and the climb, but it could not be flown at full power horizontally because at the very high speeds it reached it had structural flutter problems.' Even by 1945, however, the development problems of the BMW 003 had not been fully resolved (it will be remembered that at one time this engine was to have powered the Me 262). Kappus had a very lucky escape on 29 March 1945 during a flight from Burg in the 15th prototype, an Ar 234B fitted with two BMW 003s for development trials. He had just taken off, when:

'I noticed a sudden increase in engine noise and an apparent surge in power. I noticed to my amazement that the tachometer of my No 2 engine indicated 11,000 rpm. I instinctively cut the power. This was critical, since I had just taken-off and was only about 200 feet off the ground. Then I thought about it, and concluded that to have such an excessive engine speed (9,600 rpm was maximum revolutions) the engine would have shed all of its compressor and turbine blades immediately. Therefore the failure had to be in the tachometer itself — the engine could not possibly be turning so fast! And, because the airplane was still 'dirty' — gear and flaps down — I confidently advanced the throttle again to get her around the field. That was my big mistake.'

Line up of Ar 234s at Burg.

Suddenly the engine burst into flames, trailing a blazing tail longer than the aircraft itself, though it is probably fortunate that Kappus, in his enclosed cockpit, never saw it. He pulled the Ar 234B round in a tight circuit and forced it down on the runway; as the aircraft came to a stop a crash truck screeched to a halt beside him and the crew began playing their fire extinguishers on the engine. Once out of the cockpit, Kappus was horrified to see that all of the turbine blades of his port engine had gone, as had the jet nozzle. The flying blades had shot out in all directions, shredding the flap on that side in the process: he afterwards pulled one of the blades out of the self-sealing rubber jacket of the rear fuselage fuel tank.

In fact, the tachometer had been reading correctly the whole time! The fault was tracked down to the shaft of the fuel governor, sensing that the engine revolutions had fallen, poured in more and more fuel to the combustion chambers and the engine revolutions ran away out of all control. Kappus had indeed had a lucky escape — had his flight lasted only a few more seconds, the fire would have cut through the aircraft's flying controls and then nothing could have saved him.

During March 1945 Soviet troops advanced on Alt Loennewitz and the Arado plant was blown up to prevent it falling into enemy hands. When production halted, a total of 210 Ar 234Bs and fourteen Ar 234Cs had been delivered to the Luftwaffe.

The Ar 234 continued in action for a few weeks after production terminated. On 5 April the remaining bombers of KG 76 moved to Kaltenkirchen near Hamburg. Often under severe pressure from Allied fighters, the unit now found itself being sent to attack targets on both the Western and the Eastern Fronts. The unit's war diary recorded the final missions:

**6.4.** 6th *Staffel*: attack on (British) armoured units west of Achmer. Following this attack, the 6th *Staffel* ceased operations until 12.4 in order to regroup.

III. *Gruppe*: shallow dive attack, from 1200 m to 800 m, on the canal bridge at Vinte, SW Achmer.

One interesting idea tried out as a means of increasing the radius of action of the Ar 234 bomber was a towed V1 flying bomb, with the warhead, engine and tailplane removed and a wheeled undercarriage fitted, to serve as a container for extra fuel. The trials did not reach an advanced stage.

**7.4.** III. *Gruppe*. Attack (on Soviet troops) in the area Jueterbog-Zossen south of Berlin.

**10.4.** III *Gruppe*, evening. Target: Autobahn between Bad Oeynhausen and Hannover.

**13.4.** III *Gruppe*. Due to the presence of (enemy) low flyers, 4 Arados were unable to take-off for a mission.

**14.4.** 6 *Staffel*, mid-day. Attack on (British) vehicle concentration in the bridgehead over the Aller (river) at Essel, 30 km ENE Nienburg.

**15.4.** 6 *Staffel*, morning. Attack on (British) vehicles at Meine, 11 kms of Gifhorn, and armoured columns on the autobahn Hannover-Brunswick. Four enemy fighters made a vain attempt to chase Lt Croissant over Gifhorn. Due to the presence of fighters he flew at low altitude to Ratzeburg south of Lübeck.

During the landing at Kaltenkirchen a fighter, believed to have been a Tempest, shot down Ofw Luther of the 6 *Staffel*. He made a crash landing and suffered severe injuries (the loss links with a claim by two Tempest pilots of No 56 Squadron).

**18.4.** Early afternoon. Weather reconnaissance of the area of the bridges over the Aller near Rethem, 17 km north east Nienburg (over which British troops were advancing). Attack on the bridges from 500 m. Defended by fighters and flak of all calibres.

**19.4.** Mid-day, operation as on previous day. *Major* Polletien, Ia (Operations Officer) of the *Geschwader*, returning to Lübeck-Blankensee from an operation in the Berlin area, and despite a radio warning from the airfield he was shot down by an English fighter and killed.

**20.4.** III. *Gruppe* at Kaltenkirchen, evening. Shallow dive attack from 2500/1000 m on (Soviet) tanks and vehicles on the road between Zossen and Baruth, south of Berlin. Negligible defences. The flight to the target began with an easterly flight over the Baltic before heading from there to the area of Berlin.

**26.4.** Stab. Morning. Target: Russian tanks at the Hallenschen Tor in Berlin. Ofw Breme reported: the area from Tempelhof — Neu Koeln — Hermannplatz is already occupied by the Russians, here one could see no firing. North of the Hermannplatz blazed, flames reaching up to 300 m. By the Hallenschen Tor was a sea of fire. I did not wish to drop my bombs there so I jettisoned them into a lake ESE of Schwerin.

**29.4.** Stab Morning. Target Berlin.

Evening. Shallow dive attack on (Soviet) armoured column east of Berlin. Ofw Breme praised the way in which Fw Woerdemann in the control tower at Blankensee airfield kept watch on the air situation (for patrolling enemy fighters) and guiding him safely by means of radio calls and light signals.

**30.4.** Stab, afternoon. Target: government district of Berlin. Due to attacks by five enemy fighters Fw Woerdemann was forced to jettison his bombs.

**3.5.** III. *Gruppe*: Fw Drews, 8 *Staffel*, flew from Leck during the afternoon on the last recorded operation by KG 76: shallow dive attack from 1500 m to 800 m on vehicles S of Bremerfoerde, strong flak defences.

Despite the undoubted bravery of those who flew it, the Ar 234 achieved little in the bomber role. Certainly its high speed and general invulnerability impressed its enemies, but that was not what it was there for. The purpose of the attacks was to destroy targets, and there were never sufficient Ar 234s to achieve this. Even during the largest attack on a single day, on 27

The four-engined Arado 234C was on the point of entering service when the appoach of Red Army ground forces brought an end to production at Alt Loennewitz. The increased power from the BMW 003 engines greatly improved the bomber's performance, though even at the end of the war this engine was still not reliable

February, the 18½ tons of bombs carried by the 37 aircraft involved was too little to cause more than a minor inconvenience to the troops in dispersed positions. Allied bomber forces carried many times this load, even against targets of relatively minor significance. Nor did the Ar 234 achieve much as a makeshift night fighter. In its original, reconnaissance role, however, the Ar 234 was consistently successful in photographing installations and returning with the precious pictures, usually undetected by the enemy. The irony was that by the time the Luftwaffe possessed this capability, the German armed forces lacked the strength to exploit it.

**Arado 234B**

**Power Units**: two Junkers Jumo 004B axial-flow turbojets each rated at 900 kg (1,980 pounds) static thrust.
**Armament or military load.** Bomber version: usual bomb load carried on operations was a single 500 kg (1,100 pound) bomb or small bomb container under the fuselage; Ar 234s were test flown carrying up to three times this bomb load, but never on operations; normally the Ar 234 bomber carried no gun armament, though a few late production aircraft (like the one in the drawing), carried two fixed rearwards-firing 20 mm Mauser MG 151 cannon with 200 rounds per gun. Reconnaissance version: usually two Rb 50/30 aerial cameras in the rear fuselage, splayed outwards across the line of flight at 12°; no guns.
**Performance**: maximum speed (clean) 742 kph (461 mph) at 6,000 m (19,500 ft); with 500 kg bomb, 692 kph (430 mph) at 6,000 m. Range at 6,000 m carrying 500 kg bomb, no reserves 1,560 km (970 miles). Climb to 6,000 m carrying 500 kg bomb, 12 mins 48 secs.
**Weight Empty**: equipped 5,200 kg (11,460 pounds); normally. loaded, with two take-off booster rockets and a 500 kg bomb, 9,465 kg (20,870 pounds).
**Dimensions**: Span 14.4 m (46 ft 3½ in), Length 12.64 m (41 ft 5½ in), Wing area 26.4 sq m (284 sq ft).

# CHAPTER 5

# The Yokosuka Ohka

By the spring of 1944 the Japanese forces had lost the initiative in the Pacific War, and the U.S. island-hopping campaign had started to make deep inroads into areas that previously had been securely held. In a desperate bid to reverse the trend, Japanese Army and Navy officers produced a plethora of ideas for schemes and weapons whose successful application depended on the willingness of their men to die for the Emperor. The Imperial Headquarters gave its approval for

Crew of a Mitsubishi G4M2e 'Betty' mother aircraft of the 721st Kotutai awaiting the order to take-off. The Ohka manned suicide weapon is just visible, semi-recessed into the fuselage of the bomber. *(US Naval Institute)*

*tan* (sincerity-loyalty) missions involving air attacks on targets at distances beyond round-trip range of the aircraft taking part. Since these crews had no chance of surviving the mission, *Jibaku* (self-crashing) attacks became increasingly common.

Division Leader Kentaro Mitsuhashi salutes before he and the other Ohka pilots board the 'Betty' mother aircraft on 21 March 1945 to attack the US carrier task force. All fifteen of the 'Bettys' carrying suicide weapons were shot down before they got within launching range of the US warships. *(US Naval Institute).*

Following on from this there were several schemes for the use of manned suicide aircraft, explosive motor-boats and even manned torpedoes. While most of these ideas centred on modifications to existing service equipment, a few of them called for the use of purpose-built systems. In the summer of 1944 one of the latter was submitted by Navy Ensign Shoichi Ota, a navigator flying with a Japanese Navy transport unit. Ota proposed a small rocket-boosted suicide plane with an explosive warhead as an integral part of the nose structure, for use against enemy shipping. Carried into action under a twin-engined bomber, the weapon was to be released when it was gliding range of the target.

Ota had no formal training in aeronautical engineering, so in preparing his proposal he elicited help from Professor Taichiro Ogawa of the Aeronautical Research Department at Tokyo Imperial University. Another member of the university staff, Hidemasa Kimura, undertook the basic design of the aircraft and even built a model and tested it in a wind tunnel.

Armed with the drawings and the results of the wind tunnel tests, Ota presented his ideas for a 'sure-hitting' guided bomb to Lieutenant-Commander Tadanao Miki who headed the future aircraft design section at the Yokosuka Naval Aeronautical Research Laboratory. Miki later commented that he was horrified at the idea of sending men to certain death in this way, but since suicide attacks were now part of official policy he had to repress his personal feelings. The scheme was presented to the Naval General Staff on 5 August 1944 and Air Staff Officer Minoru Genda greeted the proposal with enthusiasm. At his bidding, chief of staff Admiral Koshiro Oikawa ordered the tiny plane into production.

The task of developing Ota's ideas into a working weapon system was handed to Tadanao Miki who, despite his reservations, spared no effort to produce the necessary detailed drawings of the aircraft as rapidly as possible. Since the machine might be flown by volunteers with limited flying experience, ease of handling was of the utmost importance. The aircraft had also to be capable of being mass-produced by semi-skilled or even unskilled labour, and wherever possible wood and other non-critical materials were to be used in its construction.

The programme received the official designation Navy Suicide Attacker Model 11. The initial test aircraft were assigned the designation MXY7, but later that term was dropped in favour of the more evocative Ohka (Exploding Cherry Blossom) for the operational versions.

Detailed design work was completed within a few days and the construction of prototype aircraft began immediately. At launch the Ohka would weigh 4,718 pounds. Since no part of the plane's operational profile required it to fly at speeds lower than 200 mph, only a small wing was necessary. That fitted to the Ohka had a span of 16 feet 9¾in and an area of just over 64 square feet, giving the weapon an extremely high wing loading of 73 pounds per square foot when it left the mother aircraft. The length of the fuselage was 19 feet 10¾in, and the rear section contained three solid fuel rockets, each of which generated a thrust of 588 pounds and had a burning time of about ten seconds. The pilot could fire the rockets individually or in unison, at any time during the flight.

The 2,646 pound warhead took up the whole of the nose of the aircraft and accounted for more than half of the Ohka's all-up weight. To ensure a very high probability of detonation, the main charge was fitted with five separate fuses: one in the nose and four in the rear plate. The pilot armed these fuses by pulling a handle in the cockpit, once he was well clear of the mother-plane. A series of fuse settings was available, ranging from instantaneous firing to a maximum delay of 1.5 seconds after impact, the latter to give the warhead time to penetrate deep into a ship's hull before it detonated. Unusually for a Japanese aircraft, the pilot was reasonably well protected from enemy fire; the steel jacket of the warhead gave protection from rounds coming from ahead, and there was a strip of steel armour plate about ¾-in thick beneath the pilot's feet and another to protect the upper part of his back. The steel casings of the three rocket units provided a degree of protection for the pilot's lower back and legs.

The twin-engined Mitsubishi G4M ('Betty') medium bomber was chosen for the role of mother aircraft for the Ohka. The necessary modifications resulted in the G4M2e version with cut-away bomb doors, a strong suspension hook with a quick-release and restraining pads to hold the flying bomb securely in place under the belly.

By the end of September ten Ohka operational airframes had been completed at the Yokosuka Arsenal. Without waiting for the results of flight trials the Navy ordered the weapon into production, aiming to have the first hundred ready for action by the end of November 1944. Rear Admiral Jiro Saba, director of the Naval Laboratory's Aircraft Section, approached Lieutenant Commander Yokei Matsurra at the Munitions Ministry and asked him to arrange for a private industrial company to mass-produce the Ohka. Like Tadanao Miki, Matsurra was appalled at the concept of the weapon and replied 'There is no way we could assign this project to private firms. Besides the security problem, they would think the Navy had gone crazy. Production must be done inside the laboratory, in secret.' Despite his relatively junior rank, Matsurra's view prevailed and a production line was set up at the Yokosuka Arsenal to build the planes.

Although westerners tend to view the use of suicide weapons as an inherent part of some

ABOVE AND RIGHT:
Model II Ohkas captured by US Marines at Yontan (later Kadena) airfield, Okinawa. When they were found these aircraft were in fully operational state and ready for use. More than half of the tiny plane's 4,718 pound weight at launch was taken up by the 2,646 pound still-encased warhead in the nose. *(Campbell and USMC, via Robert Mikesh)*

monolithic Japanese military culture, in reality there were many Army and Navy officers in senior positions who were horrified at the idea of sending men into action with absolutely no chance of survival. These officers made their feelings known at the time, but they could not prevail against the general mood that the use of such tactics, though disagreeable, was essential if the nation was to overcome enemy forces with enormous numerical and technical superiority.

As has been said, at no time during its operational flight was the Ohka required to reduce speed below 200 mph. The design made no provision for the plane to make a soft landing nor for it to fly more than once. It was necessary to carry out flight testing and train pilots to fly the machine, however, and Tadanao Miki designed a special non-operational version of the Ohka to cater for these requirements.

The non-operational version of the plane was fitted with a landing skid and wing flaps, and a metal wing and tail to withstand the impact of landing. In place of the warhead and the rocket motors were tanks holding water ballast to give the aircraft the same all-up weight and wing loading as the operational machine during the launch and the high speed descent. As he neared the ground the pilot pulled levers to release some 3,000 pounds of water ballast. With the ballast gone the plane's wing loading fell to a reasonable 27 pounds per square foot, allowing the pilot to make a more-or-less normal landing on the skid.

Also during September 1944 the Japanese Navy began to assemble a force of pilots to fly the Ohka and other types of suicide aircraft. Air units were canvassed for pilots willing to volunteer for 'special attack' missions; although the suicidal implications of this term were well understood in that service there was no shortage of takers. Those

I-13
22

who were single parents, only children, first sons or who had heavy family commitments were immediately rejected, the remainder were sent on to prepare themselves for the grim combat role. The volunteers had varying levels of flying experience, and the best of them were selected for the initial training courses.

In October the first Ohka unit began forming, the *Jinrai Butai* (the nearest English translation is 'Thunder Gods Corps', (which is closer to the Japanese term than the 'Divine Thunderbolt Corps' given in other accounts). Organizationally the unit was listed as the 721st Naval Flying Corps under Commander Motoharu Okamura, based at Konoike near Tokyo. A veteran combat pilot who had long advocated suicide attack operations as a means of turning the tide of the war, Okamura brought considerable energy to the task of building up his force. The unit was established with two squadrons of G4M2e 'Betty' bombers, the 708th and 711th, each with eighteen planes modified to carry the Ohka. Also part of the Corps was a squadron of A6M5 Zero fighters modified for the suicide attack role, and two squadrons of Zero fighters to escort the suicide planes and mother aircraft during operations.

When the volunteer suicide pilots began arriving at the Konoike, training began in earnest. Initially this comprised a series of gliding descents in an A6M5 Zero fighter, with the engine idling to familiarise pilots with the long attack glide of the Ohka.

Also during October the Ohka began its flight trials at Sagami, commencing with an unmanned glide into the ocean during which the aircraft behaved as predicted. On the final day of the month Lieutenant Kazutoshi Nagano made the first manned test flight in the aircraft. With water ballast in place of the warhead and the fuselage rockets, the Ohka was fitted with a rocket under each wing to boost its speed. The test aircraft left the mother plane at 11,500 feet and went into a stable glide. When the pilot fired the rockets, their unequal thrust caused the machine to yaw and he was forced to jettison the units. The rest of the gliding descent went off without incident and after releasing the water ballast Nagano made a smooth landing on the skid.

During November Ohkas made a number of unmanned flights with full rocket boosting, and in the course a near-vertical dive one of them exceeded 600 mph. The flight trials revealed that the Ohka's range after launch was somewhat less than its proponents had expected. This aircraft was *primarily* a glider and only *secondarily* was it a powered plane. If launched from 19,500 feet in a steady descent at 230 mph holding a constant glide angle of about 5½ degrees, the Ohka had an absolute maximum range of about 37 miles. This absolute maximum had no relevance in combat, however, for under operational conditions the maintenance of a constant glide angle would be out of the question. Under combat conditions the launching aircraft would have to close to within about 15 miles of the target for an effective Ohka attack. When the pilot fired the rockets their thrust increased the range of the Ohka only by about three miles.

If he was intercepted by enemy fighters after launch the Ohka pilot could fire one of the rockets to boost his speed to 400 mph, which was sufficient to outrun a Grumman Hellcat. But after the rocket finished burning the suicide plane's speed dissipated rapidly. If the pilot fired all three rockets simultaneously as he entered a steep final attack dive, the Ohka could reach a speed of around 580 mph. At that speed the suicide plane would be almost unstoppable.

The first Ohka training flight, on 13 November 1944, ended in disaster. Lieutenant Tsutomu Kariya was launched from 9,800 feet and everything went according to plan until he pulled the handle to release the ballast. Kariya made the error of releasing only the water from the nose tank, while that in the rear fuselage tank remained in place. That threw the aircraft badly out of trim and the nose of the plane reared up. Then it stalled and smashed into the ground, cartwheeling end

OPPOSITE:
The cockpit of the operational version of the Ohka was the ultimate in simplicity, since the aircraft was not designed to return from its single mission. The instrumentation comprised a compass, an airspeed indicator, an altimeter and a rate of sink indicator. The selector switch for the three rockets was on the lower left side of the panel and allowed the pilot to fire the rockets simultaneously or independently. The T-shaped handle at the top left of the instrument panel was pulled to arm the warhead once the Ohka was safely clear of the mother aircraft. Note the simple ring-and-bead sight in front of the windscreen, to assist the pilot to align the aircraft on the target during the final attack dive.
*(USAF via Robert Mikesh)*

over end. The pilot sustained fatal injuries and died a few hours later. The Ohka had claimed its first victim. Tsutomu Kariya was buried with military honours and the training programme continued.

The flight test programme also continued, and on 20 November an unmanned Ohka with a live warhead was launched and the latter detonated when the aircraft crashed into the sea. During a manned test flight a few days later Kazutoshi Nagano fired one of the rear-mounted rockets and reached a speed of over 400 mph without encountering any difficulties, then landed safely.

By mid-December a total of 151 Ohkas had been completed at the Yokosuka Arsenal, which now shifted its efforts to building much-needed trainer versions. Series production of the next six hundred operational flying bombs was transferred to the naval aeronautical arsenal at Ibaragi.

In the mean time the *Jinrai Butai* was declared ready for operations and assigned to the Combined Fleet. The Navy also began moves to deploy Ohkas to the Philippines, where they were to be stored at Clark Field until needed. If it became necessary to launch strikes from the airfield, the suicide pilots would be flown there aboard the Bettys that were to carry their Ohkas into action. Fifty flying-bombs were loaded on the newly-commissioned 70,000-ton aircraft carrier *Shinano*, the largest in the world, together with a large quantity of supplies and aviation equipment destined for the islands. On the 28th the behemoth set sail on her maiden voyage from Tokyo Bay, but early the following morning *Shinano* was hit by four torpedoes from the submarine USS *Archerfish* and sank a few hours later. In December a further attempt was made, with a batch of thirty Ohkas aboard the carrier *Unryu*, but this also came to nothing when the vessel was torpedoed and sunk by the submarine USS *Redfish*. Following the loss of the two valuable carriers and their loads of Ohkas, the Japanese Navy gave up the idea of positioning these weapons on the Philippines.

The attempt to move Ohkas to Formosa (now Taiwan) was more successful. Early in January the aircraft carrier *Ryuho* slipped past the American submarine blockade and reached the island with a load of fifty-eight suicide bombs. Formosa was not one of the islands on the U.S. agenda of invasion, however, and the weapons sent there would sit out the war in their camouflaged hide-outs. A few Ohkas also reached Okinawa, Singapore and other overseas bases.

During January 1945 the *Jinrai Butai* received orders to move to Kanoya Air Base on southernmost Japanese island of Kyushu, and prepare to mount combat operations from there. At that time the Corps' Ohka strength stood at about 160 flying-bombs and a similar number of pilots trained to fly them, and 72 modified Betty mother planes; in addition the unit possessed 108 Zero fighters modified for the *kamikaze* role. If these aircraft could fight their way through the defences and deliver a concentrated attack on an enemy Task Force, there was no doubt that they could cause considerable mayhem.

By now there were severe morale problems among the Ohka pilots, however. Following their hasty training for the macabre role they had been kept waiting for months on end with little to do but consider their ultimate fate. These were men who had no qualms about going to their deaths in a blaze of glory, provided they saw a good chance of inflicting havoc on the enemy in the process. But the pilots were unwilling to throw away their lives in what looked increasingly like a useless enterprise. Carrying the Ohka semi-recessed under the fuselage and burdened with additional armour, the maximum speed of the unwieldy Betty mother plane was around 200 mph. Given the likely strength of the enemy fighter cover, it needed little imagination to see that the Ohkas would not have much chance of getting within attack range of a U.S. Task Force. Lieutenant Commander Goro Nonaka, the unit's attack leader, did not mince words in expressing his loathing for the Ohka. In his view that it was a poor weapon and a waste of brave pilots that could be far better employed flying elsewhere. The strain of the situation was now beginning to tell on the pilots and there were several cases of insubordination and drunkenness.

Due to the stranglehold imposed by the U.S. Naval and air blockade, the *Jinrai Butai* was effectively confined to the Japanese home islands. Unable to deploy outside the area to seek worthwhile targets, the Corps had to wait for a force of enemy ships to venture within its reach.

The Corps spent several weeks waiting, until the opportunity to go into action finally came in March

1945. On the 18th and 19th, U.S. carrier planes of Task Force 58 mounted large scale strikes on airfields and naval bases on the Japanese home islands. Task Force 58 was exactly the sort of target for which the *Jinrai Butai* had been created: the powerful U.S. battle group comprised ten large and six small aircraft carriers, with an escort of eight battleships, sixteen cruisers and more than sixty destroyers.

During the first two days of the action the warships came under heavy attack from Japanese bombers and 'conventional' suicide planes, which caused damage to five aircraft carriers and put one of them out of action. On the third day, 20 March, the Task Force stood off to the east of Japan to allow its destroyers to refuel. Despite aggressive patrolling by U.S. Navy fighters, Japanese reconnaissance planes maintained contact with the armada throughout the day.

The Model 22 Ohka was a smaller version of the flying-bomb, designed to be carried by the twin-engined Yokosuka P1Y1 Ginga 'Francis' high speed bomber. The diminutive aircraft had a wing area of only 43 square feet and the weight of the warhead was reduced to 1,323 pounds. Power for the Model 22 came from a Tsu-11 jet developing 440 pounds thrust. This unusual engine had no turbine to drive the compressor, the latter was turned by a Hitachi four-cylinder piston engine. The absolute maximum range of the aircraft was about 80 miles and its effective attack range would probably have been about half that. The Model 22 was credited with a maximum speed of 276 mph in horizontal flight, but during an operational mission its speed would be much increased by maintaining a progressively steepening descent as the plane neared its target. *(via Robert Mikesh)*

At dawn on 21 March part of the American force was reported about 370 miles off the south-eastern tip of Kyushu, and the *Jinrai Butai* was ordered to prepare for immediate action. The main attack force was drawn from the 721st Kokutai and comprised fifteen modified Bettys carrying Ohkas. Two further Bettys, without bombs but carrying radar, were to fly ahead of the force to locate the enemy ships and guide the mother planes into position to launch their flying-bombs. There was an emotional ceremony at Kanoya airfield that morning, as the Ohka pilots prepared to go to their deaths. Vice-Admiral Matome Ugaki, commander of the Fifth Naval Air Fleet, was the senior officer present and he poured the sake for each suicide pilot to drink a toast to the success of the mission.

Shortly after noon the Bettys took off individually, assembled into formation and headed out to sea in the direction of the enemy force. From then on the mission rapidly turned sour, however.

Under the original plan there should have been about eighty A6M5 Zero fighters to cover a large scale Ohka operation of this type. Following the heavy air fighting of the past three days many of the fighters were in a poor state, however. Several turned back after take-off with technical problems, and when the escorting force headed out to sea it was down to only thirty Zeros. At Kanoya there was a heated discussion on whether the Ohka strike should be called off but Vice Admiral Ugaki, aware that a recall would further depress the already brittle morale of the suicide pilots, ordered the attack to continue.

The Japanese force was 80 miles to the northwest of the U.S. force when it was first detected by the ships' radars. The Ohkas' assigned target was Task Group 58.1, comprising the large aircraft carriers *Hornet*, *Bennington* and *Wasp* and the smaller *Belleau Wood*, with an escort of two battleships, four cruisers and nearly a score of destroyers. The ships' guns would play no part at all in the one-sided battle about to follow, however.

Immediately the attack force was been detected the four carriers scrambled every serviceable fighter on deck, and soon 150 Hellcats and Corsairs were airborne and moving into positions to block the approach of the Japanese planes. For the carriers' fighter control officers this was a straightforward medium-level interception, and they had little difficulty vectoring their charges to within visual contact of the enemy.

The first to engage the raiders, while the latter were still 70 miles from the ships, were a couple of dozen Hellcats on standing patrol belonging to VF-17, VBF-17 and VF-30 from *Hornet* and *Belleau Wood*. Within ten minutes more than half of the slow and unwieldy Bettys had been knocked down, while several of the survivors jettisoned their Ohkas and made spirited attempts to get away. As more American fighters joined the battle the Bettys were picked off one by one, until all had been shot down. Among those who went to their deaths was the outspoken Goro Nonaka.

The Corsairs and Hellcats also made mincemeat of the Japanese fighter escort, destroying fifteen Zeros for a loss of one Hellcat. When the American fighters returned to the carriers their pilots were elated by the ease with which they had defeated the enemy raiding force. Pilots reported that the Japanese bombers appeared to be carrying some sort of small winged weapon beneath the fuselage, and this was confirmed when films from the fighters' combat cameras were developed. Initially it was thought that the weapon might be a Japanese anti-shipping weapon similar to the German V.1 flying-bomb.

The few Zeros that survived the action returned to Kanoya, bringing the harsh news of the débâcle to those waiting expectantly at the airfield. According to one report, when Vice-Admiral Ugaki heard of the massacre of his attack force he broke down and wept.

As the Japanese crews had foreseen, the Achilles' Heel of the Ohka was the extreme vulnerability of the Betty mother-planes to fighter attack. None got close enough to the target ships to release its suicide weapon. And even if a few had done so, given the huge concentration of fighters the chances Ohkas reaching the warships were extremely low. Taking these factors together, it was clear that the Ohka was less likely to penetrate well-managed enemy fighter defences than the conventional fighters and bombers being used in the *kamikaze* role. The only advantage the Ohka had over the latter was that if it did get through to a target, its larger warhead would inflict considerably more damage.

The failure of the mission on 21 March led to re-evaluation of the tactics for using the Ohka, and never again would the Bettys be sent out in a single large formation. Henceforth the mother-planes would approach the target area individually and from different directions, endeavouring to sneak through the defences by exploiting cloud cover, poor visibility and the element of surprise.

On 1 April 1945, following a long preparatory bombardment, American troops stormed ashore on beaches of Okinawa. The strategically important island lay within 400 miles of the southern tip of Kyushu, and in recognition of this the Japanese forces threw in everything they had to defeat the invasion. Vice-Admiral Ugaki ordered the *Jinrai Butai* into action against the enemy fleet early that morning. Six Ohka-laden aircraft took off and made their way individually into the target area. One aircraft failed to penetrate the defences and returned with its Ohka, another was attacked by American fighters and forced to jettison its flying-bomb into the sea, a third crashed into high ground.

Nothing more was heard of the other Bettys, but at least one launched an Ohka for a successful attack. The battleship *West Virginia* had a flying bomb ram into one of her main 16-in gun turrets, where the warhead exploded causing severe damage and numerous casualties. The attack transport *Alpine* and the cargo ships *Achernar* and *Tyrrell* also suffered damage during *kamikaze* attacks at about the same time, though it is unclear whether Ohkas were involved in any of these incidents.

At last the true nature of the Ohka was recognised by American intelligence officers. In an attempt to denigrate its military importance they nick-named the weapon the *Baka* (Japanese for 'idiot' or 'fool'). But those on board the threatened ships failed to see the joke and, as people will when they are on the receiving end of a new enemy weapon, in assessing its capability they gave it the benefit of every possible doubt. Seen in that light the Ohka was indeed a fearful weapon.

The third Ohka attack took place on the afternoon of 12 April. Embedded in a large scale *kamikaze* air attack on shipping off Okinawa were nine Bettys. Only one damaged mother-plane returned from the mission, and its crew provided the first eye-witness report of an Ohka attack. Taking advantage of cloud cover along the route and in the target area, the bomber arrived off Okinawa. The crew sighted an American warship and closed to attacking range. Ensign Saburo Dohi was launched in the Ohka from 19,600 feet at a point just over 11 miles from the target. The crew of the Betty watched the suicide plane gliding towards the warship, and leave a smoke trail as the pilot fired the booster rockets. The smoke trail ended in an eruption of flame as the weapon smashed into the target and detonated.

Dohi was credited with sinking an American battleship. So was another Ohka pilot, after his mother plane reported by radio before it ditched that the weapon had scored a direct hit on one of these vessels. Two other Betty crews reported by radio that their Ohkas hit unspecified enemy warships, before these bombers also crashed into the sea.

U.S. Navy records provide no corroboration for the claims against the battleships. Although the battleships *Idaho* and *Tennessee* suffered damage on that day, in each case their assailants were 'conventional' *kamikaze* aircraft.

Four attacks by Ohkas on that day can be identified, however. One was on the radar picket destroyer *Mannert L. Abele*, dead in the water after suffering damage during an earlier *kamikaze* attack. A single Ohka slammed into the starboard side of the ship almost amidships, the warhead detonated, and the destroyer broke in two parts which rapidly sank. The destroyer/minesweeper *Jeffers*, on her way to rescue survivors from the *Abele*, also came under attack from an Ohka. As the suicide plane closed in rapidly, however, the vigorous anti-aircraft fire from the ship's gunners appeared to score hits. The damaged Ohka crashed into the sea and exploded about 50 yards from the warship. Even at that distance the detonation was powerful enough to cause damage to the upper deck, and *Jeffers* was forced to leave the area for repairs.

The destroyer *Stanly* also had a lucky escape, after being targeted by two Ohkas. One levelled out low over the sea and ran in at high speed, engaged by the ship's anti-aircraft guns. The suicide plane struck the vessel close to the bow just above the waterline, and its warhead went clean through the hull and emerged on the far side. The charge detonated several yards away, causing remarkably little damage to the ship. The other Ohka also made a horizontal attack run and passed close over the top of *Stanly*, and carried away her ensign before it crashed into the sea and detonating safely clear.

On 14 April there was yet another determined attempt to strike at shipping off Okinawa, when seven Ohka-carriers formed part in a large *kamikaze* operation escorted by more than a hundred fighters. None of the 'Bettys' returned from this operation and there is no evidence that the Ohkas achieved any successes.

Two days later, on the 16th, more than a hundred *kamikaze* planes, including six Bettys, were launched against the concentration of shipping. Two mother-planes returned from the mission but there were no claims of hits.

On 28 April a force of 80 *kamikaze* planes, including four Ohka-carriers, attempted a night attack on shipping off Okinawa. Only one Betty returned and again there were no hits claimed.

On 4 May seven Bettys took part in a morning strike by about 120 *kamikazes*. The visibility around Okinawa was poor that day, enabling several of the attackers to penetrate the defensive fighter screens. A lone Betty was sighted about 5 miles from one of the American radar picket destroyers, but before fighters could be vectored to the scene the bomber launched its Ohka. With Ensign Susumu Ohashi at the controls, the flying-bomb was first seen about a mile from the light minelayer USS *Shea*, closing rapidly. Undaunted by the hail of anti-aircraft fire, the Japanese pilot crashed his plane into the starboard side of the bridge and the warhead detonated. With 27 of her crew dead and 91 wounded, the badly damaged *Shea* remained afloat but she had been damaged beyond repair. Also that morning, the minesweeper *Gayety* suffered minor damage when an Ohka exploded nearby. Only one Betty returned from the mission.

On 11 May the Ohka achieved what was to be its final success. With more than a hundred *kamikaze* planes, four Bettys headed for Okinawa. One of the bombers descended to low altitude and launched a suicide plane at the destroyer *Hugh W. Hadley*, which had suffered damage during an earlier attack. The Ohka scored a hit or a very near miss which added to damage and caused severe flooding. A determined effort by the destroyer's damage control team saved the vessel, but although she was towed to safety she was judged beyond repair.

To blunt the force of the *kamikaze* attacks, on 24 May U.S. Navy carrier planes delivered a series of heavy attacks on airfields on Kyushu from which the Japanese planes were launched. Kanoya, the home of the *Jinrai Butai*, was one of the primary targets and several of its aircraft were destroyed on the ground.

Despite this pummelling, the Corps continued in business. On the next morning eleven Bettys took off and headed for Okinawa, the largest attack by the unit since the catastrophic mission on 21 March. Flying individually, the Bettys arrived off Okinawa to find rain squalls and poor visibility which forced several of them to abandon the mission and return. One crew proved more determined than the others, however, and ran in at low altitude below cloud looking for a target. Gunners on the destroyers *Braine* and *Anthony* engaged the plane, and shot it down before it could release its Ohka.

On 22 June, as the fighting on Okinawa was nearing its close, six Bettys took off for the island. Only two Bettys returned from what would be the final operational mission with this weapon, and no hits were claimed.

On Okinawa American troops captured four intact Ohkas hidden in blast shelters ready for use. For the first time U.S. intelligence officers were able to examine the unusual weapon that Navy fighter pilots had first reported four months earlier.

Meanwhile the Yokosuka arsenal had begun production of an advanced version of the Ohka, the Model 22. With a warhead half the weight of that of the Model 11, the all-up weight of the Model 22 was one third lighter and the wing proportionately smaller with an area of only 43 square feet. The Ohka Model 22 was powered by the Tsu-11 jet developing 440 pounds of thrust. This unusual engine was not fitted with a turbine, and the compressor was driven by a Hitachi four-cylinder piston engine. The absolute maximum range of the aircraft was about 80 miles and its effective attack range would probably have been about half that. The Model 22 could attain 276 mph in horizontal flight, but during an operational mission its speed would be much increased by progressively steepening of the descent as the plane neared its target. The Model 22 was tailored to fit under the fuselage of the Yokosuka P1Y 'Francis', a twin-engined bomber that was much smaller and faster than the 'Betty' and able to fly higher.

As in the case of its predecessor, production of the Model 22 began before this version commenced flight testing. The flight handling characteristics of the diminutive plane were expected to be difficult, and with a stalling speed of over 200 mph even when its fuel was burnt a soft landing was impossible. Each test flight was to end with the pilot baling out of the machine and landing by parachute. Katusohi Nagano, the redoubtable Navy pilot who had carried out much of the Model 11 test programme, made the first manned flight in the Model 22 on 26 June 1945. As predicted, he found the aircraft unstable in flight and difficult to handle. He succeeded in escaping from the plane, but his parachute was only partially open when he hit the ground and he suffered fatal injuries. Fifty Model 22s were built during the final months of the war but the weapon was never used in action.

At the end of June the greater part of the *Jinrai Butai* moved to Komatsu on the main home island of Honshu, where it began the intensive training of a batch of new Ohka pilots in readiness to meet the expected Allied invasion. The Army and Navy had combined their aircraft reserves into a 5,000-plane force that was to be used primarily in *kamikaze* attacks against the American fleet, with 230 Ohka Model 11s and 22s held in readiness for operations at five separate points around the home islands.

Trainer version of the Ohka, photographed on exhibition at the US Navy Memorial Museum at Washington DC. This differed from the operational version in being fitted with a landing skid, wing flaps, and water tanks in the nose and tail containing jettisonable ballast in place of the warhead and rocket motors. The trainer version was also fitted with metal wings and tail, in place of the wooden appendages on the operational version, to enable it to withstand the shock of repeated landings. *(via Robert Mikesh)*

The Yokosuka arsenal had plans to build new and hopefully more practical versions of the Ohka. Probably the most effective from the tactical point of view would have been the Model 43B powered by an axial flow turbojet engine, designed to be catapulted into the air from a ground launcher. But none of these projects left the drawing board.

The Japanese efforts were halted in their tracks on 15 August, 1945 when, following the atomic bomb attacks on Hiroshima and Nagasaki, Emperor Hirohito broadcast to his people ordering them to cease fighting and accept the Allied terms of unconditional surrender.

During the plane's short career in combat, Ohkas were sent on just under eighty combat sorties. In supporting these operations, all of which were flown from bases on the Japanese home islands, the Betty mother-planes suffered a debilitating average loss rate in excess of *70 per cent per mission*. In other words, the chances of the crew of a mother plane surviving any one operation were only marginally better than those of the Ohka pilot.

Because they usually operated in conjunction with large numbers of 'conventional' suicide planes, it is often difficult to assign individual hits to the air-launched bombs. On the best available information the Ohka can be credited with sinking one destroyer, and damaging another destroyer and a minesweeper so seriously that they had to be scrapped. Ohkas also inflicted serious damage to a battleship, two destroyers, a minesweeper, an attack transport and a cargo ship.

Off Okinawa the Allied fleets were indeed hit hard, but the overwhelming majority of the damage was caused by standard service planes converted for the *kamikaze* role. Total Allied naval losses off Okinawa to all *kamikaze* attacks during the period between 20 March and 13 August 1945 amounted to: nine destroyers, six transports and five smaller ships sunk; and ten battleships, sixteen aircraft carriers, four cruisers, 81 destroyers, 44 transports and 62 smaller ships damaged. The Ohka's contribution to that catalogue of damage was insignificant. Given the usually overwhelming strength of the American fighter defences, the manned flying-bomb never had much chance of success. The effort expended in developing and producing it, and in modifying the mother-planes and training the crews, was in no way commensurate with the meagre results it achieved in action.

**Yokosuka Model 11 Ohka (Exploding Cherry Blossom)**
**Power Unit:** three Type 4 Mark 1 Model 20 solid-fuel rocket motors each developing 588 pounds of thrust.
**Armament:** nose mounted warhead weighing 2,646 pounds.
**Performance:** maximum speed in a steep dive, 580 mph. Absolute maximum gliding range when released from 20,000 feet, about 37 miles. Maximum practical range in combat, 15 miles.
**Weight (at launch)** 4,720 pounds.
**Dimensions:** span 16 feet 9¾ inches; length 19 feet 10¾ inches; wing area 64.6 sq ft.

The definitive trainer version of the Ohka was the Model 43, fitted with two separate cockpits. Only two examples were built before the war ended. *(via Robert Mikesh)*

# CHAPTER 6

## The Heinkel 162

The prototype of the Heinkel He 162, pictured shortly after its roll-out at Vienna/Schwechat early in December 1944.

In September 1944 the German Air Ministry issued a requirement for a new type of jet fighter, the so-called *Volksjaeger* (people's fighter). The concept was for a cheap and unsophisticated lightweight fighter with many parts made from wood and other non-strategic materials, and a simple structure capable of being manufactured by semi-skilled and unskilled labour. A further requirement of the *Volksjaeger* was that it should be easy to fly, and there was even a bizarre idea that pilots whose only previous flying experience had been in gliders might be able to operate the new fighter effectively in combat.

*Generalleutnant* Adolf Galland and other senior officers in the fighter force expressed vehement opposition to the *Volksjaeger* project, regarding it as a useless diversion of resources away from the Me 262 and other more-effective programmes. Galland pointed out that it was a fallacy to expect an aircraft designed and built to such a short time scale to be easy to fly, and the notion that half-trained pilots could handle it effectively in action was nothing short of ludicrous. But the idea of the lightweight fighter that could be turned out in very large numbers had strong support from Goering, Armament Minister Albert Speer and Otto Saur in

On 10 December 1944, during a high speed run over the airfield at Schwechat to demonstrate the new fighter before senior Nazi party officials, the prototype He 162 suffered a structural failure of the starboard wing and aileron. The aircraft plunged into the ground killing pilot Gotthold Peter.

charge of the fighter production. Galland could only look on in frustration, as his reasoned objections to the new fighter were overruled.

On 10 September 1944 the German Air Ministry wrote to leading aircraft manufacturing companies inviting them to tender design proposals for the *Volksjaeger* competition. The single-seat fighter was to be powered by one BMW 003 turbojet and have an all-up weight of around 4,400 pounds, less than one-third that of Me 262 and considerably less than any Allied fighter type it might meet in combat. The specification called for a maximum speed of at least 466 mph at sea level, an operational endurance of at least half an hour and a take-off distance in still air of no more than 500 metres (545 yards). The aircraft was to be armed with two 20 mm cannon each with 100 rounds, or two 30 mm cannon each with 50 rounds. Time was of the essence, and companies offering designs had to submit their draft proposals within ten days. The winning design had to be ready to enter large scale production by 1 January 1945.

Since it was clear that the fighter chosen would be built in huge numbers, the competition aroused considerable interest. Arado, Blohm und Voss, Fieseler, Focke Wulf, Heinkel, Junkers and Siebel all submitted designs for the *Volksjaeger*. Heinkel had a head start over its rivals, however, for the company had been working on preliminary designs for its own lightweight jet fighter since the early summer. The design team headed by Siegfried Guenther and Karl Schwaerzler quickly revised their projected fighter to enable it to meet the new requirement, and offered it as their submission.

Siegfried Guenther was one of the outstanding aircraft designers of the era and his previous creations included the Heinkel 51 and He 100 fighters, the He 70 high speed transport and reconnaissance aircraft and the He 111 and He 177 bombers. Schwaerzler had served as Chief Engineer on several of the projects. The design of a fighter to meet the difficult requirement tested the abilities of the two talented men to the full.

Stills from a cine film of the take-off of 6th prototype He 162, which made its maiden flight on 23 January 1945. This aircraft retained the wing shape of the first prototype without the drooped wing tips.

Following the break-up in mid-air of the first prototype, the wing structure of the production He 162 was re-designed and strengthened. One of the changes introduced was the distinctive turned-down extension at the end of each wing tip, to reduce the net dihedral of the wing.

Close-up of the rear of the BMW 003 turbojet. The 'acorn' fitted to the nozzle had to be extended after the engine was started, and the ground crewman checked that it reached the vertical lines marked on the fairing beneath the engine. The extension at the trailing edge of the wing where it joined the fuselage was a modification fitted to production aircraft to postpone the onset of buffeting at high speeds.

OPPOSITE:
The sparsely appointed instrument panel of the He 162, in keeping with the planned goal of simplicity of operation. The bulged extension forward of the control column housed the nose wheel when the latter was retracted.

Achtung!
x100°C
1M4
1M1

A brand new He 162, probably photographed at the Heinkel works at Marienehe, being prepared for flight. *(via Creek)*

Ground crewman working on an He 162 of 1st *Staffel* of JG 1.

ABOVE:
One of the few photographs to survive showing an operational He 162 airborne, seen with its flaps lowered and about to land.

BELOW:
Pristine He 162 in the markings of 1st *Gruppe* JG 1.

The Heinkel design submission was for a clean-lined high wing monoplane, with the single podded jet engine mounted above the fuselage and mid-way along it. To keep the tail out of the way of the jet efflux the aircraft was fitted with twin fins and rudders. The fuselage was of light alloy construction, with a moulded plywood nose cap. The wing was to be made in one piece and constructed primarily of wood, with a plywood skinning. The tailplane, elevators and rudders were of metal construction, the fins were made of wood. With the wing and engine set close behind the cockpit, a pilot abandoning the aircraft in flight had little chance of doing so without striking one or other of these. To enable the pilot to escape from the jet fighter in an emergency, the aircraft was fitted with a rudimentary ejector seat designed by the Heinkel company and powered by an explosive cartridge.

At the end of September the Heinkel design was officially selected for production as the *Volksjaeger*. In an effort to confuse the Allied intelligence services the fighter was officially designated the Heinkel 162, the low type number intended to suggest that it had been allocated much earlier in the war. Initially two production versions of the aircraft were to be produced in quantity: the He 162 A-1 bomber-destroyer with an armament of two Mk 108 30 mm cannon each with 50 rounds of ammunition, and the A-2 air superiority fighter with two MG 151 20 mm cannon each with 120 rounds.

With the acceptance of the design came an order for one thousand of the lightweight fighters to be delivered by the end of April 1945, with production scheduled to rise to two thousand aircraft per month by the end of May. To achieve such figures within the required time scale the planners at the *Jaegerstab* (fighter production committee) had to short-circuit many of the accepted practices in aircraft manufacture. The tasks of detailed design, construction of prototypes and tooling up the factories for mass production were to take place simultaneously and begin almost immediately. Final assembly of the fighter was to take place at the Heinkel plant at Marienehe, the Junkers plant at Bernberg and underground production facility at Nordhausen. A vast number of sub-contractors dispersed throughout the country was to feed these plants with the necessary sub-assemblies and components.

At the Heinkel factory at Vienna work began on the construction for the initial batch of thirty-one aircraft. By mid-November the fuselage and wings of the first prototype were nearing completion and the engine and the remaining sub-contracted parts were about to be delivered.

At the beginning of December the prototype was ready for engine running and taxying trials. On the 6th Gotthold Peter took the aircraft up for its maiden flight from Vienna/Schwechat — a remarkable 90 days since the conception of the programme. In this course of the 20 minute flight Peter reached 522 mph at 19,600 feet, and found that in general the aircraft handled reasonably well though there was some longitudinal instability and a tendency towards excessive side-slip. The only moderately serious problem, and the one that brought the initial flight to a hurried conclusion, was that a wooden door for the undercarriage broke away. After the aircraft landed it was found that this was the result of defective bonding of the glued joint.

Disaster struck four days later, when Peter gave a demonstration of the He 162 over Schwechat for the benefit of senior Nazi party officials. During a high speed run over the airfield part of the leading edge of the starboard wing came adrift, followed by the starboard aileron and wing tip. As other parts of the wing broke away the fighter rolled out of control and dived into the ground with the unfortunate pilot still in the cockpit.

The subsequent investigation revealed that the cause of the structural failure was another and a more serious case of defective glue bonding of wooden components. As a result of these findings the wing of the second prototype, then virtually complete, received a more thorough inspection. The wings for subsequent aircraft were re-stressed with a revised structure giving increased strength.

Despite the loss of the first aircraft, work on the various aspects of the He 162 programme continued with undiminished vigour. On 22 December, less than two weeks after the accident, Heinkel director Carl Francke took the second prototype into the air. The flight passed off without incident, though because the aircraft was fitted with the original-type wing Francke had to observe a speed restriction of 310 mph. This

Senior commanders of JG 1 pictured at Leck immediately after the cease-fire, awaiting the arrival of British forces. From left to right: *Major* Werner Zober commanding 1st *Gruppe*, *Oberst* Herbert Ihlefeld the *Geschwader* commander, *Hauptmann* Heinz Kuenneke commanding 1st *Staffel* and *Oberleutnant* Emils Demuth commanding 3rd *Staffel*. (Demuth)

aircraft was armed with two 30 mm cannon and undertook the initial air firing trials.

The third and fourth prototypes, both of which flew on 16 January 1945, were fitted with the new strengthened wing. These and subsequent aircraft also featured a number of modifications to improve their handling in the air, with additional lead ballast to the nose to bring forward the centre of gravity and slightly larger tail surfaces. The most obvious external change to these aircraft was the turned-down plates fitted to the wing tips, a move that reduced the effective dihedral angle of the wing and was intended to cure the tendency to side-slip (had this programme been run to normal time scales, the dihedral angle of the wing would have been reduced before the type went into production; but with more than a hundred wing sets already in an advanced state of assembly Guenther had to adopt a quick if rather inelegant solution to the problem).

During the air firing tests with two Mk 108 30 mm cannon it was found that recoil forces were too great for the original nose structure to absorb. For this reason few He 162 A-1s were built. The early production aircraft were A-2 versions fitted with two Mauser MG 151 20 mm cannon. The first production version with a strengthened nose structure and 30 mm cannon armament was to be the A-3.

Flight tests revealed that the He 162 A-2 had a maximum speed 553 mph at sea level, and 562 mph at 19,500 feet. With the various modifications to strengthen the aircraft and

improve its handling, the original all-up weight of around 4,400 pounds specified for the *Volksjaeger* had been quickly exceeded. The take-off weight of the He 162 A-2 in the operational configuration was 6,184 pounds or more than one-quarter more. That was still a magnificent effort by its designers, however. Since the maximum speed of the fighter exceeded the requirement by a handsome margin, the excessive weight was quietly forgotten.

By the end of January 1945 six He 162s were flying, including two production aircraft. Although the flight test programme was only in its initial stages, the type was in full production and the trickle of aircraft was scheduled soon to become a flood. At the end of January the first Luftwaffe unit, *Erprobungskommando* 162 based at Rechlin/Roggenthin, was formed to assist with the testing of the new fighter and to speed the introduction of the type into front line units. The unit's commander was *Oberstleutnant* Heinz Baer, a highly respected fighter leader with more than 200 aerial victories to his credit. Early in February the first production He 162s arrived at the unit and

Hans Kuenneke pictured in front of his aircraft. The machine is one of the few He 162 A-1s to go into service, fitted with two Mk 108 30 mm cannon instead of the 20 mm weapons carried by the A-2. *(Demuth)*

Baer and his pilots began to evaluate the fighter for combat.

During the course of February forty-six He 162s were delivered to the Luftwaffe, sufficient for the first operational unit to begin re-equipping with the new fighter. Ist *Gruppe* of *Jagdgeschwader* 1 received orders to turn over its FW 190 fighters to the IInd Gruppe, and withdraw to Parchim where it was to re-equip with the He 162. Parchim lay within 50 miles from the Heinkel works at Marienehe, one of the centres where the assembly of the jet fighter was in full swing. At the plant the unit's pilots and ground crews gained their first hands-on experience with the aircraft. Also in February, five pilots from I./JG 1 travelled to Schwechat to gain flying experience in the new fighter under instruction from works test pilots.

During March further production He 162s arrived at Parchim and the unit could begin pilot training in earnest. By this time, however, the collapse of the Third Reich was already in sight and Allied forces were thrusting deep into Germany from both the east and the west. For Luftwaffe units the situation was becoming increasingly chaotic with each day that passed, with the transport system under almost continual attack from the air leading to severe shortages of spare parts and aviation fuel at the airfields. As a result there were severe delays in converting I./JG 1 into an effective fighting unit with the He 162.

On 7 April the airfield at Parchim came under attack from a force of 134 Flying Fortresses of the 8th Air Force, during which it suffered such heavy damage that two days later the jet fighter *Gruppe* was forced to abandon the airfield and move to that at Ludwigslust nearby. The unit continued its operational work-up with about fifteen He 162s on strength, with about ten available for flying on any one day. After less than a week at Ludwigslust the unit moved again, this time to Leck in Schleswig Holstein close to the Danish border. At the same time the IInd *Gruppe* of JG 1 gave up its FW 190s and moved to the Heinkel works airfield Marienehe to re-equip with the jet fighter, receiving brand-new aircraft as they came off the production line.

During the work-up period He 162 pilots had orders to avoid enemy aircraft whenever possible. With Allied fighters conducting frequent offensive sweeps over every part of the territory still held by German troops, however, such contacts were inevitable. On 15 April *Leutnant* Rudolf Schmitt of I./JG 1, a pilot straight out of flying training making his fourth flight in the He 162, reported that he encountered a Spitfire but successfully avoided combat.

On 19 April a He 162 pilot was credited with the first aerial victory while flying the new jet fighter, shortly before the same aircraft became the first He 162 lost in air combat. *Feldwebel* Guenther Kirchner of Ist *Gruppe* was credited with shooting down a British aircraft, after the pilot of the latter was taken prisoner and told his captors that he had been shot down by one of the new jet fighters. On his way back to base, however, Kirchner's own aircraft crashed and he was killed. That is the German side of the story.

The 2nd Tactical Air Force lost a number of aircraft over enemy territory on that day and from

Emil Demuth pictured beside his personal He 162. The sixteen victory bars painted on the fin referred to aircraft that he shot down earlier in his career. *(Demuth)*

He 162s of JG 1 lined up at Leck imediately after the cease fire, shortly before their capture.

LEFT AND ABOVE:
He 162s of JG 1 lined up at Leck following the surrender.

British records it is not possible to confirm or refute the claim that one of them was shot down by a He 162. The loss of the German jet fighter does find confirmation from British records, however. During a strafing attack on Husum airfield Flying Officer Geoff Walkington, flying a Tempest of No 222 Squadron, reported encountering an unidentified jet aircraft with twin fins and a single engine — obviously an He 162. Walkington went after the enemy machine but it was very fast at low altitude and even at 360 mph he was unable to close the distance. The German pilot got safely clear, but then he made the fundamental mistake of entering a sweeping turn to starboard which allowed the Tempest to close to within firing range. Walkington fired a series of short bursts at the German aircraft and saw his opponent suddenly enter a spin which continued until it crashed into the ground.

*Leutnant* Rudolf Schmitt ejected from an He 162 on 20 April, to make what is believed to be the first and perhaps the only successful emergency use of the jet fighter's ejector seat. Schmitt's flying logbook has survived and this confirms his escape but makes no mention of whether he was shot down or if enemy aircraft were involved in the incident. The logbook gives the duration of the flight as 25 minutes, which was close to the maximum for the new fighter at low altitude. Possibly the inexperienced pilot had become lost and ran out of fuel.

On 23 April I./JG 1 was placed under the control of *Luftflotte* Reich and the unit received official clearance to commence flying combat missions. Two days later the redoubtable Schmitt was again airborne, seemingly none the worse for his ejection five days earlier. He took off as one of a pair of He 162s scrambled in an unsuccessful attempt to engage low-flying Mosquitoes reported near Flensburg.

Due to its over-hasty development the He 162 retained some nasty vices when it went into service, and several aircraft were lost in flying accidents. On 24 April *Hauptmann* Paul-Heinrick Daehne, the commander of I. *Gruppe*, was on a training flight over Leck when he entered a tight turn at low altitude. Observers on the ground saw the aircraft suddenly enter a violent yaw, then parts broke away. The machine went out of control and crashed into marshy ground nearby, taking the pilot to his death. It appears that the cause of the crash had not been determined before the end of the war halted the investigation.

On 26 April *Unteroffizier* Rechenbach was credited with the destruction of an unspecified enemy aircraft and his victory was confirmed by at least two independent witnesses. Again, this was a day when the 2nd Tactical Air Force lost several aircraft over enemy territory and the claim cannot be confirmed or refuted from British records.

On 30 April *Leutnant* Alfred Duerr ran short of fuel and was killed when he attempted an emergency landing on a strip of autobahn near Lübeck. The poor endurance of the jet fighter was a constant source of difficulty and it is known that the unit lost at least one other pilot to this cause.

Early in May II./JG 1 moved to Leck to join the Ist *Gruppe*, and on the 4th the two *Gruppen* amalgamated into a single operational He 162 unit, *Einsatz-Gruppe* JG 1 under the command of *Oberst* Herbert Ihlefeld. That morning Rudolf Schmitt claimed the destruction of a Typhoon near Rostock, and this time there is clear verification of the victory from British records. The 'Typhoon' was in fact a Tempest of No 486 Squadron piloted by Flying Officer M. Austin, who parachuted to safety and was taken prisoner. The fact that the novice German pilot had been able to shoot down one of the Royal Air Force's best fighters illustrates the Heinkel's formidable combat potential.

On 5 May a cease-fire was declared in north-western Europe and JG 1 was confined to the ground. When British troops arrived at Leck the next day they found thirty-one of the jet fighters drawn up in neat rows on either side of the runway, most of them with cockpit and engine covers tied neatly in place.

In total the Luftwaffe formally accepted delivery of about 120 He 162s; possibly half as many again were collected from the factories by service pilots, but in the chaos of the final collapse the records were lost. Around two hundred more of these aircraft had been completed and were awaiting collection or flight testing when the end came.

One pilot who flew the He 162 with I./JG 1, *Oberleutnant* Emil Demuth, later commented that in his opinion the He 162 was a first class combat aircraft and much faster than any Allied machine he had encountered. Demuth was an experienced fighter pilot with 16 previous victories to his credit, however. In the hands of less experienced pilots the jet fighter had an appalling flight safety record. During the three-week period between 13 April and the end of the war, I./JG 1 lost a total of thirteen aircraft and ten pilots. At least one and possibly three of the losses were due to enemy action but the rest — an average of one every two days — resulted from flying accidents. The most common causes of loss were engine flame-outs and pilot error; in addition, as we have seen, there was at least one case of structural failure in flight and there may have been more.

After the war several captured He 162s were test flown in Great Britain, France, the U.S.A. and the Soviet Union. As the Royal Navy's Chief Test Pilot at Farnborough, Lieutenant-Commander Eric Brown had the opportunity to fly examples of each captured enemy aircraft brought to the establishment. The authors are indebted for his permission to quote comments he made on his first flight in the He 162, which set the jet fighter in a revealing light and confirm Emil Demuth's views on the machine:

'The take-off was much longer than I had expected, and any attempt to pull the aircraft off prematurely under 118 mph resulted in a tendency to wing dropping. Ideally the nosewheel was lifted off at about 105 mph and the aircraft allowed to fly itself off . . . With the aircraft cleaned up, I eased the throttle back to the recommended 9,200 rpm and stabilised the climbing speed at 215 mph. The He 162 proved very stable in the climb, and reached 5,000 ft in 1½ minutes, at which I levelled out and gently brought the throttle back to 8,900 rpm which gave a cruise of 300 mph with an engine temperature of 450°C . . . Stability checks showed the He 162 positive about the longitudinal and directional axes but neutral laterally. Harmony of control was excellent with the rudder perhaps just a shade too light. It was soon evident that the Germans had got the original stability problems licked, but I wondered if they had cured the sideslip trouble. Application of rudder caused large amounts of slip and skid, and considerable dipping of the nose, and no more than three quarter rudder could be applied if a steady flat turn was desired; beyond this the rudders began to judder and buffet, and looking aft I could see vortices streaming back from the tops of the fins, the turn becoming jerky. The danger

The He 162 was scheduled to be produced in large numbers, and more than a thousand of these aircraft were in various stages of construction when the war ended. This assembly line for fuselages was situated underground, in a disused gypsum mine at Moedling near Vienna.

signals were loud and clear. On the credit side, however, the aircraft had excellent directional snaking characteristics, making it a good gun platform. From this aspect it was the best jet fighter of its time, and I was certainly in a position to judge, having flown every jet aircraft then in existence.'

At 30,000 feet Brown found that the fighter had very good stability and control characteristics. He then tried out the He 162 into a high speed dive.

'There was no buffeting or vibration, and a check on the rate of roll at 400 mph revealed the highest that I have ever experienced outside the realm of hydraulically-powered ailerons, and the stick force demanded to produce these exhilarating gyrations was delightfully light.'

As Brown had discovered, the He 162 was intolerant of over-harsh use of the rudders. Possibly the break-up of *Hauptmann* Paul-Heinrick Daehne's aircraft had followed a failure of the tail structure in flight. Certainly this was the case in November 1945, when Flight Lieutenant Robert Marks was flying a He 162 in a display of captured aircraft at Farnborough. During a high speed fly-past at low altitude he made the mistake of pushing on too much rudder to increase the jet fighter's already excellent rate of roll; that overstressed the tail and one of the fin and rudder assemblies broke away. The aircraft dived out of control and smashed into the ground.

The knowledge that the aircraft was liable to suffer a structural break-up led to a general reluctance to attempt to fly the He 162 to its limits. As an air superiority fighter the aircraft was also marred by its novel layout, with the engine air intake situated immediately behind and above the cockpit. It would be difficult to think of a more effective way of denying a pilot a view of what was happening in the all-important 'six o'clock' position to the rear. During operations this would have made its pilots feel extremely vulnerable if, for any reason, they had to reduce speed much below 450 mph.

The other fundamental weakness stemmed from the aircraft's very short endurance when flying at high speed: a mere 30 minutes at sea level or 48 minutes at 20,000 feet, and that was without any operational reserve in case a diversion was necessary due to bad weather or the presence of enemy aircraft over the base airfield. Several He 162s were lost because their pilots failed to get them back on the ground before the fuel ran out.

Some previous accounts on this aircraft have made rather too much of the plan by Goering and others to send pilots with minimal flying experience into action in the He 162. To be sure it was a silly idea and one that would not possibly have succeeded, but that was not the fault of the aircraft or its designers. Certainly the He 162 would have been a death-trap in the hands of half-trained pilots. The same can be said for any other state-of-the-art fighter plane.

When the He 162 entered service it still had several faults that needed to be corrected. Despite this, and despite the disadvantages of its novel layout, in the hands of an experienced pilot it could have been an effective little fighter. Had the war continued for much longer, there is little doubt that it would have made a name for itself as a formidable foe in combat.

**The Heinkel 162 A-2**

**Power Unit:** one BMW 003 axial-flow turbojet rated at 2,028 pounds thrust.
**Armament:** two Mauser MG 151 20 mm cannon each with 120 rounds of ammunition.
**Performance:** maximum speed 553 mph at sea level, 562 mph at 19,500 feet. Range 242 miles at sea level, 385 miles. Initial climb 3,780 feet per minute.
**Weights:** Empty, Equipped: 3,875 pounds. Normal Loaded: 6,184 pounds.
**Dimensions:** span 23 feet 7½ inches; length 29 feet 8¼ inches; wing area 120 sq ft.

After the war captured He 162s were tested flown by pilots from each of the victorious nations. This example was tested at the French Air Force test centre at Mont de Marsan.

## Heinkel He 162A-2 cutaway key

1 Pitot tube
2 Moulded plywood nose cap
3 Nosewheel retraction mechanism
4 Spring-loaded nosewheel extension assembly
5 Shock absorber scissor
6 Nosewheel
7 Nosewheel fork
8 Nosewheel leg
9 Nosewheel door
10 Gun trough
11 Nosewheel well
12 Rudder pedal
13 Window panel (visual nosewheel retraction check)
14 Wooden instrument panel
15 One-piece moulded windscreen
16 Revi 16G gunsight (interchangeable with the Revi 16B)
17 Jettisonable hinged clear vision canopy
18 Ventilation disc
19 Heinkel cartridge-operated ejection seat
20 Ejection seat handle grip
21 Throttle control quadrant
22 Retractable entry step
23 Gun barrel shroud in cockpit wall
24 Port 20mm MG 151 cannon
25 Ammunition chute
26 Main oxygen supply bottle (3.5 pint/2 litre capacity)
27 Explosive charge ejector rail
28 Pilot's headrest
29 Canopy hinge
30 Ammunition box behind cockpit (120 rounds per gun)
31 Flexible main tank (153 Imp gal/ 695 litre capacity)
32 Fuel lines
33 FuG 25a IFF radio compartment
34 Beech plywood wing skinning
35 Jet intake
36 Riedel two-stroke starter motor bullet
37 Oil tank
38 BMW 003E-1 Sturm axial-flow turbojet
39 Riedel starter fuel tank
40 Seven-stage axial compressor casing
41 FuG 24 R/T homing loop
42 Annular combustion chamber
43 Exhaust centre body
44 Exhaust outlet
45 Jet efflux fairing
46 Heat-resistant aft dorstal decking
47 Light metal tailplane
48 Starboard fin housing R/T receiver aerial
49 Starboard rudder
50 Rudder tab
51 Elevator
52 Elevator tab
53 Tailcone (movable through +3° to −2°)
54 Port tailfin structure
55 Rudder structure
56 Tailplane/tailfin attachment

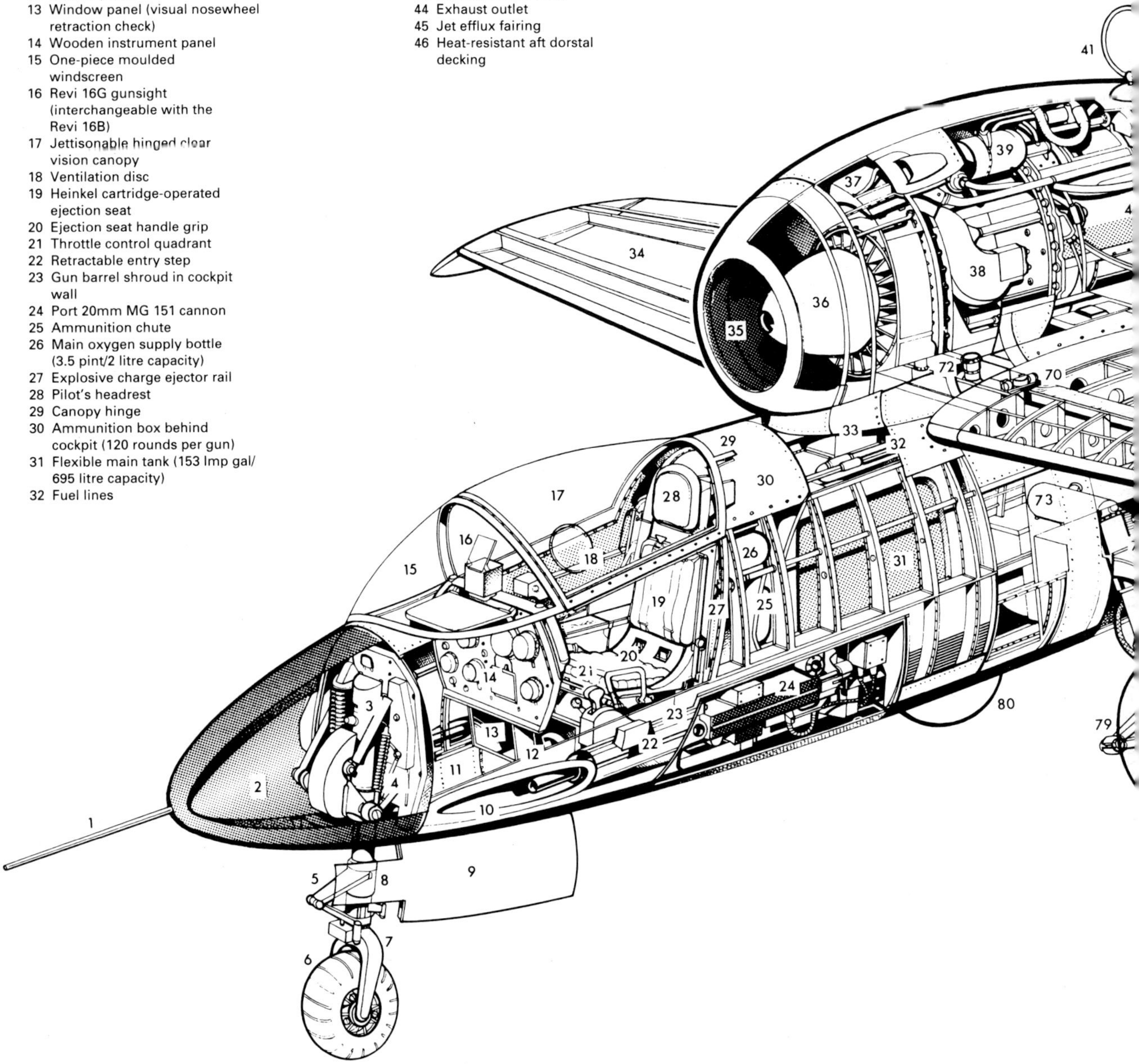

57 Port tailfin upper and lower plates (housing R/T transmitter and IFF aerials)
58 Tailskid
59 Dural fuselage skinning
60 Monocoque fuselage construction
61 Control cables
62 Downswept wing root fillet
63 Hydraulically-operated flaps
64 Port aileron

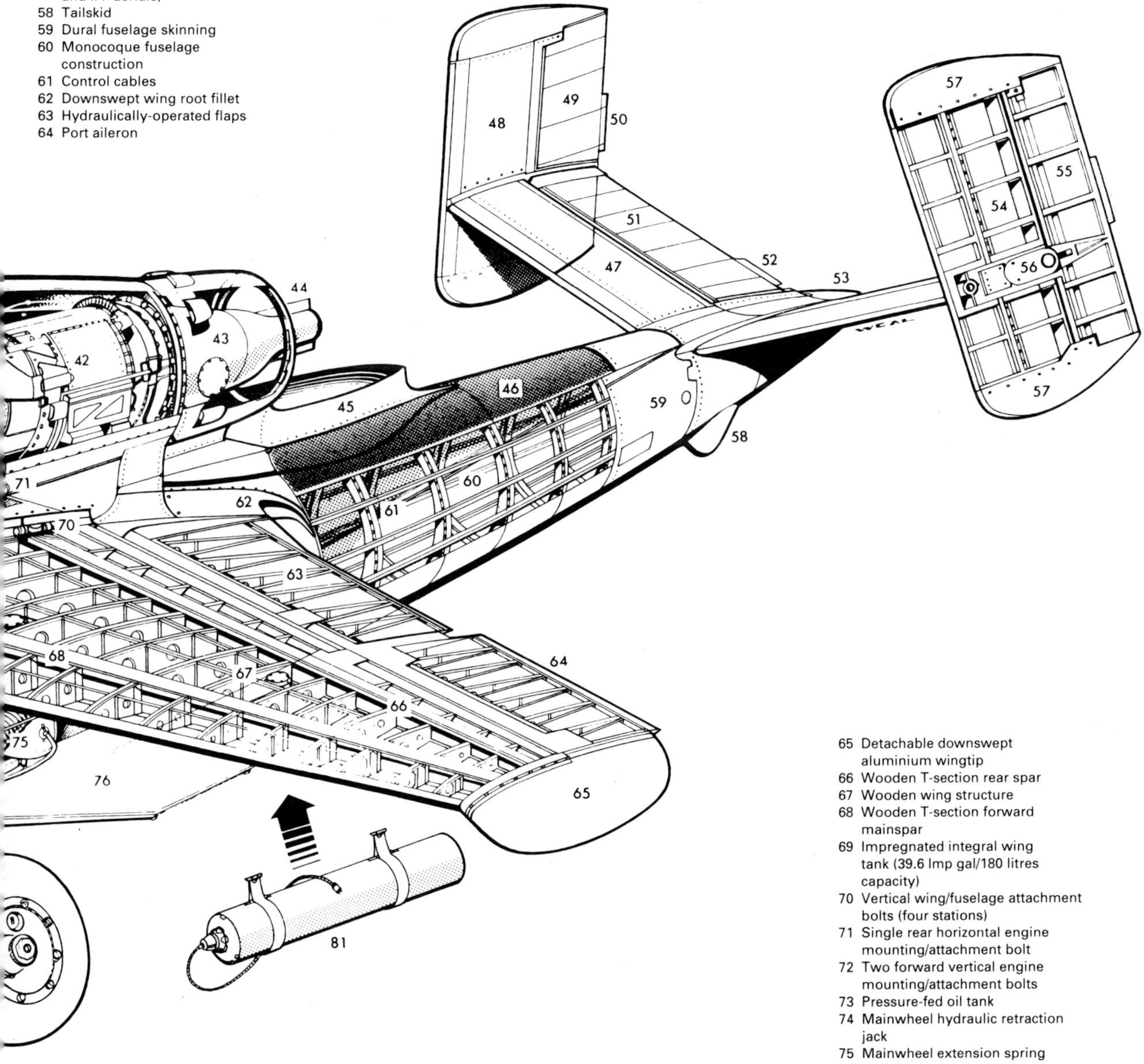


65 Detachable downswept aluminium wingtip
66 Wooden T-section rear spar
67 Wooden wing structure
68 Wooden T-section forward mainspar
69 Impregnated integral wing tank (39.6 Imp gal/180 litres capacity)
70 Vertical wing/fuselage attachment bolts (four stations)
71 Single rear horizontal engine mounting/attachment bolt
72 Two forward vertical engine mounting/attachment bolts
73 Pressure-fed oil tank
74 Mainwheel hydraulic retraction jack
75 Mainwheel extension spring
76 Wooden mainwheel door
77 Mainwheel leg
78 Mainwheel tyre (660mm x 190mm)
79 Shock absorber scissor
80 Narrow-track main undercarriage assembly
81 Assisted take-off rocker unit (attached to fuselage immediately aft of mainwheel well)

YIPPEE

# CHAPTER 7

# The Lockheed P-80 Shooting Star

The first jet-propelled aircraft built in the U.S.A., the Bell XP-59A Airacomet, made its maiden flight in October 1942. Eventually some seventy Airacomets were built, and production aircraft were armed as fighters with one 37 mm cannon and three .5-in machine-guns. The aircraft's disappointing maximum speed was only 413 mph, however, and it was slower than the latest piston-engined fighter types then flying. Although it was unsuitable for use as a combat aircraft, the P-59A provided the U.S. industry and the Army Air Forces with useful experience in the construction and operation of jet aircraft.

Once it was clear that the P-59A was unsuitable for front-line service, the Army Air Force sought a more effective jet fighter type. In May 1943 the Lockheed Aircraft Company was invited to tender to build a fighter aircraft powered by the new British de Havilland Halford H-1 Goblin engine which developed 2,500 pounds of thrust. One month later the company's Chief Research Engineer, Clarence L. 'Kelly' Johnson, submitted a design proposal for a smooth-lined low-winged aircraft, with the jet engine mounted in the fuselage. The design received immediate approval and the Army issued a contract for the construction of a prototype of the jet fighter, to fly within 180 days of signature. Now with the official designation XP-80, the fighter was to carry a nose-mounted armament of six .5-in machine-guns.

To achieve the extremely tight deadline, Johnson demanded and received authorization for the 128 personnel assigned to the project to be isolated from the rest of the company. That way, he argued, his people could work without hinderance from the companys' normal bureaucratic restrictions. The move paid off and by the time the first Goblin engine arrived at Burbank early in November 1943, the airframe of the XP-80 was almost finished. The work of installing the turbojet began without delay and the new fighter was rapidly completed. The prototype was then disassembled and loaded on to a truck. Hidden under tarpaulins and protected by an armed guard, the precious aircraft was moved to Muroc Air Base in California's Mojave desert where it was to undergo flight testing safe from too many prying eyes.

After re-assembly at Muroc, the XP-80 began its ground engine runs with more than a month to go before the contracted date for the first flight. Then, after the remarkably smooth progress enjoyed by the ambitious project, the new fighter suffered a major setback. During what was to have been one of the final engine runs at full power before the first flight, one of the engine air intake ducts collapsed. Johnson had underestimated the suction forces that were produced in a long intake duct, when a turbojet was running at maximum power. Pieces of metal torn away from the duct were drawn into the engine compressor, where they caused serious damage and necessitated an engine change. It took more than a month for a replacement engine to arrive from England, during which the XP-80 was fitted with redesigned and strengthened intake ducts.

More than seven weeks elapsed before the XP-80 was again considered ready to fly. Nicknamed *Lulu-Belle*, she was painted in an attractive green and grey colour scheme. As Milo Burcham prepared to get airborne on the morning of 8 January 1944, Kelly Johnson's advice to his Chief

OPPOSITE:
Lockheed Chief Test Pilot Milo Burcham carried out the initial test flying of the P-80. Burcham was killed while test flying a YP-80A on 20 October 1944, when his engine flamed-out within a minute of taking off from Burbank airfield. Burcham is here seen beside a P-38 Lightning fighter, another of Kelly Johnson's successful designs. *(via Warren Bodie)*

*Lulu-Belle*, the prototype Lockheed XP-80, with Lockheed test pilot Tony LeVier at the controls. *(National Archives via Jay Spenser*

Test Pilot was simple: 'Just fly her, Milo. Treat her nice . . . and find out if she's a lady or a witch.' Burcham lifted the prototype into the air and started to climb away. Then he levelled out, returned to the airfield and landed almost immediately. As the aircraft taxied in there were fears that the aircraft had some handling problem. Burcham told the onlookers that the reason for the early return was that he could not get the landing gear to retract; it transpired that he had not operated the novel safety catch fitted to the operating handle. The test pilot also said that the fighter's hydraulically boosted ailerons were much more sensitive than expected, but Johnson assured him that they were behaving normally.

Burcham re-started the engine, took off again and climbed away and for a time the jet was out of sight of the watchers on the ground. When the new fighter next came into view it was sweeping low over the dry lake at 475 mph indicated, and as it shrieked past the stunned audience the pilot pulled into a series of aileron rolls. Such a display of exuberance with a prototype during an early flight would be frowned on today, but it was typical of what took place during test flights in the 1940s. Burcham then returned to the airfield and landed normally, leaving no doubt that in his view the XP-80 was a 'pilot's aircraft'.

Allis-Chalmers, the company chosen to build the H-1 Goblin under licence, was having a lot of difficulty with getting the turbojet into large-scale production and the programme was suffering delays. In the meantime, however, the new General Electric I-40 engine was developing an impressive 3,850 pounds of thrust — an increase of more than one-third over the Goblin. In February 1944 the Army issued an amendment to its earlier contract, calling for the construction of two XP-80A airframes revised to take the larger and heavier new engine. Just over a week later, the Army Air Force approved the construction of thirteen YP-80A pre-production aircraft; and a week after that the service placed a production order for five hundred P-80A fighters.

While this was happening, the intensive flight testing of *Lulu-Belle* continued. Following recommendations from both company and service test pilots, the sensitivity of the fighter's ailerons was reduced. The XP-80 was found to be very manoeuvrable even at altitudes up to 40,000 feet, and it became the first American aircraft to exceed

500 mph in level flight (its maximum speed was 502 mph at 20,500 feet).

In June 1944 the first I-40-powered XP-80A was delivered to Muroc, nicknamed *Gray Ghost* because of its high gloss grey colour scheme. Again Kelly Johnson's secluded team had pulled off a coup, for the much-revised aircraft was ready to fly a remarkable 139 days after signature of the contract for the installation of the new engine. Although at first glance it closely resembled XP-80, in fact the XP-80A was somewhat larger all round. The loaded weight of the latter was 13,780 pounds, more than 4,500 pounds heavier than *Lulu-Belle*. To accommodate the much larger engine the internal structure of the rear fuselage of the XP-80A had to be re-designed, and it was extended by 18 inches. The wing area was enlarged to compensate for the extra weight, and the span was increased by 22½ inches. To restore longitudinal stability after these changes, a larger fin with a rounded top was fitted to the aircraft.

Test pilot Anthony W. 'Tony' LeVier was chosen to head the test programme of the XP-80A and make the first flight, and in preparation for this he was checked out in *Lulu-Belle*. He remembered the aircraft with great affection, and recalled that the check-out was:

'. . .the most pleasurable of my flying career. The handling qualities were outstanding — and the speed was over 500 mph [on the] level . . . The original XP-80 was really a delightful little plane. The Halford engine, though underpowered, was fairly well developed.'

After the death of Milo Burcham, Anthony W. 'Tony' LeVier became the company's Chief Test Pilot and took over the P-80 test programme. He is seen here boarding the second XP-80A prototype *Silver Ghost*. Note the early type 'bone dome'. *(via Warren Bodie)*

ABOVE:
Kelly Johnson, the brilliant designer who headed the P-80 design team (left) pictured with Hal Hibberd, Chief Engineer at Lockheed. *(via Warren Bodie)*

Despite its outward resemblance to the earlier aircraft, the XP-80A was a good deal less pleasant to fly. When the new fighter took to the air for the first time on 10 June 1944, the I-40 still needed a lot more development work to make it into a reliable power unit. LeVier later commented:

'After operating the engine and making the usual brief taxi and brake tests, I became fully aware that this aircraft was much heavier [than the XP-80], and I became concerned as to whether the bird would take-off at all at the [manufacturer's mandated] reduced take-off thrust and high ambient air temperature. Normally I would have used the great expanse of the dry lake bed, but with this aircraft I knew a better surface was needed. I decided to use the Northbase runway [at Muroc] which was slightly downhill from west to east and was ramped down to the lake bed. This would give us an extra margin of safety in case of an emergency . . .'

Even with that assistance *Gray Ghost* was reluctant to get airborne. LeVier continued:

'I thought the bird would be similar to the original and docile XP-80 on take-off, but it suddenly became cantankerous and ornery, with a tendency to over-rotate, and I hopped, skipped, and jumped down the runway. Once airborne, I realized this aircraft was not only unstable in pitch but the heat pouring into the cockpit was almost unbearable . . . When I reduced power after lift-off the aircraft would hardly accelerate, and it took several minutes before I obtained VI [velocity indicated] to commence the climb. Struggling to 10,000 feet over Muroc Dry Lake, I proceeded to run off the list of test items on my knee pad. As I started the flaps down test, the plane began to roll upside down. Unable to correct the split-flap condition I said, "Nuts to this — I am getting down before I lose this whole can of worms." Using almost full right stick, I made a fast flat approach and landed on the dry lake bed safely. I was in despair. That little "jewel" the XP-80 had turned into a "dog."'

Some of the problems had been corrected a few days later, when LeVier took the aircraft up on its second flight. Stability in pitch was improved slightly by adding ballast in the nose. Since the first flight General Electric had been able to reduce its limitation on the maximum thrust that could be used, and that improved the plane's performance noticeably. Still there were surprises in store for LeVier, however:

'During descent, and without warning, a loud rumbling and grinding sound appeared to be coming from behind the cockpit, accompanied by a rapid and uncontrollable snaking of the plane. I assumed the engine was chewing itself to pieces and I promptly pulled up and prepared to bale out! However, as speed decayed, the rumpus in the engine area subsided to its normal smooth hum. With my fright subdued and a semblance of tranquillity in the cockpit, I landed to report my new findings. After careful analysis of all data, including the intrepid pilot's report, the noise in the engine area was determined to be "duct rumble," a brand new troublesome, but not dangerous, problem. It was caused by stalled inlet ducts, resulting in an "organ pipe" effect. The airplane snaking was attributed to alternating reverse air flow through the ducts.

'The third test flight was to see how fast she would go. With all squawks worked off (they said), I launched and climbed to 10,000 feet. I was now allowed to cob the engine, pulling maximum thrust at 11,500 rpm. I headed east from Lancaster in the Antelope Valley with the throttle to the wall, but within minutes I had to abort the flight. The heat coming into the cockpit was so scorching I was unable to grasp either the throttle or the control stick. I nudged the stick and throttle back and slowed down so that I could crank the sliding canopy open to cool things off. I was soaking wet from perspiration, but surprisingly enough, I felt okay except for my left forearm which later on developed blisters.'

'We discovered the cause of the heat to be a faulty cockpit pressurization valve which allowed 325 deg F air directly into the left side of the cockpit. It's a small

BELOW:

During Operation 'Extraversion' at the end of the 1944 the U.S. Army Air Force shipped four YP-80A pre-production aircraft to Europe, two to England and two to Italy. The aircraft were not cleared for combat and their main purpose was to boost morale by giving demonstrations to show U.S. forces that the answer to the German jet aircraft would not be long in coming. In this photo two of the YP-80As are seen flying past Mount Vesuvius in Italy in early 1945. *(USAF)*

wonder I wasn't fried. The average cockpit temperature was 185 deg F, just right for a "sauna bath."'

'With better prospects, we tried that speed run again and hit more than 565 mph, which was pretty darn good for the fourth flight, considering all the trouble we had had . . . Elated with our first real significant milestone, I peeled off to the left to head for home. I had exhausted most of my fuel, and was not paying attention to my speed when suddenly I felt a very high frequency vibration. Startled again, I looked to my left and thought I saw aileron flutter. I pulled off power, and lowered my speed brakes to reduce speed and the flutter stopped. My "pucker factor" went back to normal.

'Later analysis proved it was not flutter, but another brand new problem called "buzz". This new bug was caused by the aircraft reaching the critical Mach number, about Mach 0.8, wherein a supersonic enclosure developed on the wing and the resultant "shock waves" caused the ailerons to "buzz".'

Clearly a lot more needed to be learned about the handling of the new fighter before its high maximum speed could be utilised under combat conditions.

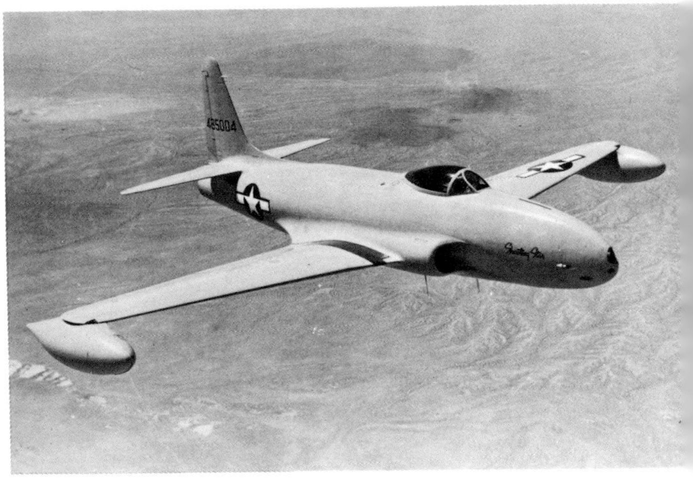

ABOVE AND BELOW:
An early production P-80A Shooting Star seen in flight, bearing the light grey paint scheme which was standard on these aircraft. Quantity production of the fighter was in full swing by March 1945, only 21 months from the beginning of design work. *(Norm Taylor Collection)*

Early production P-80A pictured at Edmonton, Canada during cold weather testing at Ladd Field, Fairbanks, Alaska in November 1945. The boundary layer bleed intakes, clearly visible just inside the air intakes, were a modification to carry away the low energy air and solve the problem of 'duct rumble'.
*(Logan L. Coombs)*

At this time U.S. intelligence officers expected the large scale deployment of jet fighters by the Luftwaffe to be imminent. To gain data on how best to counter them, the Army Air Force conducted four-day series of tests over Muroc at the end of July 1944. The raiding force comprised a formation of B-24 Liberators escorted by P-38s, P-47s and P-51s. The defending force was made up of P-59A Airacomets, the XP-80 and the XP-80A. The tests revealed that the best way to prevent enemy jet fighters reaching the bombers was to provide an escort of jet fighters. Failing that, the best tactic for propeller-driven escort fighters was to create a large, very flexible formation close to the bombers. That would restrict the enemy jet fighters to making high speed slashing and diving attacks on the bombers, with very high closing speeds that would allow only short firing passes.

The second XP-80A, nicknamed the *Silver Ghost* because it was left in bare aluminium, flew for the first time in August 1944. Intended primarily as an engine test bed, the aircraft had a second seat fitted in place of the rear fuel tank to accommodate a test engineer. The provision of the second seat allowed Kelly Johnson to fly in his brainchild, and for the first time he heard the mysterious organ-like duct rumbling.

Kelly quickly determined the cause of the problem, and solved it by fitting boundary layer bleed intakes just inside the ducts to carry away the low energy air. Another of the XP-80A's problems, that of aileron buzz, was partially cured by increasing the tension of the aileron cables.

During an engine acceleration test at 40,000 feet in *Silver Ghost*, with an engineer aboard, LeVier suffered a flame-out. As he headed back to Muroc for a dead stick landing the aircraft lost electrical power and the hydraulic power failed before he could extend the landing gear. Fortunately the engineer was able to squeeze forward and operate the hydraulic hand-pump lever, and get the gear down and locked just as LeVier flared out for the landing.

Like those in other nations, the early American jet engines required extremely careful handling. Tony LeVier wrote:

'Those early fuel controls were so undeveloped; nothing but the utmost caution in handling of the throttle would prevent melting the engine hot section into a spewing white-hot molten mass of hardware. Throttle bursts were strictly forbidden. A ground start was so difficult only selected personnel were allowed to run an engine. When the engine would "light-up", you had to nurse the throttle between idle and cut-off to prevent flames shooting 20 feet out from the tail pipe. The Turbine Inlet Temperature (TIT) would go off the scale in the "blink of an eye."'

By now U.S. aircraft over Europe had encountered both the Messerschmitt 163 and the Me 262 in combat. Ignorant of the problems that faced the German jet pilots, American fighter pilots felt that technically they were now outclassed by the enemy. Their demands for an aircraft of equivalent performance added to pressure to get the P-80 into operational service as rapidly as possible, despite the latter's failings.

The first YP-80A made its maiden flight in September 1944, and in the weeks to follow a succession of these aircraft joined the test programme. Then, on 20 October, Milo Burcham was killed in the third YP-80A, when the aircraft crashed following an engine flame-out within a minute of taking-off from Burbank. The cause of the loss was found to be a sheared drive shaft in the fuel pump which, along with a malfunctioning overspeed governor, caused the engine to flame-out. To prevent a recurrence, all aircraft on the production line aircraft were fitted with an electric emergency fuel pump to serve as a backup. Tony LeVier was promoted to Chief Test Pilot to replace Burcham, and the test programme continued.

Still there was enormous pressure to bring the jet fighter into service in a combat theatre, no matter how limited its role. Towards the end of the 1944 the Army Air Force ordered Operation 'Extraversion': the shipping to Europe of four YP-80As with ground crews, spares and equipment. Two of the jet fighters were to go to England and two to Italy. The aircraft were not authorized for use in combat, their role would be to carry out demonstration flights to teach American fighter and bomber crews the optimum tactics to employ against the German jets. An important though unstated aim of the exercise was to raise morale among American aircrew, by demonstrating that the Army Air Force also had a jet fighter in service and the technical advantage currently enjoyed by the enemy would soon be nullified.

The YP-80s were shipped to Europe in December, and by the end of January 1945 the first had been reassembled and was flying over England. Then, during a test flight over England on 28 January, a YP-80 broke up in mid-air killing its pilot. The cause of the accident was found to be the failure of the attachment of the jet tailpipe to the tail cone. The three remaining YP-80As would continue to perform demonstration flights over England, France and Italy until the war in Europe came to an end.

Also during the final week in January, and despite the numerous unsolved technical problems with the aircraft, the Army Air Force asked Lockheed to plan for a much greater rate of production of the P-80A. The requirement was for one thousand of these fighters to be delivered before the end of the year. The eventual requirement was for five thousand aircraft, with production scheduled to reach thirty aircraft per day during 1946. To provide a second source of supply, North American Aviation Inc was brought into the programme with an order to build a thousand P-80Ns, and the Allison Division of General Motors was to build the I-40 engines.

At that time only eleven XP-80s and YP-80s were flyable — and three of the latter were in Europe and far removed from the programme to test modifications intended to cure faults on the production aircraft. The first production P-80 flew in February 1945, and in the weeks that followed these aircraft began to trickle into the test programme. Several Army pilots now became involved in the expanding P-80 programme, assisting the Lockheed pilots with the massive workload of test flights.

On 20 March 1945 Tony LeVier had a close shave while flying the first XP-80A, *Gray Ghost*. He had levelled off at 10,000 feet preparatory to a maximum speed run to test a redesigned air intake duct when suddenly the aircraft shook, the nose pitched down violently and the fighter tumbled out of control. The pilot fought his way out of the cockpit and parachuted to safety, but he landed heavily and suffered back injuries. Examination of the wreckage revealed that the rear fuselage and the entire tail unit had parted company from the rest of the aircraft. The root cause of the incident was a faulty casting in the turbine wheel which broke up at high speed. The massive centrifugal forces hurled chunks of superheated metal at high velocity into the surrounding structure, weakening the fuselage to such an extent that the latter snapped in two. Later LeVier commented, 'I can say with all sincerity, there is nothing worse for an aviator than to lose his tail . . .'

Following the surrender of Germany in May 1945, the U.S. government cancelled the contract with North American Aviation to build P-80s. The two YP-80As in Italy were shipped back to the U.S.A., while the surviving machine in England was passed to Rolls-Royce to serve as a flying test bed for the new Nene engine.

The war in the Pacific continued, however, and there was no let-up in the pressure to get the P-80 into front-line service. The 412th Fighter Group, the Army Air Forces' first jet fighter unit and the only one to operate the Bell Airacomet, moved to Muroc and began to re-equip with P-80s. In June the Group received notice that as soon as it was combat ready it was to deploy to the Pacific Theatre. One of the Group's constituent squadrons was to operate the photographic reconnaissance version of the P-80A, fitted with nose-mounted cameras in place of the guns and designated the F-14 (F for Photographic).

Already the testing and production programmes of the P-80 had been pushed too far and too fast, however, and many of the plane's defects had not received the attention they deserved. As more of these aircraft became available, and they were flown by a wider cross-section of pilots, it was almost inevitable that there would be a spate of accidents.

On 1 July a production P-80A crashed on take-off due to pilot error. On 2 August a YP-80A exploded in mid-air and crashed, killing the pilot. Then on 6 August, on the same day that the atomic bomb exploded on Hiroshima, Major Richard I. Bong, the Army's leading fighter ace with 40 victories, was killed when the engine of his P-80 flamed-out after take-off and the aircraft plunged into the ground.

This early P-80A-1 has its nickname on the nose, in stylized Lockheed fashion, and the duct rumble fix just outside the intake. It carries an extended pitot head protruding from the port wing tip. *(Norm Taylor Collection)*

P-80A-1 with the underfuselage airbrake extended.
*(Norm Taylor)*

Coming at a time when the end of the war was in sight, the death of Richard Bong delivered a severe blow to the P-80 programme. Previously the fighter's poor safety record had been hidden in the name of national security. Now the aircraft suddenly came under the media spotlight and it was being damned as a killer. The Army Air Force had to defend the aircraft before Congress, at a time when funding for almost every large contract was being brutally slashed or cancelled altogether. Voices were being raised to cut funding for the development of the 'dangerous' jet aircraft to go the same way. In a telex to those running the testing of the P-80, General Hap Arnold made clear what he required if he was to keep the programme alive: '. . . there will not be an accident. I repeat, there will not be an accident.'

Following the death of Bong all P-80s were grounded, pending detailed investigations of each of the fifteen accidents suffered by experimental, pre-production and production aircraft. In eight cases the plane had been completely destroyed, in four it suffered major damage and in three cases there was minor damage. So far the programme had claimed the lives of six pilots.

At the beginning of September 1945, although all of the accidents had not yet been fully investigated, the order grounding the P-80 was partially lifted. After each had received a particularly thorough check, test flying resumed using five Shooting Stars that had been modified to the latest standards. Flights were permitted only by experienced pilots and were to take place only within the aircraft's proven safe flight envelope. During September each of the five jets flew more than a hundred hours, and there were no incidents. By then the surrender of Japan had removed the wartime pressure for rapid operational deployment of the P-80 at any cost. Armed with this proof that the jet fighter was not intrinsically unsafe, General Arnold was able to gain the Congressional support needed to keep the P-80A programme going though the production order was reduced to 917 aircraft.

Lockheed engineers pushed ahead with modifications to rectify the aircraft's other failings. The restrictions on flying the jet fighter were lifted, though from now on the programme proceeded more slowly and with a good deal more care than had previously been the case.

Sadly, the reason for the flame-out of Dick Bong's engine was traced to the same malfunction that had caused the death of Milo Burcham nearly ten months earlier: a failure of the main fuel pump. Bong's aircraft was fitted with the back-up emergency fuel pump, but the fighter ace had omitted to switch it on prior to take-off and he paid for the oversight with his life.

The P-80 made its official public debut at the end of September 1945, and General Arnold ordered a series of spectacular flights to establish in the public mind the jet fighter's superb performance. The first of these was a coast-to-coast high speed dash involving three P-80As. Each aircraft was modified to carry a total of 954 Imp gallons of fuel, 50 per cent more than the standard fighter version. Two of the P-80As were to make refuelling stops during the flight, but one was to attempt to fly the distance non-stop and jettison its external tanks over the desert when they were empty. On 26

BELOW:
Top scoring U.S.A.A.F. fighter ace Major Richard Bong pictured in the Lockheed P-38, the type in which he scored his 40 aerial victories. Bong was killed in a P-80A on 6 August 1945 after his engine flamed-out immediately after take-off. Following Bong's death all P-80As were grounded pending a detailed review of the aircraft's safety record. *(via Warren Bodie)*

January 1946 Colonel William Councill took off in his heavily laden P-80A from Long Beach, California. Assisted by a powerful tail wind, he covered the 2,453 miles to La Guardia Field, New York city non-stop in 4 hours, 13 minutes at an average speed of just over 580 mph. Although they were slowed by the need to land to refuel along the route, the other two P-80s also broke the previous record for a flight between the two points.

Hap Arnold's ultimate goal for the P-80 was to capture the World Absolute Speed Record, then held by the British Gloster Meteor at 616 mph. The P-80R was specially modified for the purpose, fitted with a more powerful J-33 engine and a cutdown more-streamlined canopy. After several setbacks, on 19 June 1947 Colonel Al Boyd achieved at average speed of 623 mph during four runs over the Mojave desert, to regain the coveted record for his country for the first time in 24 years.

While the exploits of the much-modified and strictly non-fighting Shooting Stars captured the newspaper headlines, comparative tests between captured Messerschmitt Me 262s and P-80As revealed that in one-versus-one combat the latter failed to outperform the older German machine. The secret report on the tests stated with candour:

'Despite a difference in gross weight of nearly 2,000 lb, the Me 262 was superior to the average P-80A in acceleration and speed, and approximately the same in climb performance. The Me 262 apparently has a higher critical Mach number, from a drag standpoint, than any current A.A.F. fighters.'

The Shooting Star appeared just too late to fight in World War II, but after the conflict it became the primary jet fighter type of the new U.S. Air Force. Production of the P-80A ran to 677 aircraft, including 114 modified for the FP-80A unarmed photographic reconnaissance role. The next version, the P-80B, featured a thinner wing, ejection seat and a more powerful version of the J-33 engine; it was followed into production by the definitive day-fighter version, the more refined P-80C. All told, production of the day-fighter and reconnaissance versions of the P-80 ran to 1,717 aircraft.

BELOW:
The 412th Fighter Group formed in 1944 with Bell P-59As to introduce jet flying to the U.S. Army Air Forces, and the unit was the first to receive the P-80A in the summer of 1945. In this line-up of aircraft of 412th, taken in 1946, the aircraft carry the pilots' previous victory tallies, nose art and leaders' stripes on the fuselage. With the coming of peace these personal markings would soon be removed. *(Peter M. Bowers, via Norm Taylor Collection)*

ABOVE:
The photographic reconnaissance version of the P-80A had the armament removed and revised nose contours to accommodate the cameras. It was initially designated the F-14A, and later re-designated the FP-80A. There were plans to deploy a reconnaissance squadron equipped with these aircraft to the Pacific Theatre late in 1945, but the end of the war led to their cancellation. *(Norm Taylor Collection)*

The P-80C flew large numbers of combat missions during the Korean war, in the course of which one of them achieved the first-ever jet-versus-jet victory when it shot down a MiG-15. The type remained in front-line service until 1954.

The Lockheed F-94, a two-seat radar-fitted night and all weather fighter developed from the P-80 design, formed the backbone of the North American air defence system during the early 1950s. More enduring, though less spectacular, was the success achieved by the two-seat trainer version of the fighter. Initially designated the TF-80 and later the T-33, it remained in production from 1948 to 1959. Total production by the parent company, and under licence in Canada and Japan, ran to more than 6,750 aircraft. During the past forty-five years countless military pilots all over the world have gained their first experience of handling a jet aircraft in the cockpit of a 'T-Bird'. Many continue to do so, for at the time of writing some 400 of these aircraft remain in service with a dozen air forces.

The production of the P-80 and its derivatives ran to a staggering total of just over 9,900 aircraft spread over fifteen years, making it one of the most successful jet aircraft ever built. The fact that the prototype was designed and built in less than 150 days serves to confirm, were confirmation ever needed, the virtuoso brilliance of Kelly Johnson and the team of engineers that worked with him.

**Lockheed P-80A Shooting Star**

**Power Unit:** one General Electric I-40 (later re-designated J33) developing 3,850 pounds thrust.
**Armament:** six Colt Browning M2 .5-in machine-guns mounted in the nose, provision to carry two 1,000 pound bombs or (on 100th subsequent aircraft) ten 5-in rockets under the wings.
**Performance:** maximum speed 558 mph at sea level, 492 mph at 40,000 ft. Range (with two 137 Imp gal drop tanks) 1,100 miles. Time to climb to 20,000 feet, 5 mins 30 seconds. Service Ceiling 45,000 feet.
**Weight (empty, equipped)** 7,920 pounds; (normally loaded) 11,700 pounds.
**Dimensions:** span 38 feet 10½ inches; length 34 feet 6 inches; wing area 238 sq ft.

One of the early XFR-1s in flight near San Diego, fitted with the original small vertical tail surfaces.
*(Ryan via Hal Andrews)*

# CHAPTER 8

# The Ryan FR-1 Fireball

In December 1942 the U.S. Navy began to study the possible use of jet propelled fighters from aircraft carriers. As the test reports on the early Allied experimental jets became available, the Fighter Plans department at the Bureau of Aeronautics learned that there were serious problems to overcome if these machines were to operate from ships' decks. The early jet aircraft all had sluggish acceleration at low speed (which meant long take-off runs), high landing speeds (long landing runs), and extremely high fuel consumption (poor range and endurance); these attributes were the very antithesis of what made a successful naval aircraft. It seemed that if jet aircraft were to operate from carriers the latter would need to have much longer decks, more powerful catapults and greatly increased storage capacity for aviation fuel (later, of course, that would prove to be the case).

At that time the U.S. Navy was committed to a hard-fought war of attrition to stem the Japanese advance in the Pacific, and clearly this was no time to undertake a major redesign of existing carriers or those under construction. With this in mind the Bureau of Aeronautics decided that it would enter the jet age on the back of a compromise, with a composite-powered fighter fitted with both a piston engine and a turbojet. Compared with an aircraft powered by jet engine alone, such a machine would have better acceleration for take-off and in case it was necessary to abort a deck landing at the last moment; also, by shutting down

Ryan Aeronautical Co. test pilots fly two XFR-1s over the southern California mountains, with two different versions of the enlarged vertical tail surfaces. Eventually the shorter of the two, on the aircraft nearest the camera, was fitted as standard. *(Ryan via Hal Andrews)*

An XFR-1 aboard the escort carrier USS *Charger* during the fighter's initial carrier trials. *(USN via Hal Andrews)*

the turbojet and cruising on the piston engine alone, the aircraft would have a reasonable range and endurance for a fighter type. With both engines running at maximum power the aircraft promised to have a horizontal speed as high as, and a climbing performance better than, existing piston-engined fighters.

The Bureau of Aeronautics invited tenders from nine manufacturers for the design of a single-seat lightweight fighter powered by one piston engine and one turbojet. The requirement called for an aircraft with a high top speed, a reasonably low landing speed, a high rate of climb, an extensive cruising radius, exceptional manoeuvrability and the ability to operate from the decks of the small escort carriers (CVEs) then entering service in large numbers. Although the Ryan Aeronautical Corporation had never previously built anything for the Navy more ambitious than a primary trainer, the Bureau judged that its proposed Model 28 fighter offered the best engineering compromise to the conflicting set of requirements.

In February 1943 the Bureau of Aeronautics issued a letter of intent to purchase three prototypes of the Ryan Model 28, plus an airframe for static testing. The experimental fighter received the official designation XFR-1. The aircraft was to be fitted with a Wright Cyclone R-1820, a nine-cylinder radial developing a modest (for a fighter) 1,300 horsepower, and a General Electric I-16 developing 1,600 pounds thrust. As well as the novel arrangement of the power plants, it was the first aircraft designed for carrier operation with a low-drag laminar-flow wing, and the first to have flush riveting over the entire external surface. It was also one of the first carrier-based aircraft with a tricycle landing gear, and powered folding wings to assist stowage on board ship. The armament comprised four .5-in machine-guns, and there was provision to carry underwing racks for two bombs, two external fuel tanks or four rockets. To get the programme moving as rapidly as possible, in December 1943 before the prototype had flown the Navy placed an order for a hundred production FR-1s.

On 24 June 1944, Ryan Chief Test Pilot Robert Kerlinger took the XFR-1, by now named the Fireball, on its maiden flight on the power of the piston engine alone. The General Electric turbojet was not yet ready for installation in the aircraft, which carried ballast in lieu during the flight. The I-16 was fitted a few weeks later and full testing of the composite-powered fighter could begin. The second XFR-1 joined the test programme in September 1944.

Initially the XFR-1 carried separate fuels for each type of engine, high octane gasoline for the piston engine and kerosene for the turbojet. This inflexible arrangement would have caused serious problems in operational use, and early in the test programme the jet engine was adjusted to operate on high octane gasoline. From then on both types of engine ran on the same type of fuel.

A production FR-1 Fireball at the Ryan plant in San Diego under test with an auxiliary fuel tank on the right shackle. *(Ryan via Hal Andrews)*

Describing the performance of the Fireball, Company President T. Claude Ryan commented:

'The front engine is rated at 1350 horsepower. This is sufficient for normal take-offs, the FR requiring no more than other planes of comparable power and weight. However, as a safety factor against engine failure on take-off, it is good practice to have the jet engine idling, so that it can be opened to full thrust in an emergency. The Wright Cyclone Model R-1820 engine is extremely economical on fuel and makes possible maximum range for cruising. It is fitted with a Curtiss Electric fast-feathering three-blade constant speed propeller. A heavier, more powerful engine is not necessary since the jet unit is available when the pilot requires superlative performance . . . With the *front engine only*, the Fireball can climb at 2,880 feet a minute from sea level. And its most economical cruising speed with that engine is 207 miles an hour . . . Once in flight, the *jet unit operating alone* will thrust the Fireball along at about 300 miles an hour . . . The conventional engine provides maximum thrust and efficiency at slow and medium speeds and the jet provides maximum thrust at high speeds. Used together, they give the best balance of performance for all requirements. . . . With both engines operating at full power, the FR can climb a mile in a minute at the exceptionally high indicated air speed for best climb of 220 miles an hour.'

ABOVE:
An FR-1 over the Chesapeake Bay during flight tests from the Naval Air Station Patuxent River, Maryland, in July 1945. Though the wing was not radical in plan form, its laminar flow airfoil gave the Fireball very clean aerodynamic characteristics. Pilots found the fighter light on the controls and it was an exceptionally stable gun platform. *(USN via Hal Andrews)*

Mr. Ryan's view of his company's product was, of course, highly subjective, but the Fireball could easily outclimb the Grumman F6F Hellcat and the Vought F4U Corsair, the two best Navy carrier fighters at that time. Moreover, the composite-powered prototype's maximum speed of 430 mph made it considerably faster than the Hellcat and nearly as fast as the latest version of the Corsair.

In October 1944 the prototype XFR-1 was judged ready to move to the Navy flight test facility at Patuxent River, Maryland, for testing by service pilots. On the 13th of that month Bob Kerlinger was making a routine test flight in preparation for the move, when the Fireball disintegrated killing the pilot. At the time the cause of the loss could not be determined, though company officials speculated that Kerlinger might unintentionally have exceeded the aircraft's limiting Mach number during a dive. As a very clean aircraft, it was likely that Fireball would encounter problems with compressibility.

OPPOSITE:
A service test Fireball over the Pacific performing the fighter's favourite party trick: flying with the R-1820 engine stopped and the Curtiss Electric propeller feathered running on the GE jet engine alone.
*(USN via Hal Andrews)*

ST37

ST37

Following the accident Al W. Conover, the company's new Chief Test Pilot, conducted a carefully staged series of test dives with the XFR-1 with incremental increases in speed to investigate the plane's 'compressibility limits'. That appeared to settle the question, but on 25 March 1945 test pilot Mickey McGuire pushed a Fireball into a high speed dive from 35,000 feet and never pulled out. Examination of the wreckage revealed that the aircraft hit the ground in one piece with no evidence of a structural break-up. Again the loss was put down to the pilot having exceeded the plane's limiting Mach number and lost control as a result.

A Fireball of VF-66 ascending on the elevator during one of the unit's carrier deployments. The plane's Wright piston engine was ticking over to warm the motor for a rapid take-off as soon as possible after reaching the deck. *(via Hal Andrews)*

Although these unexplained accidents cast a cloud over the programme, flight testing and large-scale production of the Fireball continued. The fighter lived up to its performance expectations, though there was a problem with the piston engine overheating and production aircraft were fitted with radiator cowl flaps. Also, to improve stability, the aircraft was fitted with enlarged tail surfaces. The Bureau of Aeronautics continued to support the programme and in January 1945 it placed an order for six hundred examples of the FR-2 version of the Fireball, fitted with the Wright R-1820-74W engine developing 1,450 horsepower.

In March 1945 the first production Fireballs came off the assembly line and were issued to Navy squadron VF-66 based at San Diego. Conversion training began. Leading the unit was Lieutenant-Commander John F. Gray, a Hellcat ace credited

with the destruction of eight enemy planes in the air and sixteen on the ground, and most of the pilots had considerable experience of combat.

The pilots found their new mounts exceptionally light on the controls and very manoeuvrable, and the view from the forward-placed cockpit with its large bubble canopy was excellent. Gray was very enthusiastic about the Fireball and commented:

'We can run rings around anything I've seen in the air . . . The combination of the jet unit and the conventional gasoline engine in the nose is an ideal one, especially since it is all contained within a fighter as small as, or even smaller, than most of the other fighter planes the Navy is now using. We found nothing freakish or tricky about the plane. It flies like any other fighter, and it's exceedingly light on the controls at all speeds.'

A line-up of Fireballs of VF-66, running-up at the Ryan factory. In the background are some of the FM-2 Wildcat fighters assigned to the squadron to enable its pilots to maintain proficiency until it received its complement of FR-1s. *(Ryan via Hal Andrews)*

On 5 April 1945 another Fireball was lost. Test pilot Dean N. Lake was making a high speed run past the Ryan factory at Lindbergh Field in the third XFR-1, when he felt an unusual buffeting and noticed a section of the skin lifting away from the wing. Moments later the plane's canopy blew off and the aircraft went into an uncontrollable roll. Lake leapt clear of the aircraft before it plunged into the ground, and landed by parachute.

An investigation revealed the lower skin of the wing had peeled away due to the failure of several countersunk rivets. As the wing came apart, high speed air was ducted along its length producing an overpressure in the fuselage which caused the canopy to blow off. There was evidence to suggest that Kerlinger's Fireball might have been lost to the same cause, for the pilot's autopsy revealed that he suffered a heavy blow to the head that could have resulted from the canopy coming adrift.

During work-up Gray often encountered other Navy aircraft which took a keen interest in the new bird. On one occasion, while cruising over the Pacific using only the piston engine, four Hellcats pulled into formation to him:

'With only the front engine going, naturally my cruising speed was not as high as that of the others and they had to throttle down to stay alongside me. The leader signalled for an echelon, to be followed by a peel-off. I opened up the jet and the old Fireball shot ahead and far out of reach of the other planes. I left them standing back there bewildered. Adding insult to injury, I pulled alongside another fighter, feathered my prop and sailed on past him with the jet.'

During subsequent structural tests on the ground, it was discovered that when subjected to extreme stress, in some parts of the wing the rivets were liable to sheer and then the thin skinning could tear loose. The solution was to add extra rivets in highly stressed areas of the wing.

Despite this setback the Navy was particularly keen to get VF-66 operational as soon as possible, for the Fireball was seen as a useful counter to the high speed *kamikaze* planes being employed by the Japanese against Allied shipping. The new fighter made its first shipboard arrested landing on 1 May 1945, when three Fireballs were detached to USS

*Ranger* for deck qualification tests. During these tests the aircraft's nosewheel assembly was found to be insufficiently strong for carrier landings, a problem that was to dog the aircraft throughout its service career. It was normal practice for U.S. Navy pilots to make 'firm' deck landings, and they did so in other types of aircraft without difficulty. But if the Fireball was landed at all heavily it tended to bounce, and when its hook then caught a wire the aircraft slammed heavily down on onto the deck. This often resulted in damage to the nosewheel leg, and sometimes the propeller struck the deck causing damage to both it and the engine.

Lieutenant D.M. "Whitey" Kreuger and Lieutenant-Commander William McClendon worked out a special deck landing technique for the Fireball. If the pilot put a slight forward pressure on the stick just before touch-down, a serious bounce could be prevented. 'This called for a fine touch on the part of the pilot,' Kreuger later explained, 'and was just the opposite of what the pilots of the period were used to doing.'

As VF-66 gained more experience with the Fireball, John Gray and his pilots were able to establish a set of standard operating procedures for use with the type. The squadron commander wrote:

'We can cruise upstairs for hours feeding the nine-cylinder Cyclone engine — using about 30 to 35 gallons per hour — then start and stop the jet several times during the flight when extra bursts of speed are needed. This is considered the normal operation or best use of the engines, which are highly efficient for patrol and long-range cruising. On the approach to a target, when a surge of speed is needed, pilots start and idle the [jet] engine before making the approach. Although primarily designed to provide increased power in combat or emergencies, the jet engine also can be employed on take-offs or misjudged landings . . . It is the rate of climb, however, that makes the Fireball [so] spectacular. With both engines giving full power, a pilot can actually shoot to 6,000 feet in a little over a minute at an angle of 19 degrees.

'Using the jet and reciprocal engines on take-off, the brakes are held and the jet engine accelerated to full power, and then the brakes are released and the throttle applied to the forward engine. For normal cruising the forward engine alone is used. The jet engine starts much more easily in the air than on the ground, and accelerates faster, but the rate of acceleration with the jet is always slower than the rate possible with a conventional aircraft engine.'

Gray and his fighter pilots were confident that the Fireball would prove a good combat aircraft, and certainly it was a very stable firing platform. In April 1945 the squadron took its FR-1s to Twenty-Nine Palms for a month's gunnery training, during which a couple of pilots both came within one point of breaking the all-time West Coast gunnery record. Despite two fatal crashes during June, VF-66 pushed ahead with its preparations for an early operational deployment.

The Japanese surrender in the middle of August stopped in its tracks the programme to rush the Fireball into front-line service. By then sixty-six FR-1s had been completed, but the Navy immediately cancelled its order for the remaining 634 aircraft.

In October 1945 VF 66 was decommissioned. The Fireballs and the unit's personnel transferred to VF-41 and John Gray assumed command of that unit. The testing of the new fighter continued and in November the unit embarked fifteen pilots and eight FR-1s on USS *Wake Island* to undergo carrier qualification. It was the first time a full squadron of Fireballs had put to sea. In a six-day period the unit carried out a total of 89 arrested landings, and all but one of the pilots qualified to deck-land the new aircraft.

The most noteworthy incident during the work-up occurred on 6 November when, shortly after getting airborne, Ensign J.C. "Jake" West found that his Fireball's piston engine was losing power rapidly. He started up the jet engine and returned to the carrier using that one alone. Coming in fast, the Fireball took the No.6 (final) wire and came to a halt in the crash barrier. Although it had not been his intention to make such a landing when he took off, it must be recorded that West was the first pilot to make a 'jet only' landing on the deck of an aircraft carrier.

Although the technique of moving the stick forward before touch-down reduced the incidence of Fireballs suffering damage during deck landings, if the aircraft did land heavily it was likely to suffer damage to the undercarriage. Usually this could be repaired on the carrier, though it imposed an additional workload on the maintenance personnel. Ryan FR-1 project engineer W.T. Immenschuh explained the problem:

The XFR-4 was an improved version of the Fireball fitted with a Westinghouse J34 developing 4,200 pounds of thrust, involving an 8-inch extension of the fuselage. The aircraft was also fitted with flush entry air inlet ducts for the jet engine just aft of the piston engine, and was used to develop features being considered for the turboprop-powered XF2R. *(Ryan via Hal Andrews)*

'Continued operation [of the FR-1] will result in three failures of the airplane components. Very hard landings (common with new pilots) will cause the spokes in the magnesium alloy nose wheel to fail and the main gear axle will deflect and sometimes take a permanent set, causing the rim of the wheel to rub against the shock strut. The tendency of the airplane to fall back on the tail bumper after the run out of each arrested landing will cause wrinkles in the tail cone skin surrounding the bumper.'

On March 1946, VF-41 embarked on the USS *Bairoko* for a full-scale operational evaluation. This involved a week of intensive flying, during which so many Fireballs suffered damage that evaluation had to be halted. The evaluation also revealed a major fault with the plane's aileron control system, and this and evidence of partial structural failure of some of the aircrafts' wings led to the temporary grounding of all of these fighters.

After modifications to the aircraft, flying was resumed. Then, in June, VF-41 lost two of its leading pilots under particularly tragic circumstances. On the 3rd of the month, as aircraft of VF-41 were returning to San Diego in formation after taking part in an air show at Los Angeles, the wing of John Gray's aircraft started to fold in flight. The Fireball swung out of control and smashed into Jake West's aircraft and both planes went down, taking their pilots with them.

The Ryan XF2R-1 Dark Shark .was the ultimate development of the composite-powered fighter concept. The aircraft was fitted with a General Electric GE XT31 1700 shaft horsepower turboprop in the nose, which produced an additional 500 pounds of thrust from the exhaust at the rear of the engine. A General Electric J31 turbojet developing 1600 pounds of thrust was fitted in the rear fuselage. Despite its maximum speed of nearly 500 mph, by the time it made its maiden flight at the end of 1946 in the XF2R-1 was outclassed by pure-jet naval fighter types then flying. *(Ryan, USN via Hal Andrews)*

In November 1946 VF-41 was redesignated VF-1E but the unit continued operations as before. Following further modifications to its aircraft, in the spring of 1947 the Fireball squadron went to sea on board the USS *Badoeng Strait*. Yet again there were cases of planes suffering nosewheel damage as a result of heavy landings. During the course of this carrier deployment one Fireball was lost and four were damaged.

In spite of these problems, VF-1E again put to sea on *Badoeng Strait* in April 1947, and on the USS *Rendova* in June. The problem of structural damage had still not been solved, however, and after a very heavy landing on *Rendova* one of the Fireballs broke in two. That was the death-knell of the plane's service career. The FR-1 was again grounded, and in the following month the type was officially withdrawn from Fleet service. A few Fireballs would continue to fly at test establishments, before the last was finally grounded in April 1948.

The company proposed several improved versions of the Fireball, but following the end of the war none of them aroused much official interest. The XFR-3 was to have had a General Electric I-20 jet engine developing 2,000 pounds of thrust, but this variant was never built.

The ultimate expression of the composite-powered fighter theme to take the skies was the XF2R-1, unofficially nicknamed 'The Dark Shark'. This was the fifteenth production Fireball airframe, with a turboprop fitted in place of the piston engine and a more powerful type of jet engine. The aircraft made its first flight in November 1946 with a General Electric XT31 turboprop developing 1,700 horse power and 550 pounds of thrust; the turboprop drove a steel four-bladed airscrew whose blades could be fully feathered or moved rapidly perpendicular to the airflow, the latter to serve as an effective airbrake to shorten the landing run. A General Electric J-31 developing 1,600 pounds of thrust was installed in the rear fuselage. To compensate for the lengthened nose of the fighter, it was fitted with an enlarged dorsal fin. The XF2R-1 was credited with a maximum speed of over 497 mph at sea level, an initial rate of climb of 4,850 feet per minute and a service ceiling of 39,100 feet. A still more-powerful projected variant, the XF2R-2 powered by the same turboprop and a Westinghouse J-34 turbojet developing 4,200 pounds of thrust, was never built.

Had the war in the Pacific not ended when it did, and had Allied forces launched their planned invasion of Japan, there is little doubt that the Fireball would have taken part in that operation. In that event pilots would undoubtedly have accepted the type's failings in return for its excellent rate of climb and its high speed and relatively good endurance, for these were the qualities required to blunt the expected massed attacks by Japanese suicide planes.

The end of the war, coupled with improvements in turbojet design that came at about the same time, stifled the Fireball programme. The rationale for the composite-powered fighter had been that its jet engine provided a high maximum speed and a good high altitude performance, while the piston engine provided the good acceleration at low speed. But by 1945 the latest types of jet engine had a somewhat less sluggish response than their predecessors. Moreover, following the Japanese surrender, the requirement for high performance fighters to operate from small escort carriers quickly came to an end, as all of these ships either passed out of service or were relegated to second-line tasks.

By the spring of 1945 the first naval fighter powered by turbojet engines alone, the twin-jet McDonnell FH Phantom, was in production. Considerably faster than the Fireball, the new plane was able to conduct limited operations from the larger US Navy carriers. Its successors in the design stage would be able to do so with considerably greater safety margins. Faced with such competition the Ryan composite-powered fighter, which had come close to carving a niche in aviation history, became just another of those good ideas that ended up as flotsam in a backwater of technology.

**Ryan FR-1 Fireball**

**Power Unit:** one Wright Cyclone R-1820-72W radial engine developing 1,350 horsepower; one General Electric I-16 (J31) developing 1,600 pounds thrust.
**Armament:** four Browning MG 53 .5-in machine-guns mounted in the wings, provision to carry two 1,000 pound bombs or four 3-in rockets under the wings.
**Performance:** maximum speed (on both engines) 426 mph at 18,100 feet; (piston engine only) 295 mph. Initial rate of climb, 4,800 feet per minute. Service ceiling 43,100 feet. Range (with one 125 Imp gal drop tank) 1,430 miles.
**Weight (empty, equipped)** 7,915 pounds.
**Dimensions:** span 40 feet 0 inches; length 32 feet 4 inches; wing area 275 sq ft.

## CHAPTER 9

# The Bachem Ba 349 *Natter*

The Bachem *Natter* (Viper) semi-expendable rocket-powered interceptor was an aircraft quite unlike any other to enter service during the long history of military aviation. One of several 'weapons of desperation' that made their appearance in Germany during the final months of the war, the machine was designed to provide point defence for important targets against daylight bombers flying at altitudes around 20,000 feet. The concept of the weapon was essentially that of a 'manned surface-to-air missile'.

*Natter* with the nose cone removed, to show the method of installation of the battery of twenty-four Foehn 73 mm spin-stabilized unguided rockets. These weapons were to be ripple-launched in a single firing pass at one bomber then the *Natter* dived away and the pilot began his escape procedure. *(Dressel)*

The planned mode of operation was as follows. With an all-up weight of 2½ tons the *Natter* was to take off vertically from a railed launcher, and accelerate to a speed of around 400 mph going almost straight up. When the fighter neared the altitude of the enemy bomber formation the pilot was to take control of the machine, level out and manoeuvre into a firing position behind one of the enemy aircraft. From a range of about 200 yards he would ripple-fire his battery of unguided rockets in a single attack, then he would dive away using up the last of the volatile chemical fuels for the rocket motor. When the rocket motor cut-out he was to continue in a gliding descent with the speed decaying steadily. As the *Natter* passed through an altitude of about 4,500 feet, he was to release his seat harness and slip the catches that held in place the

An early test version of the *Natter* on its simple transporter trolley.

nose of the aircraft. The entire nose section in front of the pilot, including the windscreen, would then fall away and as it parted company from the rest of the machine a cable would eject from its housing a large recovery parachute attached to the rear fuselage. The rear part of the aircraft would then slow up suddenly, and the pilot's weight would carry him safely clear of his seat allowing him to complete the descent using his own parachute.

After the main part of the aircraft reached the ground the most expensive parts — the rocket motor and the autopilot in particular — were to be removed for re-use. The mainly wooden airframe was not built to withstand the stresses of landing, and was to be scrapped after each flight.

Although the operational concept might appear quaint to modern eyes, it is worth pointing out at this stage that the *Natter* was the world's first practical design for a fighter capable of vertical take-off and landing performance (the former under rocket power, the latter by parachute).

The first proposal for vertically-launched manned rocket-powered interceptor came from Dr Wernher von Braun, who described a much heavier machine in a memorandum that he wrote to the German Air Ministry in the summer of 1939. Although the idea was rejected at the time as being both unworkable and unnecessary, *Dipl-Ingeneur* Erich Bachem of the Fieseler company was one of those who saw the merits of such a weapon. During the war Bachem produced a series of design studies for vertical take-off rocket-propelled fighters, but these also came to nothing.

In the spring of 1944 the German Air Ministry issued a requirement for a small and inexpensive interceptor of mainly wooden construction, to provide for the point defence of important targets. Junkers, Heinkel and Messerschmitt submitted design proposals for such an interceptor, as did Bachem who offered as his solution the BP 20 *Natter* semi-expendable fighter. Initially the Luftwaffe Technical Office was lukewarm towards the proposal, especially that part which required the pilot to end each sortie on the end of a parachute. The more-conventional

ABOVE AND RIGHT:
Unmanned *Natter* being prepared for the first vertically-launched take-off, on 22 December 1944. *(via Heise)*

Heinkel P 1077 *Julia* rocket fighter design was its preferred choice.

All that changed when Bachem managed to secure support for his proposed interceptor from an unusual quarter. Then nearing the height of his power, SS *Reichsführer* Heinrich Himmler continually sought ways to extend his influence in government and the armed forces. Bachem's rejected interceptor offered him the chance of a toehold in the nation's air defence system, and Himmler placed an order for 150 of the rocket fighters using SS funds. In order to retain control of its own programme, the Luftwaffe had no alternative but to place an order for a further fifty *Natters*. The semi-expendable fighter was officially incorporated into the emergency fighter production programme and received the official designation Bachem Ba 349.

Detailed design work on the *Natter* began in earnest in August 1944, at a small requisitioned factory at Waldsee in the Black Forest. The airframe was almost entirely of wood, the metal parts being restricted to load supporting attachments, hinges and control push rods. Cruciform fins at the rear carried the aircraft's control surfaces which acted in the normal sense as elevators and rudders and, operating differentially, as ailerons. The small rectangular stub wing, made in one piece with no moveable control surfaces, had a span of 19 feet 9 inches and an area of just over 50 square feet.

The power unit for the Ba 349A, the initial development version, was a Walter 109-509A-2 liquid-fuel rocket motor developing 4,400 pounds of thrust. This unit was similar to that fitted to the Me 163, except that it was modified to operate when the aircraft was in the tail-down or the normal horizontal flight position. Two tanks for the rocket fuels were mounted in the fuselage behind the pilot, one for 96 Imp gallons of *T-Stoff* mounted above the wing spar and one for 42 Imp gallons of *C-Stoff* mounted below the spar.

To provide the necessary additional thrust for the vertical take-off and the initial part of the climb, the aircraft had four Schmidding solid-fuel booster rockets mounted on the rear fuselage;

Ba 349A *Natter* airframes under construction at the Bachem works at Waldsee in the Black Forest. *(via Heise)*

these provided a total of 4,400 pounds of thrust for 10 seconds, after which the burned-out containers were jettisoned and the aircraft continued its climb on the power of the Walter 509 alone.

The launcher for the *Natter* was just over 75 feet high, with three channelled rails to hold each of the wing tips and the lower fin and maintain the aircraft at the correct attitude. The launcher pivoted at the base, to enable it to be lowered to the horizontal so that the fighter could be loaded into place.

Ground crewman filling the *C-Stoff* tank prior to the first unmanned launch of a *Natter* with full rocket power, on 25 February 1945.

During the launch and the 10-second boost phase, the aircraft's control surfaces remained locked in the fore-and-aft position. Following the release of the boosters, the controls were unlocked and the mid-part of the climb continued under radio control from the ground, with correction signals being fed into a Patin three-axis autopilot to hold the *Natter* on the planned flight path. The pilot had the facility to disengage the autopilot any time he required to assume control of the aircraft.

The designers considered various types of weapon for use with the interceptor. The armament finally chosen consisted of a battery of unguided rockets, *either* thirty-three R4M 55 mm folding-fin rockets, *or* twenty-four *Foehn* 73 mm spin-stabilized rockets.

By November 1944 the *Natter* was ready to begin flight tests, initially as an unpowered glider. A prototype was ballasted to a weight of 3,750 pounds, representative of the fighter in the climb after the booster rockets had been jettisoned. A Heinkel 111 bomber took the aircraft to 18,000 feet and released it, with *Flugkapitaen* Zueber at the controls. The pilot found that the plane's heavy wing loading of 74 pounds per square foot made it extremely stable in flight. Descending at a steep gliding angle, Zueber found the controls crisp and effective throughout the speed range between 435 mph and to 125 mph. As the aircraft passed through 3,000 feet the pilot initiated the escape procedure and both he and the aircraft completed the descent by parachute.

The first successful vertical launch of a *Natter*, a much-lightened unmanned aircraft powered only by the four booster rockets, took place on 22 December. Ten further prototypes were launched in this way using only the booster rockets. The first modified Walter 509 rocket motor did not arrive at Waldsee until February 1945. On the 25th of that month a fully loaded aircraft made a vertical launch and climbed to altitude on the thrust of the main rocket unit and four boosters, carrying a dummy pilot. The test flight went off exactly as planned and at the end of it the dummy pilot and the main part of the airframe made soft landings on their respective parachutes.

The success of that trial cleared the way for the first manned test flight. *Oberleutnant* Lothar Siebert volunteered to conduct the maiden flight in the *Natter*, and on 28 February he climbed aboard the diminutive interceptor poised on its launcher. Leaving a trail of black smoke from the four Schmidding powder rockets, the aircraft climbed slowly at first. At the end of the boost phase the four burned-out rockets fell away and the interceptor continued its vertical climb. Then, shortly after the aircraft passed 1,500 feet and as it was accelerating to high speed, observers on the ground saw the canopy come adrift. The nose tilted and the aircraft continued its climb at a shallow angle on its back, before it arced into the ground with the Siebert still in the cockpit. The subsequent investigation failed to determine the cause of the accident. There were suspicions that the canopy had not been properly locked in place and the pilot had been knocked unconscious when it tore away, but that did not explain why the aircraft had deviated so violently from the intended vertical flight path while under autopilot control.

Despite the tragic loss of the pilot during the first manned launch, there was no shortage of volunteers willing to fly the novel interceptor. By the end of March the aircraft had completed three successful manned test flights, and it was decided to conduct a full operational evaluation of the *Natter*.

Early in April an operational air defence site was set up at Kircheim to the east of Stuttgart, with ten launchers. The diminutive rocket fighters and their pilots stood-to each day, ready to engage the next enemy bomber force to come within range. In the event an American tank unit reached the area before the bombers, and the rocket fighters and launchers were blown up to prevent capture.

The Ba 394B *Natter*, intended as the main production version, was fitted a Walter 109-509C rocket motor with an auxiliary cruising chamber to provide reduced thrust over a longer period and increase the plane's endurance at high altitude from 2¼ minutes to 4½ minutes. The motor's additional plumbing necessitated some redesign of the rear fuselage. Also, to shift the centre of gravity rearward to improve handling during the early part of the climb, the booster rockets of the 'Berta' were positioned further back along the fuselage and slightly higher than those on the 'Anton'. Three Ba 349Bs were built before production ended, and one was test flown.

Altogether a total of thirty-six *Natter* airframes of all versions were built at the Waldsee plant before the approach of American forces brought production to a halt. Of that total, 22 were expended as gliders or in powered test flights, ten were blown up with their launchers at Kircheim, three were captured by American forces and one was captured by Soviet forces.

The deployment of the *Natters* at Kircheim came just too late for the aircraft to be launched into action, and the viability of the interceptor's operational concept was never proven. In retrospect, however, it is difficult to see how the rocket fighter could have achieved much. The interceptor's radius of action was even less than that of the Me 163 and, goodness knows, during operational sorties the Messerschmitt fighter usually had difficulty enough trying to manoeuvre into position to deliver an attack before the fuel ran out. Until the Bachem fighter was deployed at a very large number of sites, those planning the Allied air attack could easily have routed bomber formations so that they rarely came within reach of the *Natters*. In the unlikely event that Allies came to consider the point defence fighter as a serious threat, it would have been a relatively simple matter to send fighter-bombers ahead of the bombers to 'rough up' any launching sites that might interfere with the main attack. After the war the semi-expendable fighter idea aroused a lot of technical interest but, significantly, none of the victorious powers bothered to investigate the concept at all seriously.

OPPOSITE – TOP LEFT:
The test on 25 February was completely successful, and at the end of the flight the main part of the *Natter* airframe landed softly by parachute. *(via Heise)*

Series of photos taken on 28 February 1945, during the first manned flight test of the *Natter*.

OPPOSITE – TOP RIGHT:
The *Natter* being fuelled before the flight.

OPPOSITE – BELOW:
The pilot, *Oberleutnant* Lothar Siebert, discussing the flight with *Dipl-Ingeneur* Erich Bachem.

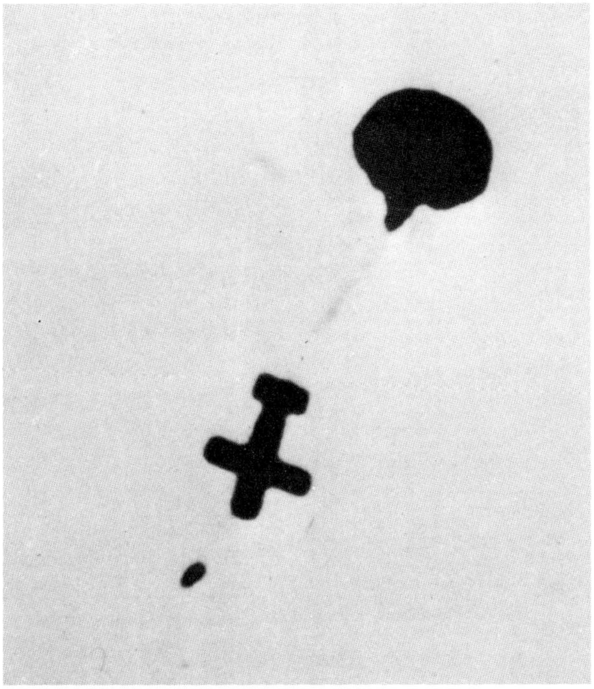

**Bachem Ba 349A Natter**
**Power Unit:** one Walter HWK 109-509 A-2 bi-fuel rocket motor developing a maximum of 3,740 pounds thrust. Four Schmidding 109-533 solid-fuel booster rockets to assist take-off, each developing 1,100 pounds thrust for 10 seconds.
**Armament:** (initial production version) thirty-three R4M 55 mm folding-fin rockets, or twenty-four *Foehn* 73 mm spin-stabilized rockets.
**Performance:** maximum speed in horizontal flight, 500 mph at 16,400 feet. Maximum range from top of climb, 25 miles from 20,000 feet. Initial climb 37,000 feet per minute.
**Weights (at take-off)** 4,850 pounds. With take-off boosters jettisoned, 3,800 pounds; with fuel expended 1,840 pounds.
**Dimensions:** span 13 feet 11½ inches; length 19 feet 9 inches; wing area 50.6 sq ft.

Lothar Siebert going through the precarious procedure for boarding the aircraft, before his last flight on 28 February 1945. *(via Heise)*

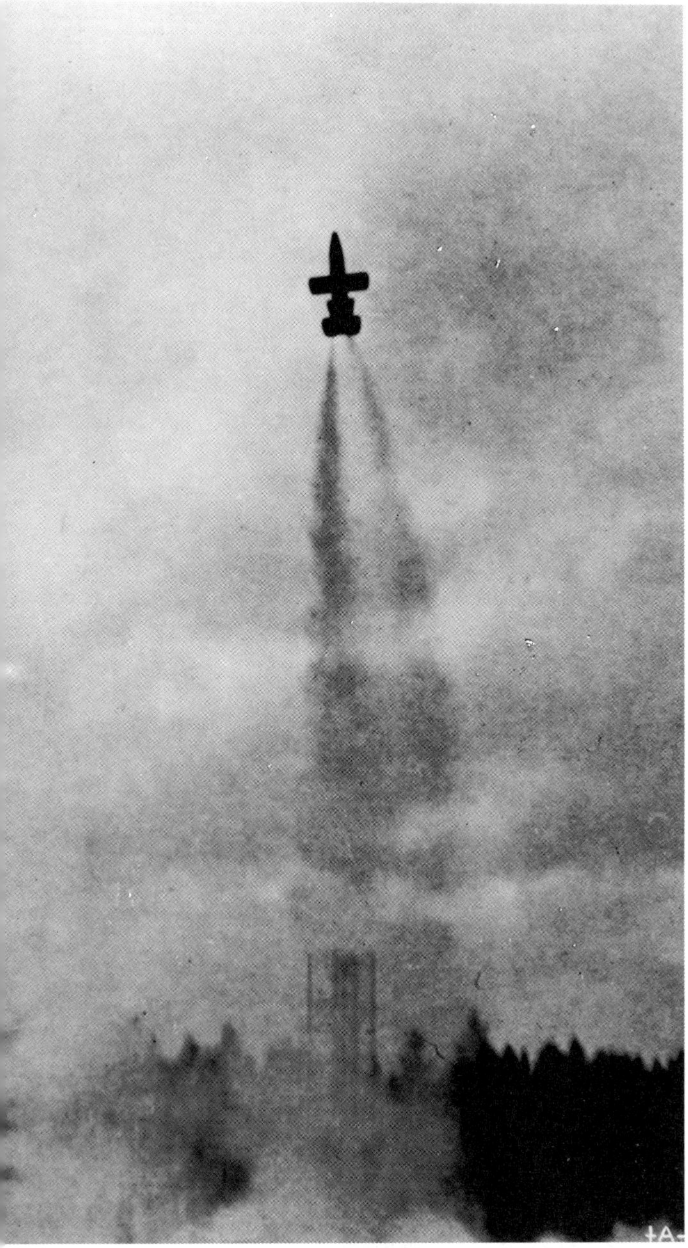

Raising a cloud of dust, Siebert's *Natter* lifted clear of the launcher . . .

. . . but then, shortly afterwards, the canopy broke away and the aircraft tilted on its back before arcing into the ground with the pilot still on board. *(via Heise)*

# CHAPTER 10

# Finale

During the final year of the war nine types of jet-propelled combat aircraft entered service with operational units in Germany, Great Britain, Japan and the U.S.A. Five of these aircraft were turbojet-powered, three were rocket-propelled and one, the Ryan Fireball, was powered by a turbojet and a piston engine.

Four types of turbojet powered aircraft flew combat missions during the conflict: the Messerschmitt 262 operated as a fighter, a fighter-bomber, a night fighter and a tactical reconnaissance aircraft; the Arado 234 operated as a bomber, a night fighter and a long range reconnaissance aircraft; the Heinkel 162 operated only in the fighter role as did the Gloster Meteor. Two types of rocket-powered aircraft also went into action, the Messerschmitt 163 fighter and the Yokosuka Ohka manned flying-bomb.

Of these aircraft, only two came close to making any serious impact on the air war. The Me 262 was by far the most effective jet fighter to go into action during the conflict. The story of this aircraft occupies the largest part of this book because it deserves to: during the conflict the Me 262 flew more operational sorties than all of the other jet propelled types *put together*. The Arado 234 enjoyed only moderate success as a bomber. But in the less spectacular role of strategic reconnaissance it was hugely successful, and roamed at will over Allied territory to photograph targets. The two remaining jet fighter types, the He 162 and the Gloster Meteor, played little part in the fighting and their effect on the conflict was negligible.

Neither of the two rocket-propelled types to go into action was able to achieve any real success. The Me 163 fighter and the Yokosuka Ohka had widely differing missions, but they had one factor in common that greatly reduced their effectiveness. Although these aircraft were capable of very high speeds, they could maintain them only for short periods and a large part of their operational flight profiles involved a gliding descent. As a result, these planes were vulnerable to attack from enemy piston-engined fighters. In the case of the Ohka this vulnerability was compounded by the need to have a slow mother aircraft to carry it to within gliding range of its target.

* * *

Apart from the single instance in March 1945 when an Arado 234 bombed Melsbroek airfield and inflicted damage on a Meteor on the ground, the opposing jet aircraft types never met in combat. Only chance kept them apart, and it is worth considering what might have happened if it had not. Without doubt the Meteor III would have been at a disadvantage in a fight against the Me 262 or the He 162. The two German jet fighters had a huge speed advantage and also greater stability at high speeds, making them more effective gun platforms. The Meteor III might have been effective against the Arado 234 when the latter carried bombs or external tanks, but once these had been released the German plane would have been difficult to catch.

* * *

If the war had continued for another nine months, how would that have affected the battle for air superiority? By the end of that time there would have been many more Me 262s and He 162s in service with front-line units, but the German fighters would have faced the Meteor 4 and P-80A Shooting Star. The introduction of the new Allied jet fighters would have made the contest a much more even affair. Yet, given the difficulties of manoeuvring at speeds close to the planes' compressibility thresholds, it is likely that most engagements between the jet aircraft would have ended inconclusively.

Had the war continued the Bachem *Natter* would also have gone into action, but as the rocket fighter with the shortest endurance of all it was unlikely that it could have achieved much.

In the Pacific Theatre the composite powered Ryan Fireball would also have seen action, though in combat the fighter was unlikely to prove any more effective than the latest piston-engined types operated by the U.S. Navy.

* * *

Two early jet fighter types went on to achieve greatness. During the immediate post-war years the Gloster Meteor served in the roles of fighter, fighter-bomber, reconnaissance aircraft, night fighter and trainer, and the type remained in front-line service in the RAF until 1961. Total production of all versions ran to 3,875 aircraft and the type saw service with ten air forces.

The Meteor carved a niche as one of the all-time great military aircraft, but even its record was eclipsed by that of the P-80 Shooting Star. The latter also went on to serve in the roles of fighter, fighter-bomber, tactical reconnaissance aircraft, night fighter and trainer, and production of all versions ran to just over 9,900 aircraft in fifteen years. Even now, in the 1990s, more than four hundred examples of the T-33 trainer version remain in service with a dozen air forces.

The P-80A and its derivatives have been in service for more than 48 years. To put that longevity into context, the type has been in day-to-day use for more than half of the period since Orville Wright made the first flight in a powered heavier-than-air machine in 1903. By any standard that is a remarkable record, all the more so if one considers that the original prototype of this aircraft was designed and built in less than 150 days . . .

# GLOSSARY

**Luftwaffe unit organisation**
The basic operational unit for fighters, fighter-bombers, reconnaissance aircraft and bombers in the Luftwaffe was the *Gruppe*. This comprised three or four *Staffeln* each with an establishment of between nine and 16 aircraft, plus a staff (*Stab*) unit of three or four; thus a *Gruppe* had a strength of between 30 and 68 aircraft. During the closing stages of the war, however, actual unit strengths were often considerably below establishment.

A feature of the jet aircraft was that in many cases these were flown by *ad hoc Kommandos* (detachments) operating independently, whose strengths varied between a small *Staffel* and a *Gruppe*.

A *Geschwader* had a nominal strength of three or four *Gruppen* and the aircraft within it were usually assigned to a single role, for example *Jagdgeschwader* (abbreviated to JG), fighters; *Nachtjagd-* (NJG), night fighters and *Kampfgeschwader* (KG), bombers. Reconnaissance units were usually independent *Gruppen*, *Aufklaerungsgruppen* (Aufkl.Gr). It should be noted, however, that no *Geschwader* ever received its full establishment of jet aircraft.

The *Gruppen* within a *Geschwader* were numbered in Roman numerals before the *Geschwader* designation; thus the Third *Gruppen* of *Jagdgeschwader* 7 was abbreviated as III./JG 7. The *Staffeln* within a *Geschwader* were numbered consecutively using Arabic numerals. Thus in a unit of three *Gruppen* each of three *Staffeln*, the 1st, 2nd and 3rd *Staffeln* comprised the Ist *Gruppe*; the 4th, 5th and 6th *Staffeln* comprised the IInd *Gruppe* and the 7th, 8th and 9th *Staffeln* comprised the IIIrd *Gruppe*. The ninth *Staffel* of *Kampfgeschwader* 76 was therefore abbreviated to 9./KG 76, and was part of III./KG 76.

The basic *fighting* element in a Luftwaffe fighter unit was the *Rotte* or pair of aircraft; two *Rotten* made up a *Schwarm* of four aircraft and three or four *Schwaerme* comprised a *Staffel*. Sometimes the *Kette* of three aircraft was employed as the basic fighting element, for example by the Me 262s of the *ad hoc* fighter unit *Jagdverband* 44 at the end of the war.

| | Luftwaffe | Royal Air Force | USAAF | US Navy |
|---|---|---|---|---|
| **Equivalent Ranks** | *Generalfeldmarschall* | Marshal of the RAF | General | Admiral |
| | *Generaloberst* | Air Chief Marshal | General | Admiral |
| | *General* | Air Marshal | Lieutenant-General | Vice-Admiral |
| | *Generalleutnant* | Air Vice-Marshal | Major-General | Rear Admiral |
| | *Generalmajor* | Air Commodore | Brigadier-General | Rear Admiral |
| | *Oberst* | Group Captain | Colonel | Captain |
| | *Oberstleutnant* | Wing Commander | Lieutenant-Colonel | Commander |
| | *Major* | Squadron Leader | Major | Lieutenant-Commander |
| | *Hauptmann* | Flight Lieutenant | Captain | Lieutenant |
| | *Oberleutnant* | Flying Officer | First Lieutenant | Lieutenant (junior grade) |
| | *Leutnant* | Pilot Officer | Second Lieutenant | Ensign |
| | *Oberfaehnrich* | Officer Cadet | Officer Cadet | Officer Cadet |
| | *Feldwebel* | Sergeant | Sergeant | Chief Petty Officer |
| | *Unteroffizier* | Corporal | Corporal | Petty Officer |
| | *Flieger* | Aircraftman | Private | Seaman |

# BIBLIOGRAPHY


Paul Allonby: *No 616 Sqn and the Meteor*, article in *Aviation News*

Manfred Boehme: *Jagdgeschwader 7*, Motorbuch-Verlag

Eric Brown: *Wings of the Luftwaffe*, Macdonald and Janes

Kenneth Chilstrom: *Test Flying from Old Wright Field*, Wright Stuff Association

Jeffrey Ethel: *Komet*, Ian Allan

Rene Francillon: *Japanese Aircraft of the Pacific War*, Putnam & Co

Roger Freeman: *The Mighty Eighth*, Macdonald and Janes

Roger Freeman: *The Mighty Eighth War Diary*, Janes Publishing

William Green: *Warplanes of the Third Reich*, Macdonald and Janes

William Green: *Rocket Fighter*, Ballantine

Bill Gunston: *The First Jet Fighters*, article in *Aeroplane Monthly*, July 1977

David Irving: *The Rise and Fall of the Luftwaffe*, Weidenfeld

Edward Maloney: *Kamikaze: The Ohka, Natter and FZG–76*, Aero Publishers Inc

Ernest McDowell: *Ryan's Fireball*, article in *AAHS Journal* Winter 1963

Eric Mombeek: *Defending the Reich*, JAC Publications

Hatsuho Naito: *Thunder Gods*, Kodansha International

Geoffrey Norris: *They Flew Meteors*, article in *R.A.F. Flying Review*

Ernst Obermaier: *Die Ritterkreuzträger der Luftwaffe*, Hoffmann

Richard O'Neill: *Suicide Squads*, Ballantine Books

Karl Pawlas: *Arado Ar 234, der erste Strahlbomber der Welt*, Luftfahrt

Alfred Price: *Battle over the Reich*, Ian Allan

Alfred Price: *Bomber Aircraft*, Cassell

Alfred Price: *Fighter Aircraft*, Cassell

Alfred Price: *The Last Year of the Luftwaffe*, Cassell

Alfred Price: *World War II Fighter Conflict*, Macdonald and Janes

Hanfried Schliephake: *Flugzeugbewaffnung*, Motorbuch-Verlag

Chris Shores: *2nd TAF*, Osprey

J. Richard Smith and Anthony Kay: *German Aircraft of the Second World War*, Putnam

J. Richard Smith & Eddie Creek: *Volksjäger*, Monogram Publications

E.T. Woolridge: *The P-80 Shooting Star*, Smithsonian Institution

Mano Ziegler: *Turbinenjäger Me 262*, Motorbuch-Verlag


In addition to the above, the authors consulted several official R.A.F. reports on the Meteor fighter now held in the Public Record Office at Kew, London.

# INDEX